Critical Thinking in Psychology

A Unified Skills Approach

D. Alan Bensley

Frostburg State University

To be

Brooks/Cole Publishing Company

I(T)P® An

Pacific Grove • A
Madrid • Melbou

Johannesburg • London
• Toronto • Washington

This book is dedicated to my family: Nancy, Mike, Kaitlin, and Zachary. Thanks for your love and patience.

Sponsoring Editor: *Jim Brace-Thompson*
Marketing Team: *Christine Davis, Lauren Harp, & Alicia Barelli*
Marketing Representative: *Diana Morgan*
Editorial Assistant: *Terry Thomas*
Production Editor: *Marjorie Z. Sanders*
Manuscript Editor: *Catherine Cambron*
Interior and Cover Design: *Carolyn Deacy*

Interior Illustration: *Jennifer Mackres*
Cover Photo: *L & M Services B. V. Amsterdam 970503*
Art Coordinator: *Jennifer Mackres*
Photo Editor: *Kathleen Olson*
Typesetting: *Bookends Typesetting*
Printing and Binding: *Webcom*

For more information, contact:

BROOKS/COLE PUBLISHING COMPANY
511 Forest Lodge Road
Pacific Grove, CA 93950
USA

International Thomson Publishing Europe
Berkshire House 168-173
High Holborn
London WC1V 7AA
England

Thomas Nelson Australia
102 Dodds Street
South Melbourne, 3205
Victoria, Australia

Nelson Canada
1120 Birchmount Road
Scarborough, Ontario
Canada M1K 5G4

International Thomson Editores
Seneca 53
Col. Polanco
11560 México, D.F., México

International Thomson Publishing GmbH
Königswinterer Strasse 418
53227 Bonn
Germany

International Thomson Publishing Asia
221 Henderson Road
#05-10 Henderson Building
Singapore 0315

International Thomson Publishing Japan
Hirakawacho Kyowa Building, 3F
2-2-1 Hirakawacho
Chiyoda-ku, Tokyo 102
Japan

Printed in Canada

10   9

Library of Congress Cataloging-in-Publication Data

Bensley, D. Alan, [date]
    Critical thinking in psychology : a unified skills approach / D. Alan Bensley.
        p.   cm.
    Include bibliographical references and index.
    ISBN-13: 978-0-534-25620-3   ISBN-10: 0-534-25620-1
    1. Critical thinking.   2. Critical thinking problems, exercises, etc.   3. Reasoning (Psychology)   4. Reasoning (Psychology) Problems, exercises, etc.   I. Title.
    BF441.B435 1997
    150'.1—dc21   97-21646
                                                        CIP

Contents

CHAPTER 5

Do We Perceive the World as It Is?   81

CHAPTER 6

The Extraordinary Claims Made About Hypnosis   95

CHAPTER 10   # Do Emotions Hinder Critical Thinking?   147

CHAPTER 11   Thinking Critically About Theories of Abnormal Behavior:
Culture and Witches   159

CHAPTER 12   Critical Thinking and Diagnosing Mental Disorders   181

CHAPTER 13

Thinking Critically About Repression and Recovered Memories of Abuse   191

CHAPTER 14

Critical Thinking and Writing   215

Preface

The Purpose of This Book

This book was written for students and instructors who are serious about the improvement of critical thinking. The specific purpose is to teach the component skills necessary for critical thinking in psychology. The emphasis is on how psychologists use critical thinking when engaging in professional activities involving scientific thinking: analyzing situations to determine causation, generating hypotheses, clinical decision making, and especially critical reading of literature reviews and critical writing. These thinking skills are taught together with coverage of important psychological concepts and fascinating psychological questions, such as whether our emotions make us irrational and whether people accurately remember previously unrecalled memories of sexual abuse.

The Theory Behind This Book

This book assumes that critical thinking in each discipline is a complex set of cognitive skills and dispositions, some of which are shared and many of which are specific to the discipline. The book also assumes that knowledge and thinking skills are often context-specific. Critical thinking skills are taught as you learn the concepts of and do the work of a particular discipline. Further, the book assumes that people use their own beliefs and commonsense theories to try to explain behaviors they observe. Research on science education suggests that these everyday theories should be taken into account when the effort is made to think critically about scientific questions.

This book defines critical thinking as reflective thinking involving the evaluation of evidence relevant to some claim so that a sound conclusion can be drawn about the claim. This definition is general enough to subsume deductive reasoning, inductive reasoning, and informal reasoning. A single definition helps organize and provide the framework for learning about a variety of kinds of thinking used in psychology.

The Approach of This Book

Because this book uses the general definition of critical thinking to create an organizational framework for teaching a set of related skills, it takes a "unified skills" approach. The exercises are designed to teach a variety of skills that support inquiry in psychology using a single critical thinking model and vocabulary. The target skills include distinguishing arguments from nonarguments, finding the central question, evaluating the kinds and quality of evidence, making predictions from theories, generating good hypotheses, and constructing good arguments. The exercises offer practice in the various components of scientific thinking in psychology. The exercises also focus on the skills that overlap in critical reading and writing. Solutions to the exercises are given in the text and in Appendix A.

The first three chapters form the basis for the remainder of the book, which has been designed to be modular. The exercises and foundational skills introduced in the first three chapters prepare students for the exercises in later chapters. To encourage readers to confront their own beliefs and "theories" about the questions critically discussed, each chapter begins by asking, "What do you think?"

The chapters and exercises differ, not only in content, but also in the kinds of target skills they are designed to develop. Several exercises (in Chapters 3, 4, 6, 8, 10, and 13) are designed to teach analytic reading skills. These primarily train students in the inductive reasoning skills that are so important to psychologists who are trying to make sense of what is known about a specific question in psychology. These are also the skills required to evaluate a psychological literature review or a textbook discussion of a question. Other chapters (Chapter 1 and 7) are designed to train students in deductive reasoning skills, the important kind of reasoning used by psychologists to make predictions from theories and to argue from theories and definitions. Chapters 2 and 11 discuss how to generate hypotheses to account for behavior.

As is appropriate for a text on critical thinking, important philosophical questions are raised in this book. For example, Chapter 3, covering whether people are basically selfish, deals with the nature versus nurture question. Chapter 4 addresses the mind-body problem. Chapter 5, on perception and illusions, deals with epistemological questions concerning the influence of perception on what we know, including a discussion of empiricism and rationalism. Chapter 6, on hypnosis, discusses issues related to whether people have free will. Chapter 10, on whether emotions make us irrational, deals with the old question of whether the passions cloud our reason. Throughout the book questions of ethics are raised: for example, in issues related to how we test people in Chapter 2, the problem of stereotyping and witch hunts, in Chapter 11; and the potential for harm to victims and those accused of sexual abuse in the "repressed memory" controversy, in Chapter 13.

Other chapters teach critical thinking through writing. In Chapter 7, students are guided through a deductive reasoning exercise in which they must justify in writing that an example from their own experience fits a definition.

Chapter 14 provides extensive training in writing responses to essay questions; in writing a short, argumentative term paper; and in writing an introduction to a research report. Chapter 14 should be covered after students have had experience with critical reading in earlier chapters.

Using This Book in Different Courses
General Psychology

The content selection, modular organization, and skills objectives of the book make it especially suitable for supporting a general psychology course. The book is filled with examples and exercises from various areas of psychology. Also, each chapter focuses on a specific topic that parallels the coverage in general psychology, such as helping behavior in Chapter 3, localization of function in Chapter 4, the definition of learning in Chapter 7, basic memory concepts in Chapter 8, introduction to judgment and decision making in Chapter 9, introduction to motivation and emotion in Chapter 10, basic issues related to identifying abnormal behavior in Chapters 11 and 12, and an introduction to the classification of mental disorders in Chapter 12. The first two chapters introduce students to how critical thinkers and scientists approach the fascinating questions that psychologists address, and the third chapter introduces critical reading. After covering the first three chapters, introductory psychology instructors may select any of the later chapters to support coverage in their own course because the chapters are independent in content and thinking skills practice. In addition to critical thinking skills, the book focuses on literacy skill development—so important to the beginning college student—in active reading in Chapter 3 and a review of the basics of writing and how to write essay question responses and short papers in psychology in Chapter 14.

Research Methods and Experimental Psychology

An important objective of this book is to help students learn how psychologists approach scientific questions; many of the chapters support this objective. Chapter 1 introduces critical thinking, basic concepts related to inquiry, and the derivation of hypotheses from theories. Chapter 2 discusses the distinction between science and pseudoscience, the evaluation of different kinds of scientific and nonscientific evidence, the advantages of science over other approaches to knowledge, the drawing of sound conclusions from reviews of the research literature, causation, and hypothetico-deductive reasoning. Chapter 3 provides instruction in the critical reading of a literature review, using the question whether people are basically selfish as an example. Several other chapters, including Chapters 4, 6, 8, 11, and 13, provide further instruction in critical reading of literature reviews. Finally, Chapter 14 discusses how to prepare for and write an introduction to a research report, returning to a study of the factors that influence helping behavior.

Cognitive Psychology

This book has several chapters that could be used to supplement a cognitive psychology course. In particular, these include Chapter 5 on perception, Chapter 6 on hypnosis and memory, Chapter 7 on behavioral versus cognitive definitions of learning, Chapter 8 on reconstruction and accuracy of memory, Chapter 9 on improving judgments and decisions, and Chapter 13 on repressed memory. In general, this book raises many issues concerning the quality of human thinking, cognition, perception, and knowledge. Taken together, these chapters discuss questions that have important implications for our capacity to know the world, to think about our experience, and to think critically. As such, this book may also be viewed as a guided tour into the territory of our mental abilities—their limits and capacities. Also, because this book discusses many implications of cognitive and educational psychology for the improvement of thinking, it could add a more personal, applied focus to cognitive psychology, a subject that often seems abstract to students.

Social Psychology

Several chapters in this book could be used to support a social psychology course. Chapters 1 and 2 use many examples from social psychology in their introduction of critical thinking concepts and in the overview of scientific methods. Chapter 3 has a lengthy discussion of altruism and prosocial behavior. Chapter 9 deals with the social basis of decisions and judgments. Chapter 10 discusses emotional and motivational influences on judgment and decision making related to issues in social cognition and uses practice problems involving analysis of social situations. Chapter 11 discusses implicit theories of personality, stereotypes, and in-groups and out-groups; it also offers a social psychological explanation of historical witch hunts and recent concern about satanic ritual activities. Chapter 14 discusses writing using examples from the study of social learning theory and the modeling of aggression and helping.

Abnormal Psychology, Personality, and Counseling

Other chapters (10, 11, 12, and 13) apply the critical thinking model to the study of abnormal psychology, personality, and clinical psychology questions and to the acquisition of important clinical thinking skills. More specifically, Chapter 10 reviews some literature on the disruptive effects of emotions such as depression and anxiety on psychological functioning. Chapter 11 discusses concepts of abnormality and whether those accused of witchcraft during the witch hunts of the 14th through 16th centuries actually had mental disorders. Chapter 13 discusses a controversial question confronting clinical psychologists: whether a person can accurately recall previously unrecalled memories of sexual abuse. At the end of Chapter 13 are exercises for analyzing client-therapist interactions in which sexual abuse is an issue.

The text also can help to simplify learning the classifications of many of the various psychological disorders found in the DSM-IV and discussed in Chapter 12. Chapter 12 relates important symptoms of disorders to a set of questions a clinician might seek to answer in coming to a diagnosis. Four sample cases are provided for practice in using the questions to come to a diagnosis.

How to Organize Your Course to Teach Critical Thinking

While instructors are free to use any of the chapters in the book after students have read the first three, some permutations of chapter use are expected to be more effective than others. For example, it is recommended that students do an additional critical reading exercise early in the course for three reasons. First, they will be able to practice with an exercise similar to one presented to them in Chapter 3. Second, students' reading skills are fundamental to their later success in the course, since much of their knowledge is acquired through reading their main textbook. Third, critical reading is probably less difficult than critical writing. Critical reading involves recognition of information (including claims, evidence, and conclusions), whereas critical writing involves at least one additional cognitive processing step: the generation of claims, evidence, and conclusions. Therefore, critical reading should precede critical writing assignments, such as the critical essay or the short argumentative term paper.

Instructors would do well to sample different types of critical thinking activities in the exercises. Such sampling will provide practice with the general model for critical thinking while introducing students to various applications of the model to psychology and will help develop component thinking skills, as well as help maintain student interest in the program. Let's examine a hypothetical example to see how a wide variety of thinking and communication skills used in psychology and academia, in general, may be covered by sampling only a few chapters. For example, if only Chapters 1, 2, 6, and 11 and part of Chapter 14 are used, these chapters would provide training in perspective taking and critical discussion, critical reading and writing, inductive and deductive reasoning, causal reasoning, hypothetico-deductive reasoning in clinical diagnosis, the application of critical thinking to students' own everyday thinking, and information about how perception and confirmation bias may distort the inferences we make about our world.

Teaching Critical Thinking

Instructors and students alike must realize that thinking critically is a complex, effortful process. It requires practice of specific kinds of thinking tasks and commitment to apply the skills learned to new situations. Everyone needs to improve his or her ability to think critically, since the purpose of critical thinking is to obtain good answers to questions that come up in psychology and everyday life.

Finally, I would appreciate the comments of both students and instructors who use the book. Write me or send in the attached comment form at the back of the book.

Acknowledgments

I would like to thank several people who have helped me with my own critical thinking and in preparation of this book. This book owes much to their help, but I take responsibility for any errors that remain.

First, I would like to thank several of my teachers who planted the seeds of my own efforts to become a critical thinker. They are Larry Sensenig of Morningside College and Mark Altom, Joel Cadwell, John A. Carpenter, Arnold Glass, Jeannette Haviland, Robert Karlin, Eileen Kowler, Kenneth Monteiro, H. Richard Schiffman, and Vicki Tartter, who were my teachers at Rutgers University.

Next, I would like to thank colleagues who made insightful suggestions and reviewed parts of the manuscript. I would especially like to thank Chrismarie Baxter, Thomas Hawk, and Ronald Reed for their influence on my work in critical thinking and their helpful comments about the book. Thanks also go to other members of the psychology department of Frostburg State University for their support while I wrote this book, many of them reading parts of the manuscript and pointing me in the right direction on various chapters. They are: Anne Bristow, Albert Crall, Cindy Herzog, Anthony LaGuidice, Kevin Peterson, Lee B. Ross, Patricia Santoro, Gabie Smith, and William Southerly. Thanks also to Gary Brosvic of Rider University, who reviewed the chapter on perception.

Brooks/Cole obtained the help of several fine reviewers who helped me in many ways to improve the manuscript; my thanks go to Bernard Beins, Ithaca College; Michael Bergmire, Jefferson College; James Calhoun, University of Georgia; M. Ann Dirkes; Robert Grissom, San Francisco State University; Kathleen Morgan, Wheaton College; Gary Poole, Simon Fraser University; and Ronald Reed, Texas Wesleyan University.

I would also like to thank other students and colleagues at Frostburg State for their help. Several graduate and undergraduate students worked on research projects related to this book, including Mary Bolton, Jill Brooks, Tanya De Both, Diane McGowan, Barb Pallardy, and Jen Post. Thanks to Dean Kenneth Stewart and to Terry Kasecamp for their comments on diagnosis and concepts of psychological disorders. Thanks also to students in my general psychology, research methods, and advanced research evaluation and interpretation courses for their useful comments on the manuscript. For helping me obtain many articles and books cited in this book, thanks go to the Ort Library staff of Frostburg State, especially Delores Miller and Carole Bodnar of the Interlibrary Loan Department. Thanks in general to Frostburg State University, which provided three different grants to help me develop parts of this book.

Finally, I would like to thank the staff of Brooks/Cole for their support and guidance on this project, especially editor Jim Brace-Thompson, his assistant, Terry Thomas, Marjorie Sanders, production editor, and Cathy Cambron, copy editor.

D. Alan Bensley

Introduction to Critical Thinking in Psychology

Learning Objectives

1. To understand the need for critical thinking and how to think more effectively in answering the questions posed in psychology and everyday living.

2. To introduce you to important basic terms and forms of arguments used in critical and scientific thinking.

3. To help you understand how the ideas and skills introduced in this chapter will help you with later chapters of the book.

What Do You Think?

Psychologists seek to answer some fascinating questions. Some of these are addressed in this book. For example: Can the moon cause people to go crazy or commit crimes? More generally, do the stars and planets influence our lives as astrology suggests? Can psychics with precognition predict the future? Should we believe someone who claims to have been abducted by aliens? What do we actually "know" about the world through our senses? Do we perceive the world as it really is? Are people basically selfish? Do people have incredible abilities when they are hypnotized? For example, can eyewitnesses after being hypnotized remember details of crimes that they could not originally remember? Did the thousands of people who were tried and executed for witchcraft in the late Middle Ages actually suffer from psychological disorders? Is there an international conspiracy of Satanists who ritually abuse, murder, and eat children? Can psychotherapists help people recover memories of sexual abuse that they have not recalled for decades? How are some people able to firewalk—that is, to walk through a bed of hot coals without apparently hurting themselves?

Critical thinking has an important role to play in answering these questions. To illustrate, let's examine the first question. A very old commonsense "theory" connects the moon's phases to abnormal behavior. For centuries, astrologers and others have claimed that the moon and other celestial bodies exert an influence on human behavior. In the 16th century, the Swiss physician Paracelsus proposed that the moon could make people crazy. The words *lunatic* and *lunacy* are based on this supposed lunar influence on psychological functioning. Many people today—in fact, approximately half of all college students—think that the moon causes people to behave abnormally, perhaps even commit crimes (Kohn, 1990). For example, one of my students told me that people at a mental health facility where she had worked were convinced that after every full moon they observed their clients behave in bizarre ways. What do you think? Does the moon make people go crazy? Pause for a moment and decide what you think about this question before reading on.

If you said, "Yes, I believe the moon does exert an influence on human behavior," then you are in agreement with many college students and perhaps some people who work at mental health facilities; however, you are most likely wrong.

Researchers have investigated a number of possible connections between various phases of the moon and human behavior, including the murder rate and the number of penalties for roughness in hockey games. Rotton and Kelly (1985) reviewed 37 different studies on the possible connection and found no good evidence that any of the phases of the moon led to increases in deviant behavior. (See Kohn [1990] for an entertaining review of studies in this area that comes to a similar conclusion.)

This example suggests that you may have an **opinion** about some question—that is, a belief, even a strongly held one, about some claim—and still be wrong. In this case, the evidence of college students' opinions and informal observations by workers at a mental health facility are at odds with the conclusions of scientific experts and their research. Whom should you believe? The critical thinker would decide whom or what to believe after a careful evaluation of the evidence. We can define **evidence** as the reasons provided in order to draw a conclusion. Your opinion, the informal observation of the mental health workers, and the research are each a kind of evidence. Sometimes, some of the evidence supports a conclusion, such as that the moon causes abnormal behavior, while other evidence does not support the conclusion. If we are to evaluate this evidence, we would be better off trusting the scientific research evidence because it is based on systematic and careful observations, rather than informal observations that could be in error and are more likely to be affected by the observer's biases. This discussion of the evaluation of evidence relevant to some question leads us to the most important objective of this book.

The Purpose of This Book

The purpose of this book is to help you learn how to think more effectively about questions. The purpose is not to tell you what to think; there are plenty of books around to do that. Rather, this book is about helping you learn how to think critically about the questions we ask in psychology. Critical thinking is important because it is what experts in psychology engage in when they are doing some of their best work. Critical thinking will also help you learn how to draw reasonable conclusions for yourself. So while obtaining answers to the interesting questions at the beginning of the chapter is important, the process of drawing sound conclusions to these questions is even more important.

All of us think. However, some types of thinking can be shown to be more effective and to lead to better conclusions than other types. In the last 20 years, educators, psychologists, and others have done considerable research on how to make thinking more effective. This research has shown that people can learn how to think more effectively with the right kind of methods and practice (Halpern, 1993). A deliberate attempt has been made to incorporate knowledge of how to improve thinking into this book. Recent research suggests that students using the methods described in this book can become more effective thinkers (Bensley, Bolton, Palardy, Brooks, & Langan, 1995; Bensley & Haynes, 1995).

The main advantage of learning how to think critically is that it provides you, the thinker, with a way of drawing the best conclusion you can for a given question. In other words, learning how to think critically can also help you to decide what to think. What you conclude in a given situation is your responsibility. That does not mean, however, that whatever you conclude is correct or true. If you draw a conclusion that is not based on the evidence, then your beliefs may simply be based on opinion or what you have heard from other people. If you draw a conclusion that is inconsistent with the facts, then you may simply be wrong. In either case, you would not be thinking critically.

Along the same lines, some theories and hypotheses can be shown to be better than others. You may have heard people say, "Oh, it's just a theory"— meaning that all theories are inherently flawed, with one just as good as another. While what people mean by the term *theory* in that statement is probably closer to what scientists call a hypothesis, the idea that theories and hypotheses are just guesses is misleading. Some theories and hypotheses are better than others. For example, while the earth is not exactly spherical, the theory that the earth is round is better than the theory that the earth is flat (Asimov, 1989). We can show that the theory that the earth is round is superior because predictions made from it would be less in error than predictions made from the theory that the earth is flat.

This idea, that one theory can be shown to be better than another, is important because people use their own informal theories all the time. Even people who have not studied psychology have their own, often conflicting and inconsistent, explanations and theories of why people think and act the way they do (Rips & Conrad, 1989). These popular beliefs are sometimes referred to as **commonsense psychology** (Myers & Hansen, 1996). For example, the common folk wisdom is that opposites attract, suggesting that people who are very different from each other may be attracted to each other. On the other hand, you have probably also heard it said that birds of a feather flock together, suggesting that just the opposite is true (Stanovich, 1996). Although people may commonly assume that both of these statements are true, they cannot both be true in the same situation. Psychological research, in general, supports the idea that people who are similar are more likely to be attracted to each other (Wade & Tavris, 1993). So, if you believed that opposites attract in personal interactions, then you should abandon or at least revise your "theory."

We will examine the differences between commonsense "theories" and scientific theories in greater detail later; but at this point you should note that in this book commonsense notions that are labeled "theories" will appear in quotation marks. This way of labeling such ideas should help you compare your own commonsense "theories" to scientific theories we discuss, so that you can revise your theory if necessary. Accordingly, this book should improve your thinking by helping you to learn to correct your own ideas when they can be shown to be faulty, limited, or in error.

You may also think of this book as a sort of user's guide to your own thinking apparatus. The book discusses a number of limitations, biases, and errors that can affect the decisions we make and the conclusions we draw. For example, Chapter 5 discusses illusions and how faulty perceptions can lead to thinking errors. Chapters 6, 8, and 13 discuss problems with the accuracy of memory. Chapter 9 discusses errors and biases in decision making and judgment. Chapter 10 discusses how strong emotions can disrupt thinking and lead to irrational behavior. Finally, Chapter 11 deals with stereotypes and the errors in social judgment that people make. Becoming aware of the biases, errors, and limitations in one's thinking is a very important part of improving thinking.

What Is Critical Thinking?

In order to think more clearly about what it is we are trying to improve, it would be useful to define critical thinking. Critical thinking is a very rich and varied concept that has developed from the thinking of many people. We will examine some of these ideas that are most relevant to this book.

Robert Ennis, a recognized authority on critical thinking, has provided an important definition of critical thinking that emphasizes its practical aspects. According to him, **"critical thinking is reasonable, reflective thinking that is focused on deciding what to believe or do"** (Ennis, 1987, p. 9). As such, critical thinking can improve both how and what people think about a variety of questions. If critical thinking really is practical, then it should help a person to decide what to believe or do on a wide range of questions: from personal decisions, such as which is the best car to buy, to more scholarly questions, such as what is the best theory of depression.

Deciding what to believe or think involves weighing the evidence about a question or claim and then using reasoning to make up your own mind about the claim. To think critically, a person must decide the best conclusion to draw in a particular situation after carefully considering the evidence, examining the reasons for believing and for not believing some claim. As Halpern (1996) points out, the term *critical* describes thinking that emphasizes evaluation, such as the evaluation of the evidence for some claim; *critical* is not being used in the sense of *negative*.

It is also useful to examine the similarities between the concepts of critical thinking and scientific thinking. Kuhn (1993) noted that critical thinking and scientific thinking both involve the coordination of theory and evidence. Lipman (1991) stated that critical thinking involves the refinement of thinking. Critical thinking is thus like science in that the idea of improving upon ideas and theories is central to most conceptions of science.

Although from time to time we will refer to each of these definitions, primarily we will use the following working definition of critical thinking: **Critical thinking is reflective thinking involving the evaluation of evidence relevant to a claim so that a sound conclusion can be drawn from the evidence.** Using this definition has two advantages with respect to the important purposes of this book. First, the definition is general enough to allow us to talk about the various kinds of critical and scientific reasoning that go on in psychology. Second, the definition will be useful in exploring the connections between the critical thinking that goes on both in reading and in writing as we inquire into psychological questions.

Because one goal of this book is to improve your critical thinking, it would also be useful to define critical thinking in terms of what it takes to become a critical thinker. Based in part on the critical thinking theories of Glaser (1985), Ennis (1987), McPeck (1981), and Perkins, Jay, and Tishman (1993), I argue that a proficient critical thinker must have four characteristics: (1) knowledge of reasoning, (2) a set of cognitive skills involved in reasoning, (3) knowledge that is relevant to the problem or question that is being thought about, and (4) a set of dispositions to think critically. For example, in order to think critically about some psychological question, such as whether or not people are basically selfish, you should know common terms, concepts, and rules used in such discussions. These include such terms as *claim, evidence, conclusion,* and *argument,* as well as the rules for reasoning about psychological questions. Second, to think critically you must have skill in identifying and using terms, concepts, and rules when analyzing an actual psychological question—something that comes from practice. Because critical thinkers seek to answer specific questions and because the reasoning they do is about something in particular, reasoning about a topic requires knowledge of it.

Knowing about reasoning, possessing reasoning skills, and knowing and understanding a subject area, however, alone do not ensure that you will be an effective critical thinker. You must also be disposed to use your knowledge and skill. A **disposition** to think critically is the tendency to use one's critical thinking skills in approaching a situation or question. For example, once you have learned basic critical thinking terminology and rules for reasoning, and have practiced using this knowledge and other relevant knowledge in analyzing actual psychological discussions, then you must also apply this knowledge and skill when you are confronted with a new psychological discussion in another situation, perhaps in a different psychology class. Another important critical thinking disposition is your tendency to ask why and to seek evidence when someone asks you to believe some claim. After reading this book, I hope you will be convinced of the need to ask why and be inclined to examine the relevant evidence carefully before you come to a conclusion. In addition, I hope that you will develop other important critical thinking dispositions, such as the disposition to be fair-minded—that is, to consider all sides of an argument and to carefully consider the evidence with which you disagree.

However, the primary goal of this book is to help you to acquire knowledge of reasoning and to develop critical thinking skills while learning about important psychological questions. In particular, we will focus on the skills of critical reading and critical writing so essential to the profession of psychology. You can help yourself acquire the knowledge and skills necessary for critical thinking by taking an active approach to your learning—that is, reading the material carefully and checking to see whether you have understood what you have read.

By now, you may have said to yourself, "This critical thinking business sounds like work to me. Why should I go to the trouble?" This question is not a bad one to ask; in fact, it may actually be a sign that you already are thinking critically. You should not agree to commit yourself to such a venture without first hearing the evidence that it is worthwhile.

Why Critical Thinking Is Important

To see why critical thinking is important, let's consider some examples of how we depend on critical thinking in our daily lives. Suppose you were accused of committing a crime. At your trial, the members of the jury said, "The evidence for and against you is mixed and confusing, but since we don't like your personality, we find you guilty." The jury did not objectively evaluate the evidence relevant to your case and so did not think critically. Or consider the research of

Kuhn, Weinstock, and Flaton (1994), who showed that subjects asked to evaluate the evidence from an actual murder trial so as to arrive at a verdict often use the evidence selectively to construct only one story (theory). A reasoned verdict, however, requires considering multiple perspectives and coordinating the varied sources of evidence with more than one theory or story.

Now, let's examine another hypothetical case. Suppose you had a serious disease, and in discussing your treatment options your doctor said, "Let's try drug X. It really is no more effective than other drugs, and it has some side effects they don't have, but I would like to try it out on you." How would you feel? Obviously, we depend on and expect a careful, objective, and complete evaluation of the relevant evidence about such serious questions. Otherwise, people might make decisions that greatly affect us for arbitrary and whimsical reasons. Even the success of a democracy depends on its citizens making well thought-out judgments concerning the claims made by the media, informed sources, politicians, and other leaders (Glaser, 1985; Paul, 1984).

Everyday examples of people's failure to think critically abound. For example, many people fail to realize that using a credit card is essentially taking out a high-interest loan. As a result of their incorrect assumption, they end up borrowing more than they can immediately pay back, so that they end up paying high rates of interest (Stanovich, 1994). Another example of a failure to think critically was the wishful thinking of investors and the uncritical evaluation of loan applications by lenders that were partly responsible for the savings and loan fiasco of the late 1980s, costing U.S. taxpayers hundreds of billions of dollars.

Research on the Need for Critical Thinking

Critical thinking is greatly needed, but much evidence suggests that students' thinking skills are not adequate to meet the challenges students face. Many educational reports including the National Assessment of Educational Progress (1981) have argued that the U.S. educational system is failing to teach many of its students how to think effectively. Langer and Applebee (1987) found that students often have difficulty in persuasive and analytic writing, two kinds of writing that require critical thinking. Using developmental tests of reasoning, McKinnon and Renner (1971) found that only one-quarter of all first-year college students they tested showed the ability to reason logically and abstractly. Although Keeley, Browne, and Kreutzer (1982) found some improvement in critical thinking resulting from students' having attended college, this improvement was not substantial. Similarly, Perkins (1985) found that schooling had some impact on students' abilities to reason about everyday questions, but not the improvement that we would hope for if students are to become proficient at critical thinking.

While no one probably wants to admit that he or she does not think critically, the abundance of everyday examples and the research evidence suggest that many people need to work on developing these skills. Even Sir Arthur Conan Doyle, a physician and the creator of Sherlock Holmes, was an uncritical dupe of mediums who claimed to be contacting the spirits of the dead (Randi, 1987). Doyle's uncritical belief in mediums and séances seems all the more ironic when we consider that Holmes, the character Doyle created, is famous for his great reasoning abilities. Along the same lines, many people today believe in channeling, the New Age method of contacting spirits. Like its predecessor, spirit mediumship, channeling is a lucrative business that nets millions of dollars per year for those who serve as channels (Kyle, 1995). The confessions of M. Lamar Keene, a lifelong medium who was on the board of directors of the Universalist Spiritualist Association, the largest of the U.S. spiritualist groups, reveal the extent of fraud involved in such groups. For example, Keene described how one medium with sexual designs on one of his female clients approached her with the promise of special spirit ministrations, then led her away from the others in the darkened room and had sexual intercourse with her. The gullible woman, who was thrilled by the experience, rushed to tell her husband how the spirits had chosen her for this special experience (Leahey & Leahey, 1983).

In summary, extensive research shows the need to improve critical thinking. Many everyday examples reveal that a failure to think critically is quite common. Moreover, unsubstantiated New Age and paranormal phenomena are widely credited as believable. This evidence suggests that many of us need to improve our ability to think critically and that this should be an important goal for teachers and students.

Why People Persist in Believing False Theories

What accounts for people's persistence in holding incorrect commonsense beliefs and "theories"? For example, if there really is no good evidence that the moon causes deviant behavior, then why do so many people persist in believing this incorrect theory? This important question illustrates that need for critical thinking in everyday life. One reason people persist in this false belief is that they have not learned how to evaluate the relevant evidence in an objective, systematic, and reasonable way. A persistent false belief like this one may be due to what is called a confirmation bias. When people fall prey to **confirmation bias,** they pay attention to evidence that confirms or supports a theory they prefer and ignore evidence that does not support or that could disconfirm their theory. For example, when the moon is full, people notice crimes they read or hear about in the news; but when no crimes occur during a full moon, they are not equally likely to notice. You are not likely to hear them say, "Hey, there's a full moon tonight, and no murder took place!" (Kohn, 1990).

Confirmation bias is a very prevalent thinking error, which also affects many social judgments. For example, Lord, Ross, and Lepper (1979) presented subjects who either favored the death penalty or opposed it with the results of two experiments of equal quality, one that supported the idea that the death penalty deterred further crime and one that did not support this idea. Consistent with the effect of a confirmation bias, they found that subjects rated the results of the study that favored their position as more convincing than the results of the study that disagreed with their theory. Furthermore, while one might expect the subjects to be less convinced of the correctness of their positions after reading the results of a study that reached the opposite conclusion, subjects instead became even more convinced of their positions.

Clinicians also fall prey to the confirmation bias in their diagnoses and treatment of clients, as discussed in Chapter 12. One would expect scientists who review journal articles for publication to be objective, not favoring articles consistent with the theories that the scientists themselves favor over submissions inconsistent with those favored theories. Mahoney (1977) found, however, that scientists do show confirmation bias in their evaluations of research, as discussed in Chapters 2 and 9. This tendency to pay attention to positive evidence and to discount negative evidence also seems to underlie belief in the moon's supposed effect on behavior.

Other reasons besides confirmation bias lead people to persist in believing the false theory of astrology. To illustrate, read over the following description of a person. To what extent does the profile below describe your own characteristics?

> It is important to you that people like you and that they admire you for who you are. But, sometimes, you tend to be more critical of yourself than other people are. While people may perceive you as confident of yourself on the outside, on the inside you are somewhat insecure. At times, you try very hard to reach your goals, but you have much unused potential. There are changes and events that are coming up in the near future that will present unique opportunities for you. Because of your personality characteristics, it is important that you watch for these opportunities so that you will not miss them.

If you thought the profile described you, then your impression is like that of participants in a study conducted by Ulrich, Stachnik, and Stainton (1963). The profile, which is similar to ones used by these researchers, provides a general description of personality that could fit many people and that people readily endorse. Likewise, horoscopes provide somewhat general descriptions of individual traits and future events. People's tendency to uncritically accept personality descriptions that do not really describe them has been termed the "Barnum effect," after that circus entrepreneur's maxim: "There's a sucker born every minute" (Meehl, 1956).

A third reason people persist in believing in astrology is that the advice provided in horoscopes may actually encourage dependency in readers. Swensen and White (1995) examined three months of a daily horoscope column and found that the messages embedded in the column appeared to promote helplessness and obedience to authority. Other research suggests that the groups of people most susceptible to astrology and other paranormal claims are those who are most uncertain about their social future, such as young people, especially young women; unmarried people; and people who rate their risk of unemployment as high (Frazier, 1992).

Finally, some people may believe in astrology because it appears to be scientific. The horoscope requires complicated calculations and appears to be based on an elaborate set of rules. The calculations are based on the position of the stars, sun, and planets during the time of Ptolemy in the second century A.D. The positions of these heavenly bodies with respect to the earth have changed considerably since then; so right from the start it is not clear why astrology does not take these changes into account. Moreover, even if astrological calculations may appear scientific, astrology is really **pseudoscience.** Although astrology and ideas like it may have the external trappings of science, believers do not take a scientific approach in asking and answering questions. In particular, believers in astrology do not seek to test their assertions with new observations as scientists do. When scientific predictions fail, scientists closely examine the theory that led to the false predictions. When astrological predictions fail, however, the theory behind the astrologers' predictions receives little examination. To the extent that astrology has been investigated scientifically, these investigations have almost uniformly found no scientific support for astrology (Crowe, 1990). In fact, 192 scientists, including 19 Nobel prizewinners, and many astronomers and physicists have disavowed astrology in a formal written statement (Bok, 1975).

You might say, "So what? Why worry about a little belief in astrology—it's just a harmless hobby." To illustrate potential consequences, let's imagine two possible scenarios. Suppose you were flying to another city; the pilot scheduled for your flight got sick and was replaced by a pilot who believed in astrology. Your new pilot is reluctant and frightened to fly the plane because his astrologer has advised him to avoid traveling. Would you want your pilot flying you in such a state of anxiety based on his unsubstantiated belief in astrology? As discussed in Chapter 10, the pilot's anxiety could interfere with his full concentration on important factors such as the weather and the state of the aircraft, factors that have been scientifically demonstrated to affect air safety.

Now, consider another scenario in which the president of the United States, the most powerful single person on the planet, regularly consults his astrologer to help decide when he will make appearances and important speeches, when he will have meetings with world leaders, and even what will be discussed at such meetings. In fact, Ronald and Nancy Reagan did consult with their personal astrologer before making these kinds of presidential decisions (Regan, 1988). The Reagans' interest in astrology went back at least to Ronald Reagan's time as governor of California. He is reported to have chosen to be sworn in for his first term as governor at just after midnight because an astrological reading had determined that this would be a propitious time (Donaldson, 1988).

In contrast, the critical thinker does not believe in "theories," like astrology, for which little good evidence exists. Instead, critical thinkers and scientists remain skeptical or at least cautious about such claims, carefully evaluating the relevant evidence in order to draw sound conclusions about such claims. To prepare you to do this, too, we will first define important critical thinking terms in more detail. Then, we will examine kinds of reasoning and the rules for drawing sound conclusions. Accompanying this discussion will be special exercises designed to help you acquire critical thinking skills. You should familiarize yourself with the terminology and rules for reasoning, but also make sure you do all the thinking exercises to get the practice you need.

How Does a Person Think Critically?

Basic Terminology

Suppose you are having a conversation about violence in our society. One of your friends says, "I think people today are very violent." Your friend is making an assertion or claim. An **assertion** is a statement claiming that someone or something has a particular characteristic or property. In this case, your friend has asserted that people have the characteristic of being violent. Claims and assertions are open to dispute and can be either true or false. It may or may not be true that people today are violent.

Like your friend, people make assertions all the time—in conversations, in newspapers, in the classroom. How are you to decide whether their assertions are true or false? One way you might decide is to take into account what other people think. Often, the truth value of an assertion depends on whether there is a consensus of opinion about it. A **consensus** of opinion occurs when there is general agreement about the truth or falsity of some claim. That many people share the same opinion as your friend might be a reason to believe your friend's assertion. Another reason for believing as assertion might be that it is based on fact. A **fact** is a commonly observed event that is taken as actual and not likely to change. A third reason for believing an assertion might be that research evidence or systematic observation supports the claim that people are violent.

Each of these reasons—consensus, fact, and research—is a kind of evidence. As such, each is a reason that might be offered in support of a claim or conclusion. Some kinds of evidence are better than others. Psychologists and other scientists especially value research evidence. You should note, however, that offering any of these kinds of evidence in support of a claim does not guarantee that it is correct.

≋ PRACTICE YOUR THINKING 1.1

Deciding on Truth Values

As noted above, a basic characteristic of assertions is that they have truth value: They can be judged as true or false. In some kinds of reasoning, like deductive reasoning, examining the truth value of statements is part of deciding whether an argument is sound. To give you some practice in deciding whether a statement should be taken as true, look at each of the following statements, and then label it as either true or false, noting your reasons.

1.   If a person has too many negative thoughts about himself or herself, then he or she will be depressed.

2.   Children are just little adults—essentially smaller versions of adults, who have not grown up yet.

3.   The more you study, the more you will learn.

4.   Psychology is the scientific study of behavior and mental processes.

Answers to Deciding on Truth Values

1.   True. You may have observed that thinking negative thoughts makes you feel depressed. Also, according to Beck's cognitive theory of depression (Beck, 1963) and research supporting it (Velten, 1968), excessive negative thoughts do lead to depression.

2.   False. Though a popular idea among many in the 19th century, Piaget and most other developmental psychologists would disagree with this statement. Children differ considerably from adults in their cognitive abilities and personality traits (Bjorklund, 1989).

3.   True. You probably know from your own experience that when you study more, you can learn and remember better. Research has also consistently demonstrated the benefits of study time for learning. This idea, called the total time hypothesis, is one of the older ones in the study of learning and memory (Baddeley, 1990).

4.   True. There is a consensus among psychologists about this definition of psychology, at least as evidenced in many psychology textbooks (e. g., Goldstein, 1995; Sdorow, 1993; and Wade and Tavris, 1996).

Returning to the example of your conversation with a friend about violence, if you examine your friend's statement more closely, you will notice that your friend has only made a claim or stated an assertion. He has offered no evidence in support of that claim. Perhaps your friend has simply forgotten to provide you with the evidence; or perhaps the claim is simply your friend's opinion. In either case, your friend has not made an argument, and you should not be persuaded by what he has said. He has not made an argument because he has not offered both a conclusion and its supporting evidence.

In the context of reasoning and critical thinking, we define an **argument** as a conclusion together with the evidence supporting it. Often, when we hear the word *argument* in everyday conversation, we think of people yelling at each other in a heated dispute. When we say that a critical thinker makes an argument, however, we mean simply that the critical thinker is making an assertion that is supported by evidence. The next time one of your teachers asks you what you think, include in your answer not just an assertion about what you believe, but also a good reason to support your assertion. Many teachers, especially those who emphasize critical thinking, appreciate this kind of answer.

≋ PRACTICE YOUR THINKING 1.2

Distinguishing Arguments from Nonarguments

In order to analyze and make arguments, you must first be able to distinguish arguments from nonarguments. See whether you can identify which of the following statements is an argument. (Simply write "yes" if the statement is an argument, or "no" if it is not, after each example.

1. The storage capacity of short-term memory is seven plus or minus two bits of information.

2. Because Mary felt very anxious just seeing a picture of a snake, her behavior therapist decided she had a phobia (irrational fear) of snakes.

3. After observing many young children trying to solve the problem, the developmental psychologist concluded that only older children and adults could solve the problem.

4. Emotions are motivated states associated with subjective experiences such as feelings, expressive behaviors such as frowning, and physiological arousal such as increased heart rate.

5. John Watson said that science requires observation of events that can be verified, but that mental states are not directly observable. Therefore, psychologists should study only behavior, not mental states, since mental states are not directly observable.

Answers to Distinguishing Arguments from Nonarguments

1. No   2. Yes   3. Yes   4. No   5. Yes

When trying to decide whether an argument has been made, it is often useful to try to locate words from the language of argumentation in the set of statements you are examining. The appendix provides an extended list of words from the language of argumentation that we will use to help identify the parts of arguments and to make arguments throughout this book. For example, in the fifth statement, the word *therefore* marks the point at which a conclusion follows. The fifth statement also contains a reason; together the premise and conclusion make an argument. In the second statement, the word *because* signals that a reason has been provided. If a conclusion is found with the reason—as it is in the second statement—then this statement is an argument. The first and fourth statements do not contain both reasons and conclusions together, so they are not arguments.

When we encounter well-formed arguments in discussions of psychological questions, in political debates, in trials, and in many everyday situations, we find evidence presented for more than one side of a question or position. In such exchanges, after one side and its supporting evidence have been presented, another side of the question will be presented with evidence that is inconsistent with the first position. This second claim and the accompanying evidence running counter to or disagreeing with the first claim are referred to as a **counterargument.** For example, suppose you are at a party talking to someone and your friend Bill bumps into you, knocking your drink over. You might say, "Bill is always clumsy," concluding that it was Bill's fault. Then another friend, Wendy, says, "No, it wasn't his fault; I saw the whole thing, and Marcia slipped and bumped into Bill, who then bumped into you." In this argument, the conclusion that it was Bill's fault is supported by the reason that Bill is always clumsy. The other position, that Bill did not cause your drink to spill, is supported by evidence inconsistent with the conclusion that it was Bill's fault.

Converging research suggests that the ability to find and make counterarguments is a hard skill to acquire. In the research on confirmation bias, we have seen that people often fail to adequately consider evidence that does not support the positions they favor. Researchers have also found that children acquire skills of argumentation in stages, with the ability to recognize and use counterarguments developing relatively late (Coirier & Golder, 1993). In fact, the research on individual differences in jurors' reasoning about a trial showed that some jurors consider only one position in an argument (Kuhn, Weinstock, & Flaton, 1994). Taken together, these various lines of research suggest that people need to practice identifying and using counterarguments. In this chapter we will practice identifying counterarguments, and in Chapter 14 we will practice writing counterarguments.

≋ PRACTICE YOUR THINKING 1.3

Identifying a Counterargument

Suppose two people are discussing the question whether people are basically selfish (which is discussed at more length in Chapter 3). One says that people are not basically selfish, offering examples to illustrate this. For instance, there's the case of Lenny Skutnik, a bystander at the scene of an air crash in the Potomac River in the middle of winter, who imperiled his own life by repeatedly diving into the frigid waters to save some of the passengers. However, people may actually help others for selfish reasons, as in a story told about Abraham Lincoln. He is said to have ordered the train he was riding to stop so that some drowning pigs he saw out the window could be saved. His motive, though, was to avoid having a guilty conscience over the matter (Batson, Bolen, Cross, & Neuringer-Benefiel, 1986).

In the spaces provided below, write the claim of the main position and the evidence supporting it and then the position of the counterargument along with the evidence supporting it.

Argument

Claim: _____

Evidence: _____

Counterargument

Other position: _____

Its evidence: _____

Answers to Identifying a Counterargument

Argument

Claim: *People are basically unselfish.*

Evidence: *The example of Lenny Skutnik, a bystander, who risked his life to help others.*

Counterargument

Other position: *People are basically selfish and help others in order to avoid feeling guilty themselves.*

Its evidence: *Abraham Lincoln helped the pigs in order to avoid feeling guilty.*

Kinds of Reasoning

Reasoning is the basic tool the critical thinker uses to come to a conclusion. Psychologists and thinkers in all disciplines use reasoning to help them think more clearly about the questions they ask and to advance the state of their knowledge. Reasoning is a powerful tool in this inquiry process because it prescribes conventional ways for us to use language so that arguments can be communicated clearly and analyzed consistently and effectively. In particular, reasoning provides us with rules for relating evidence to conclusions.

Two kinds of reasoning, inductive and deductive reasoning, are commonly used in psychology and other disciplines. In **inductive reasoning,** one reasons from specific cases to a general principle. For example, a brain scientist makes repeated observations of people with schizophrenia, a severe mental disorder involving thought disturbances such as hallucinations and delusions. She observes that schizophrenics have too much of a certain brain chemical called dopamine. The brain scientist reasons from these specific cases to the general theory that too much dopamine causes people to have the symptoms of schizophrenia.

In **deductive reasoning,** one proceeds in the other direction, reasoning from general principles to specifics. For example, a psychologist may reason deductively from the general theory that schizophrenia is caused by too much dopamine to a conclusion about a specific person, John. The psychologist concludes that if John has too much dopamine in certain areas of his brain then he will show symptoms of schizophrenia, such as thought disturbance.

While each kind of reasoning has somewhat different applications and rules, both of them use evidence to draw sound conclusions about claims. We will examine how each type of reasoning is carried out, in turn, with special attention to their use in psychology. Let's begin with deductive reasoning.

Conditional Deductive Arguments and Prediction

Deductive reasoning is used frequently for testing theories in psychology and other sciences. In psychology, "a **theory** is a set of general principles that attempt to explain and predict behavior or other phenomena" (Myers & Hansen, 1996, p. 24). Often, a theoretical prediction is put into the form of a conditional (if . . . then) deductive argument. Based on deductive reasoning from a theory, one can predict the future results of experiments and case studies.

For example, for more than 100 years it has been thought that an area called Broca's area, usually in the left frontal lobe of the brain, regulates speech production. This area was named in honor of Paul Broca, a 19th-century French neurologist who studied people with aphasia—that is, brain damage that results in language disturbances. One of his unfortunate patients with brain damage in this area was called Tan, because no matter what he tried to say it came out "tan" or "tan-tan" or "tan-tan-tan," over and over again. According to Broca's theory, this serious difficulty in producing meaningful speech is a kind of aphasia due to damage in the left frontal region of the brain (Broca, 1966).

One kind of deductive argument, called the conditional argument, is especially useful for making predictions from a theory in scientific thinking. Let's examine the following conditional deductive argument based on Broca's theory to illustrate the form of this type of argument. The conventional form of a **conditional argument** contains at least three statements. The first two statements are called **premises.** The premises of a conditional argument are divided into two parts: one called the antecedent, which goes first, often preceded by the word *if;* and a second part, the consequent, which follows and is often preceded by the word *then.* The final statement is the **conclusion,** which should logically follow from the premises. A conclusion drawn from the premises is also called an **inference.** You can see these parts illustrated in the following conditional deductive argument. The first premise is a statement of Broca's theory in "if . . . then" form. The second premise asserts that the antecedent is true for the specific case of Bill. The third statement connects the specific form of the antecedent with a specific form of the consequent in a logical conclusion. Like other kinds of deductive arguments, reasoning in the following example proceeds from the general statement in the first premise to a specific case in the conclusion.

Premise 1: If Broca's area is destroyed (**antecedent**), then speech production will be disturbed (**consequent**).

Premise 2: Broca's area in Bill's brain has been destroyed.
Conclusion: Therefore, Bill's speech will be disturbed.

When we evaluate this argument, we see that it is a **sound,** or good, argument, because it follows correct logical form and because both the premises are true and lead to a true conclusion. If speech production is disturbed when Broca's area is destroyed and if the Broca's area in Bill's brain is destroyed, then it must be true that Bill's speech will be disturbed.

When a true conclusion must necessarily follow from true premises, then we say that the argument is **valid.** In this example, the premises lead to the certain, deductive conclusion that Bill's speech will be disturbed. The valid form in this argument is called asserting the antecedent, because the antecedent of the first general premise is restated again in specific form. Deductive arguments take other valid forms besides this one, as well as invalid ones. We have focused on asserting the antecedent because it is the form used most in making predictions. For more information on valid and invalid forms of argument in deductive reasoning, the interested reader should consult Neimark (1987) or Zechmeister and Johnson (1992).

The example of Bill makes it easy to see how the conditional "if . . . then" form could be used to make a prediction. The *if* term introduces some condition that, when it is present beforehand (or in other words is an antecedent), leads to some specified result or consequent event. In other words, the antecedent predicts the consequent: *If* Broca's area in Bill's brain has been destroyed, *then* Bill's speech will be disturbed.

Conditional deductive reasoning allows researchers to test general theories by making specific predictions from them in the form of "if. . . . then" statements. Specific predictions made from a general theory are often referred to as hypotheses. A **hypothesis** is an educated guess about what will happen if we assume that certain conditions are present. For example, from the general theory that the amount of practice determines the amount of learning, we could hypothesize that *if* you study the material in your psychology course, *then* you will do well on your next exam (a test of your learning).

We can also use conditional deductive reasoning to make predictions about the outcomes of experiments designed to test hypotheses deduced from general theories. We could, for example, make a prediction about two groups differing in their amounts of study time, once again based on the theory that the amount of practice affects the amount of learning. Suppose that one group of subjects studied a list of words for ten minutes and another group studied the list for only one minute. What might we predict about each group's recall of the word list? Given that practice improves learning, we would predict that if a group studied ten minutes, then they would recall more words than a group that studied one minute.

≈ PRACTICE YOUR THINKING 1.4

Generating Hypotheses Through Deduction

To give you some practice at generating hypotheses from theories, look closely at each of the two theories that follow, and then think of a specific prediction you could make from each situation described to you. Put each of your hypotheses into "if…then" form in the spaces provided.

1. *Social Learning Theory of Aggression.* Bandura and Walters' (1959) social learning theory of aggression states that people learn how to behave in a particular way by observing other people engage in those behaviors. For example, individuals who observe others acting aggressively will themselves behave aggressively.

Based on social learning theory, make a prediction about how aggressively each of two groups will behave after one watches a violent hockey game and another watches professional bowling.

If _____

then _____

2. *Lorenz's Drive Theory of Aggression.* Lorenz (1966) proposed that humans have evolved an instinctual drive for aggression. Furthermore, because humans have few mechanisms to keep their aggressive drive in check, aggressive drive can build up to dangerous levels and then be released in violent behavior. According to Lorenz, however, dangerous aggressive drive can be drained off before an individual becomes violent by the individual observing certain events, as when spectators watch competitive sporting events, especially aggressive ones.

Based on Lorenz's drive theory, make a prediction about how aggressively each of two groups will behave after one watches a violent hockey game and another watches professional bowling.

If _____

then _____

Compare and contrast your predictions based on the first and second theories.

Answers to Practice in Making Predictions from Theories

1. According to Bandura's social learning theory of aggression, it would be expected that if people watch a violent hockey game, then they will later behave more aggressively than people who watch professional bowling.

2. According to Lorenz's drive reduction theory of aggression, if people watch an aggressive sporting event, their aggressive drive will be released and they will not become aggressive.

Notice that these two theories make opposite predictions concerning the observation of aggressive displays in sports, and so it should be possible to test both theories to see which one is supported by setting up an experiment in which one group observes violent behavior and another group observes nonviolent behavior. Most of the research has shown that observing an aggressive display or engaging in an aggressive display leads a person to further aggression (Buck, 1988). This research has fueled much concern about the dangers of viewing violence on television. On the other hand, as we will see in Chapters 3 and 14, observing a person help someone else will also lead to increases in the observer's helping behavior.

Making Assumptions and Arguing from a Perspective

Understanding and evaluating arguments would be much easier if people always stated all the premises they use in arguments. However, people frequently make assumptions in arguments; that is, they often take for granted that some premise not explicitly stated in their argument is true (Reese, 1980). The ability to identify **assumptions** is important to the ability to evaluate arguments fully. If a person makes an unwarranted assumption—that is, one that lacks reasonable justification—then that assumption may lead to a wrong conclusion. Unfortunately, there is evidence that college students are not very good at identifying assumptions in arguments (Keeley, 1992).

Let's examine an example of an assumption made in a conditional argument about the psychoanalytic notion that people repress or push unpleasant memories out of conscious awareness.

> If a person has a traumatic experience as a child, then he or she will not be able to recall it later. Jenny vomited in front of her third-grade class. When asked about the experience as an adult, she could not recall it.

Based on the psychoanalytic concept of repression, this argument appears sound. The argument has the same kind of valid form that the earlier one did. Recall that when a deductive argument has a valid form, and its premises are true and lead to a true conclusion, then the argument is sound. In this argument we assume that vomiting in front of one's class as a child is a traumatic experience. But suppose this assumption were not true: What if Jenny's vomiting was not traumatic? Perhaps Jenny did not find the experience to be traumatic because several children in her class had already gotten sick and the other students felt sorry for her. Unless we questioned this assumption, we might mistakenly conclude that Jenny could not recall her experience because it was traumatic.

≋ PRACTICE YOUR THINKING 1.5

Identifying Assumptions in Arguments

To give you more practice, find the assumption or assumptions made in each psychological argument below. Then fill in the assumption so that the argument can be analyzed.

1. Jerry could not recall the phone number from memory because he did not recite the number to himself after he heard the operator read it to him. If people do not mentally rehearse or repeat new information to themselves, then they will not be able to retrieve the information from storage in memory.

Assumption 1: _____

_____

2. If teachers clearly communicate their expectations about how to succeed, then students will be more successful. Katie tried very hard to raise her grade in Spanish, but her teacher did not make her expectations very clear, and so her grade continued to fall.

Assumption 2: _____

_____

Answers to Identifying Assumptions in Arguments

1. The presence of the word *retrieve* suggests one assumption—that is, that the human mind is like an electronic computer. This computer analogy, comparing human thinking to the way a computer processes information, has been of fundamental importance to modern cognitive psychology. Note that the phone number is referred to as information and that recall is referred to as retrieval. The validity of this argument depends on the assumption that the human mind really does function much as a computer does. If the analogy fits and the premises are true, then this argument is both valid and sound.

2. At least three assumptions are made in the second argument. First, the obstacle that seems to lie between Katie's goal of doing well and her reaching that goal suggests that Katie has a problem, because a problem is defined as the presence of an obstacle between an initial state and the goal state (Mayer, 1991). It is further assumed that one wishes to remove such an obstacle. Another assumption is that the lack of clear expectations is the only obstacle between Katie and her goal, when in fact she may not be very talented in Spanish in the first place. A third assumption is that getting good grades means you are a successful student. If you substitute in as premises the assumptions that Katie wished to remove the obstacle to her success, that this was all that was keeping Katie from succeeding, and that good grades mean success, then you could more effectively analyze this argument.

You can check whether you have missed or forgotten the main points in Chapter 1 by trying to summarize the main points. After summarizing it for yourself, check your summary against the one that follows.

Summary

Chapter 1 provided examples and other evidence to suggest the need for critical thinking in everyday living and in the pursuit of new knowledge. Critical thinkers and scientists evaluate the evidence relevant to a claim in order to draw a sound conclusion. In other words, critical thinkers make and are persuaded by arguments—that is, conclusions supported by evidence. While people frequently use commonsense "theories" to explain behavior and other events without giving much consideration to the quality of those "theories," critical thinkers realize that some theories are better than others. Specifically, theories that can account for more of the evidence and that make better predictions are superior. Moreover, critical thinkers are skeptical of new claims for which little evidence or only low-quality evidence is provided, and they do not believe claims, such as those made by astrology, for which there is no good evidence.

This chapter also introduced two kinds of reasoning: inductive and deductive reasoning. Inductive reasoning involves reasoning from specific cases and events to a general rule or principle, such as a theory, whereas deductive reasoning involves reasoning from a general rule or principle to a specific case or event. As such, deductive reasoning is useful in reasoning from a theory to a prediction, in reasoning from a definition to an example, and in analyzing some formal arguments. Deductive reasoning is also useful in that it provides us with rules for deciding whether arguments are sound by first helping us to decide whether an argument follows valid form and then by helping us to decide whether a true conclusion follows from true premises. When an argument is sound, a true conclusion must necessarily follow from true premises. So, deductive reasoning allows us to draw conclusions with certainty because, in a sense, the conclusion is implied and contained within the premises. Many everyday arguments and those that psychologists often make, however, are more like inductive arguments, which involve much more uncertainty. We turn to this kind of argument in the next chapter. Note also that you can draw a wrong conclusion if you make incorrect assumptions or omit premises from an argument.

Review Questions

What is an opinion, and when is an opinion a problem for critical thinking?

What is evidence? What is its place in critical thinking?

What is critical thinking?

From a psychological perspective, what does it take to become a critical thinker?

Why is critical thinking important, and why do we need it?

What is a theory, and what makes a good one?

What are commonsense or folk "theories," and which ones are correct?

Does an evaluation of the evidence support belief in astrology?

Why do people persist in believing false theories?

What is confirmation bias?

What is pseudoscience?

What are the basic critical thinking terms?

What is an assertion?

What is truth value and how do you decide on it?

What is an argument?

Can you distinguish an argument from a nonargument?

What is a counterargument?

Can you find a counterargument in a discussion?

How do inductive and deductive reasoning differ?

What is a conditional deductive argument, and what is it used for?

What are premises?

What is a conclusion? What is an inference?

What is a sound deductive argument?

Can you make predictions (generate hypotheses) using deduction?

What are assumptions, and can you find them?

References

Asimov, I. (1989). The relativity of wrong. *Skeptical Inquirer, 14*, 35–44.

Baddeley, A. (1990). *Human memory: Theory and practice.* Boston: Allyn & Bacon.

Bandura, A., & Walters, R. H. (1959). *Adolescent aggression.* New York: Ronald Press.

Batson, C. D., Bolen, M. H., Cross, J. A., & Neuringer-Benefiel, H. E. (1986). Where is the altruism in the altruistic personality? *Journal of Personality and Social Psychology, 50*, 212–220.

Beck, A. (1963). Thinking and depression. *Archives of General Psychiatry, 9*, 324–333.

Bensley, D. A., Bolton, M., Palardy, B., Brooks, J., & Langan, D. (1995, April). *Assessing instruction with tests of scientific and critical thinking.* Paper presented at the 66th annual meeting of the Eastern Psychological Association, Boston.

Bensley, D. A., & Haynes, C. (1995). The acquisition of general purpose strategic knowledge for argumentation. *Teaching of Psychology, 22*, 41–45.

Bjorklund, D. F. (1989). *Children's thinking.* Pacific Grove, CA: Brooks/Cole.

Bok, B. J. (1975). A critical look at astrology. In B. Bok & L. Jerome (Eds.), *Objections to astrology* (pp. 21–33). Buffalo, NY: Prometheus Books.

Broca, P. (1966). Paul Broca on the speech center. In R. Herrnstein & E. Boring (Eds.), *A source book in the history of psychology* (pp. 223–228). Cambridge, MA: Harvard University Press.

Buck, R. (1988). *Motivation and emotion* (2nd ed.). New York: Wiley.

Coirier, P., & Golder, C. (1993). Writing argumentative text: A developmental study of the acquisition of supporting structures. *European Journal of Psychology of Education, 8,* 116–180.

Crowe, R. A. (1990). Astrology and the scientific method. *Psychological Reports, 67,* 163–191.

Donaldson, S. (1988, May 8). Excerpts from a discussion of Reagan and astrology on ABC's *This Week with David Brinkley.*

Ennis, R. H. (1987). A taxonomy of critical thinking dispositions and abilities. In J. Baron & R. Sternberg (Eds.), *Teaching thinking skills: Theory and practice.* New York: W. H. Freeman.

Frazier, K. (1992). Who believes in astrology and why? *Skeptical Inquirer, 16,* 345–347.

Glaser, E. M. (1985). Critical thinking: Education for responsible citizenship in a democracy. *National Forum, 65,* 24–27.

Goldstein, B. (1995). *Psychology.* Pacific Grove, CA: Brooks/Cole.

Halpern, D. F. (1993). Assessing the effectiveness of critical thinking instruction. *Journal of General Education, 42,* 238–254.

Halpern, D. F. (1996). *Thought and knowledge: An introduction to critical thinking* (3rd ed.). Hillsdale, NJ: Lawrence Erlbaum.

Keeley, S. M. (1992). Are college students learning the critical thinking skill of finding assumptions? *College Student Journal, 26,* 316–322.

Keeley, S. M., Browne, M. N., & Kreutzer, J. S. (1982). A comparison of freshmen and seniors on general and specific tests of critical thinking. *Research in Higher Education, 17,* 139–154.

Kohn, A. (1990). *You know what they say.* New York: Harper Collins.

Kuhn, D. (1993). Connecting scientific and informal reasoning. *Merrill-Palmer Quarterly, 39,* 74–103.

Kuhn, D., Weinstock, M., & Flaton, R. (1994). How well do jurors reason? Competence dimensions of individual variation in a juror reasoning task. *Psychological Science, 5,* 289–296.

Kurtz, P., & Fraknoi, A. (1985). Tests of astrology do not support its claims. *Skeptical Inquirer, 9,* 210–211.

Kyle, R. (1995). *The New Age movement in American culture.* Lanham, MD: University Press of America.

Langer, J. A., & Applebee, A. N. (1987). *How writing shapes thinking: A study of teaching and learning.* Urbana, IL: National Council of Teachers of English.

Leahey, T. H., & Leahey, G. E. (1983). *Psychology's occult doubles: Psychology and the problem of pseudoscience.* Chicago: Nelson-Hall.

Lipman, M. (1991). *Thinking in education.* Cambridge, England: Cambridge University Press.

Lord, C. G., Ross, L., & Lepper, M. R. (1979). Biased assimilation and attitude polarization: The effects of prior theories on subsequently considered evidence. *Journal of Personality and Social Psychology, 37,* 2098–2109.

Lorenz, K. (1966). *On aggression.* New York: Harcourt Brace Jovanovich.

Mahoney, M. J. (1977). Publication prejudices: An experimental study of confirmatory bias in the peer review system. *Cognitive Therapy and Research, 1,* 161–175.

Mayer, R. E. (1991). *Thinking, problem solving, cognition* (2nd ed.). New York: Freeman.

Meehl, P. E. (1956). Wanted—a good cookbook. *American Psychologist, 11,* 263–272.

McKinnon, J. W., & Renner, J. W. (1971). Are colleges concerned with intellectual development? *American Journal of Psychology, 39,* 1047–1052.

McPeck, J. E. (1981). *Critical thinking and education.* New York: St. Martin's Press.

Myers, A., & Hansen, C. (1996). *Experimental Psychology* (4th ed.). Pacific Grove, CA: Brooks/Cole.

National Assessment of Educational Progress (1981). *Reading, thinking, and writing.* Denver: Education Commission of the States.

Neimark, E. D. (1987). *Adventures in thinking.* San Diego: Harcourt Brace Jovanovich.

Nickerson, R. S., Perkins, D. N., & Smith, E. E. (1985). *The teaching of thinking.* Hillsdale, NJ: Erlbaum.

Paul, R. (1984). Critical thinking: Fundamental to education for a free society. *Educational Leadership, 42,* 4–14.

Perkins, D. N. (1985). Postprimary education has little impact on informal reasoning. *Journal of Educational Psychology, 77,* 562–571.

Perkins, D., Jay, E., & Tishman, S. (1993). Beyond abilities: A dispositional theory of thinking. *Merrill-Palmer Quarterly, 39,* 1–21.

Randi, J. (1987). *Flim-flam.* Buffalo, NY: Prometheus Books.

Regan, D. T. (1988). *For the record.* San Diego: Harcourt Brace Jovanovich.

Reese, W. L. (1980). *Dictionary of philosophy and religion.* Atlantic Highlands, NJ: Humanities Press.

Rips, L. J., & Conrad, F. G. (1989). Folk psychology of mental activities. *Psychological Review, 96,* 187–207.

Rotton, J., & Kelly, I. (1985). Much ado about the full moon: A meta-analysis of lunar-lunacy research. *Psychological Bulletin, 97,* 286–306.

Sdorow, L. M. (1993). *Psychology.* Madison, WI: Brown & Benchmark.

Stanovich, K. E. (1994). Reconceptualizing intelligence: Dysrationalia as an intuition pump. *Educational Researcher, 22,* 11–21.

Stanovich, K. E. (1996). *How to think straight about psychology* (4th ed.). New York: HarperCollins.

Swenson, S., & White, K. (1995). A content analysis of horoscopes. *Genetic, Social, and General Psychology Monographs, 121,* 5–38.

Ulrich, R. E., Stachnik, T. J., & Stainton, N. R. (1963). Student acceptance of generalized personality descriptions. *Psychological Reports, 13,* 831–834.

Velten, E. (1968). A laboratory task for the induction of mood states. *Behavior Research and Therapy, 6,* 473–482.

Wade, C., & Tavris, C. (1993). *Critical and creative thinking: The case of love and war.* New York: HarperCollins.

Wade, C., & Tavris, C. (1996). *Psychology* (4th ed.). New York: HarperCollins.

Zechmeister, E. B., & Johnson, J. E. (1992). *Critical thinking: A functional approach.* Pacific Grove, CA: Brooks/Cole.

Inductive Reasoning and the Analysis of Psychological Arguments

Learning Objectives

1. To find out how critical thinkers and scientists use inductive reasoning, hypothetico-deductive reasoning, and causal reasoning to answer their questions.

2. To be familiar with the strengths and weaknesses of various kinds of evidence used in everyday and in scientific reasoning, such as anecdotes, statements of authorities, common sense, and evidence from research methods such as case studies, field studies, correlational studies, and experiments.

3. To learn how to evaluate inductive arguments used in the science of psychology and in everyday explanations.

What Do You Think?

You have most likely heard stories of people with psychic powers who claim to be able to predict the future accurately. Others claim to be able to communicate outside of their ordinary perceptual abilities through extrasensory perception (ESP), as in telepathy. Do you believe that there is such a thing as ESP?

Like most people, you probably have your own opinion on this question. But how are you to know whether your opinion is right? A recent national survey showed that 49% of the U.S. public believe in ESP, whereas 29% do not (Gallup & Newport, 1991). People are frequently mistaken in their opinions, however. That more people believe in ESP than do not does not mean that it exists. How are we to decide whether people actually can have ESP?

In this chapter, we will examine how we can use inductive reasoning and the methods of science to investigate this question. We will also apply these methods in this and the next chapter to address another controversial question, whether people are basically selfish. What do you think? Before examining these fascinating questions, let's look at where theories and hypotheses come from, in general.

Where Do Theories Come From?

In the last chapter we saw that scientists use theories to address questions and that some theories can be shown to be better than others. We also saw how we could use deductive reasoning to reason from a general theory to a specific case to make a prediction. Specifically, we saw that one could predict from Broca's theory that an individual with damage to the left side of the brain in Broca's area would have a speech production problem.

But where did Broca's theory come from in the first place? Although some scientific theories arise through an individual's creative insight into a question or through thinking analogously about a similar problem, scientific theories often develop through reasoning about the meaning of many repeated observations (Tweeney, 1991). For example, Broca examined hundreds of cases of brain damage and sought to correlate various types of behavioral problems with damage to various areas of the brain. From these and other observations, he generalized that a specific area of the frontal lobe, usually on the left side of the brain, was responsible for the production of speech (Kolb & Whishaw, 1990). In **generalizing,** one draws a conclusion thought to be true of all cases of a particular type, based on consistency in the cases. Through inductive reasoning, Broca reasoned from specific cases of brain damage to the general principle that speech production depended on this area's being intact. This example illustrates how we use inductive reasoning to construct theories or general principles, which must be consistent with the specific facts, cases, phenomena, research findings, and other kinds of evidence for which they are supposed to account.

A Sample Inductive Argument

To illustrate inductive reasoning in more detail, let's examine an inductive argument, based in part on literature reviews by Halpern (1993, 1996), concerning the effectiveness of programs designed to foster critical thinking. As you read through the following inductive argument, ask yourself what general principle or theory is being induced from the evidence. Then make a mental note of any differences you observe between this inductive argument and the deductive arguments discussed in Chapter 1.

> Premise 1: Thinking skills programs like those developed in Venezuela have been found to improve students' abilities to present oral arguments and to answer open-ended essay questions (Herrnstein, Nickerson, de Sanchez, & Swets, 1986).
>
> Premise 2: Philosophy for Children, a thinking skills program for children, has been shown to improve children's reasoning (Institute for the Advancement of Philosophy for Children, n.d.).
>
> Premise 3: Students report that their thinking has improved following thinking skills programs (Dansereau et al., 1979).
>
> Premise 4: Some studies show that specific instructional variables thought to be related to critical thinking have produced better test performance on the Watson-Glaser Critical Thinking Appraisal (Bailey, 1979; Suksringarm, 1976).
>
> Premise 5: Some studies of specific instructional variables thought to be related to teaching critical thinking have shown that they produce no improvement in performance on the Watson-Glaser test (Beckman, 1956; Coscarelli & Schwen, 1979).
>
> Premise 6: Students trained in thinking skills programs have shown significant gains on tests of cognitive growth and development (Fox, Marsh, & Crandall, 1983).
>
> Premise 7: Specific programs designed to teach critical thinking in college students have produced significant gains on tests of critical thinking (Bensley, Bolton, Palardy, Brooks & Langan, 1995; Bensley & Haynes, 1995; Mentkowski & Strait, 1983; Tomlinson-Keasey & Eisert, 1977).
>
> Premise 8: Specific programs designed to teach critical thinking in college students resulted in no significant gains on tests of critical thinking (Tomlinson-Keasey, Williams, & Eisert, 1977).
>
> Conclusion: Critical thinking can be taught.

Evaluating an Inductive Argument

To analyze an inductive argument, one must evaluate a number of statements to see how they bear upon some conclusion. For example, inductive arguments, like the one above, are sometimes written in the form of premises. We may define **premises** as statements that make an assertion and that are offered as individual reasons supporting the conclusion that follows. We must carefully examine the evidence presented in each premise to evaluate the degree of support it provides for the conclusion. More specifically, before we can draw a conclusion in an inductive argument, we must evaluate both the *quality* of the evidence, or how good it is, and the *quantity* of the evidence, or how much evidence exists.

A number of factors must be considered in evaluating the quality of the evidence presented in the argument that critical thinking skills can be taught. Were the research studies done well? Is the evidence supporting the claim that thinking skills can be taught as good as the evidence that does not support this notion? What kinds of evidence support each side of the question? As we will see in the discussion that follows, some kinds of evidence provide better evidence for a claim than others. For example, the self-reports of students who say that a critical thinking class helped them to think more effectively are not as good evidence as the results of more objective tests of critical thinking, because sometimes people are unaware of the changes that occur in their thinking.

Another thing to consider in evaluating the quality of the evidence is whether the source offered was a primary or secondary source. A **primary source** is the original source of some information or idea, such as the original publication of a journal article reporting on research results. Sometimes, however, people cite something written about or commenting on the original work or idea, such as a literature review that reports and interprets results of research; this is a **secondary source.** When someone cites a secondary source without looking at the original source, the quality of this source depends on the quality of the analysis and interpretations of the secondary source. If the secondary source misinterpreted a research finding, then referring to this incorrect interpretation as evidence will make for poor-quality evidence. Unfortunately, errors in thinking and mistakes are sometimes passed along this way, from one author to another, so that the ideas or findings of the original source are misrepresented. Consequently, whenever possible, we should use original sources in our own arguments, and also consider this factor in judging the quality of other people's arguments.

The critical thinker should also ask questions about the quantity of the evidence that led to a particular inductive conclusion. How many studies supported the claim, and how many did not support it? If the evidence was from a research study, as in our example, how large were the samples that showed the positive effects of the thinking skills program?

A sound conclusion in an inductive argument depends, not only on evaluating the quality and quantity of the evidence, but also on whether the argument includes all the relevant evidence. Do any other similar studies show that thinking skills programs have not been effective? For example, efforts to show an increase in intelligence through instruction in critical thinking sometimes have been shown to be effective and sometimes have not. If intelligence is thought to be directly related to critical thinking, then this evidence also should be included in the inductive argument. In practice, evaluating all the relevant evidence is very difficult. One must be able to decide which studies are related to the question and which are not, and then be familiar with all the relevant studies. While this is a daunting task, some experts are able to do it, and we must simply do our best or rely on their expertise. In this book, much of the evidence has already been gathered for you in literature reviews; your job is primarily to evaluate the evidence presented.

In summary, when reasoning inductively, the scientist and critical thinker must decide whether a claim is supported based on an evaluation of the relative quality and quantity of all the evidence, both supporting and not supporting the claim. Moreover, one must also consider whether all relevant evidence has been examined in evaluating the argument.

Drawing Inductive Conclusions: The Need for Caution

Because the conclusion one draws in an inductive argument depends on the relative quality and quantity of the evidence, we often speak of an inductive argument as having a certain degree of strength based on the support the evidence provides for a particular conclusion. The evidence from an inductive argument may be more or less strong, but it never *proves* that a conclusion is true. As a result, we approach the conclusions we draw inductively as provisional or tentative, gathering more and better evidence as we proceed to address the question. From the previous discussion of whether critical thinking skills can be taught, we may conclude at this point that the bulk of the evidence supports the conclusion that critical thinking skills can be taught, but that conclusion has not been proved.

Comparing Inductive and Deductive Arguments

Recall that I asked you to look for differences between deductive and inductive reasoning. You probably have observed some. First of all, while a number of pieces of evidence in the premises may lead us to the conclusion that critical thinking skills can be taught, some evidence did not support this claim. Unlike a deductive argument, in which a conclusion must necessarily follow from premises that are assumed to be true, the conclusion in an inductive argument may be accepted even when its premises are not all certainly true. In the present example, whereas some studies have shown increases in critical thinking after implementing specific instructional variables, courses, and programs designed to teach critical thinking, other studies have shown no positive effect on critical thinking from these. At least some of these failures can be explained by the idea that developing critical thinking ability may take very specific and extensive training. For example, Tomlinson-Keasey and Eisert (1977) failed to show any effect of their training program after one year, but Tomlinson-Keasey, Williams, and Eisert (1977) showed a significant effect after two years of training. In other words, while not all of the premises were true in the previous example, we may still be willing to conclude that critical thinking skills can be taught using inductive reasoning, especially if we can explain some of the negative evidence.

A second important difference between deductive and inductive arguments is that in deductive reasoning, if the argument was valid and all the premises were true, we are certain of our conclusion; in inductive arguments, we are typically much less certain. So using inductive reasoning, we generalize that most of the evidence supports the idea that thinking skills can be taught, but we are not completely certain.

Negative evidence may lead us to be less certain of a conclusion; it may also indicate the limits of a theory. Although critical thinkers and scientists try to develop theories that are as general as possible, negative evidence that is consistently obtained may indicate specific conditions under which the theory does not apply (Garnham & Oakhill, 1994).

Commonsense "Theories" and the Need for Caution

Because the commonsense "theories" that people use in their everyday reasoning about human behavior are often not supported by evidence, the scientist and critical thinker take a cautious approach to the claims people make. To illustrate, let's examine a very prevalent theory for explaining unusual events—that is, the theory that people have psychic powers such as ESP. Many individuals believe in ESP. For example, recently 80% of Canadian college students and 67% of U.S. students said they believed in ESP (Gilovich, 1991).

Often, however, as in the case of ESP, our personal "theories" and beliefs are supported by very little scientific evidence and instead are supported by much weaker forms of evidence. Gilovich (1991) has explored some of these kinds of evidence. For example, people may believe in ESP because of their own personal experiences of extraordinary coincidences. About two-thirds of people in the United States report that they have experienced ESP. Also, common sense is used as evidence when people hear stories from friends or others who have had premonitions that have come true. Another kind of evidence comes from the statements of so-called authorities, ranging from movie stars to scientists, who speak in favor of ESP. We also hear about extraordinary cases in the media or even research that provides evidence for ESP. But are all of these kinds of evidence equal in quality? For example, how do we know that precognition—the kind of ESP supposedly involved in knowing the future before it happens—is a good explanation for a premonition that someone had that was later confirmed? Turned around the other way, is a premonition that comes true good evidence for precognition?

One standard we frequently use to decide whether an explanation is a good one is plausibility. A **plausible** explanation is one that could conceivably account for some phenomenon using the usual assumptions we make when we are explaining. In other words, we first look for an explanation that could be true, given other things we already know about the world. We try to explain new phenomena with our established theories and knowledge before we start to consider more farfetched explanations. To illustrate, suppose you received a sealed envelope with a letter from someone who said he knew that an important event was going to occur during the next week. Then during the week, two jumbo 747 jets crash into each other, killing 583 passengers. Now, suppose that when you open the letter, the letter contains the prediction that two airplanes were going to crash in the next week. You would probably be amazed by the accuracy of this prediction. What would you conclude?

Would you conclude that the man has precognition? Many people so concluded when Lee Fried, a student at Duke University, sent such a letter, apparently predicting the air crash, to the university's president. After the successful prediction was reported, Fried admitted that he was a magician and that the successful prediction was actually a conjuring trick (Gilovich, 1991). Of 17 newspapers that covered the story, only 1 printed the plausible and correct explanation that the prediction was a trick (Randi, 1977).

This story makes three points. The first, obvious one is that people are easily fooled by tricks like these and readily offer ESP as an explanation. The second important point is that it is a good idea to eliminate other plausible explanations for apparently inexplicable events before we resort to supernatural or other extraordinary explanations. Precognition and other types of ESP violate what we know from ordinary physics; we should instead look for ordinary explanations, such as trickery, to explain ESP first, as Gendin (1981) noted. A third point to the story is that the media, by failing to report disconfirming evidence, helps to maintain a false belief in ESP among the general public (Gilovich, 1991). If the newspaper account is taken as a statement of authority, then doubts are raised about the quality of statements of authority as a kind of evidence.

Perhaps we should look to other kinds of evidence, such as scientific research, in investigating claims of ESP. Science is, at least in principle, committed to objective and impartial evaluation of all the relevant evidence. When we examine scientific research on ESP, however, we find that almost all research that supports ESP's existence has been of low quality or used fakery and fraudulent methods to obtain its results. Better-quality research has generally not supported the existence of ESP (Gilovich, 1991).

Much of the evidence for ESP comes from the statements of people who claim to be authorities and from accounts of personal experiences. This discrepancy in the evidence leaves us with the problem of deciding which evidence to believe. The argument for ESP would be stronger if better evidence supported it more consistently. Recently, more credible evidence for ESP has come from some experiments using a testing procedure from the study of perception called the Ganzfeld procedure (Bem & Honorton, 1994). More research is needed. Perhaps, if we better understood differences in the kinds of evidence people use, we would better know how to evaluate the evidence. The next section compares and contrasts these kinds of evidence in more detail.

The Critical Thinking Task

Critical thinkers and scientists often must use inductive reasoning to evaluate an argument. To do so they must evaluate conclusions they draw in terms of the quality and quantity of the evidence supporting those conclusions. The critical thinking task for inductive reasoning is summarized below; it should be committed to memory.

1. **Identify and understand the claim or question.**
2. **Gather, compare, and weigh the evidence relevant to the claim.**
3. **Draw a sound conclusion taking into account the quality and quantity of the evidence.**

Memorizing the steps of the critical thinking task is a good first step to help you improve your critical thinking, but you should also understand how to carry out these three steps. Look for opportunities to practice critical thinking in your everyday living and in your academic studies. To help you understand how quality and quantity of evidence affect the conclusions you draw, we will discuss each of these in turn.

Kinds and Quality of Evidence

We will begin by examining differences in six kinds of evidence commonly used in inductive arguments in psychology and in everyday reasoning with respect to their quality. These kinds of evidence are compared below, including their strengths and weaknesses. Accompanying this discussion, Table 2.1 summarizes the comparisons of these kinds of evidence.

Nonscientific Approaches and Evidence

Common sense consists of people's ordinary, unsystematic observations and experiences and the opinions offered to interpret these experiences. A statement of common sense proposes that "everyone knows" some claim is true. An example from social psychology should illustrate: When someone says, "Everyone knows that people are basically selfish," the person has supported the claim using common sense, or what people generally consider to be true. Of course, the claim may not be true. The majority have often been shown wrong. Moreover, the majority opinion about selfishness in a competitive country that emphasizes individualism, such as the United States, may differ from a majority opinion in a less competitive country. So while common sense has the advan-

TABLE 2.1

A comparison of potential strengths and weaknesses of some nonscientific and scientific sources of knowledge and evidence

Source	Strengths	Weaknesses
Common sense	Takes opinions of many people into account	Does not provide means of correcting incorrect opinion; cultural and perceptual bias
Anecdote	Provides a practical, familiar example	Example may be unique, not easily compared to other examples; report of example may be unreliable
Authority	When authority is an expert, then it may be informed by reason and experience	May be biased by personal or social beliefs; no means for correcting faulty beliefs
Reason (rationality)	Logical, rule-governed, consistent approach	Not corrected by experience
Experience (empiricism)	Can acquire new information through observation	Faulty perception can lead to wrong inferences; no way to evaluate and correct these
Science	Self-correcting through reason and experience	Can study only those phenomena and events that can be made observable

tage of taking many people's opinions into account, it provides no systematic means for examining these opinions or for correcting them if they are wrong.

Anecdotal evidence is based on examples, cases, or stories that illustrate a point or claim. As Stanovich (1996) noted, anecdotal evidence often starts out with a phrase such as "I know a man who . . .," which is followed by a case supporting some claim. For example, in a discussion of whether people are selfish, anecdotal stories about Mother Teresa's unselfish behavior might be provided as evidence.

Although anecdotal evidence can provide real-world examples relevant to claims, anecdotes have some serious limitations as evidence. First of all, the observations that led to the account may not be able to be produced or observed again. Therefore, the interpretation of the account is limited by the accuracy and completeness of the original observations. In addition, it is very difficult to completely account for other variables or events that may have been operating in the anecdotal situation but that were not observed. Because individual examples are unique to each case, there is no way to accurately compare them, so one cannot eliminate alternative explanations. For example, suppose that the anecdotal case of a man who gives all his extra income to charity is cited as an example of how unselfish people are. It is difficult however, to eliminate alternative explanations for the man's behavior, such as his desire to obtain a tax write-off or to be acclaimed as a philanthropist. Because of the uniqueness of anecdotes and the difficulty of reproducing them, anecdotes do not provide a good means for correcting incorrect ideas.

Statements of authority are frequently used as evidence. Appeals to authority assume that the person being treated as an authority is in a position to know important information relevant to the claim. For example, someone may claim that people are basically selfish based on the writings of some religious authority. The quality as evidence of statements of authority depends on the authority's knowledge and reliability and whether the authority's knowledge is relevant to the claim. For example, your car mechanic may be considered an authority on cars based on his or her extensive experience or training; but you probably would not go to your mechanic for an expert opinion on someone's behavior or personality.

Using authority as evidence has a number of potential disadvantages. For example, an authority's statements may be primarily based on unquestioned beliefs from the authority's culture or tradition. Also, authorities often disagree. Religious authorities disagree on the meaning of religious texts. Scientists disagree on the interpretation of research findings and theory. Who's right? If the statements of an authority are simply accepted without question or without regard for other evidence, then there is no good way to correct a belief when the authority is wrong.

A **rational** approach emphasizes the use of reasoning in explaining things. We have already examined some advantages of reasoning as an approach to knowledge. Recall that reasoning provides a systematic way of asking questions and rules for deciding whether claims are supported by evidence. Reasoning alone, however, cannot help us to arrive at sound conclusions if the reasons or premises we are arguing from are false or faulty. We need some way to correct our premises or obtain new information; reasoning alone does not provide the means.

An **empirical** approach can provide us with new information through the use of observation. We use our senses to take note of events and experiences that inform us about important conditions around us. An empirical approach provides us with new information; however, it does not provide the means for organizing and evaluating the observations that we make. Moreover, if mistakes in observation occur—such as through faulty perception—the empirical approach alone cannot help us to correct these mistaken notions.

Our comparison of these five kinds of nonscientific evidence has revealed that each has at least one advantage or strength, but that they all share similar weaknesses as approaches to knowledge. Not one of them provides an effective means for correcting mistaken ideas. The exercise that follows will give you practice at identifying these kinds of nonscientific evidence. Then we will examine science, a sixth approach to knowledge, that does provide an effective way to correct mistaken ideas.

≈ PRACTICE YOUR THINKING 2.1

Recognizing Kinds of Nonscientific Evidence

In each of the following, first identify the argument that is being made—that is, the assertion and the evidence in support of it. Then, identify the kind of evidence being used and write it in the space provided. Finally, think of a potential difficulty or limitation that each might present as a kind of evidence offered in support of a claim, and then write down the limitation.

1. During World War I, Albert Einstein, the most brilliant physicist of the 20th century, wrote letters to Sigmund Freud, the founder of psychoanalysis, arguing for peace and against the waste of life in the war.

Argument: _____

Kind of evidence: _____

Limitation: _____

2. At about the time of his correspondence with Einstein, Freud became increasingly persuaded of the view that humans have an instinct for aggression. Because Freud had great insights into human motivation, we should conclude that humans are instinctively aggressive.

Argument: _____

Kind of evidence: _____

Limitation: _____

3. In a discussion with my friend about whether mentally retarded people should be allowed to attend the same schools as people with normal intelligence, my friend said that they should not, because everyone knows that retarded people can't learn to read.

Argument: _____

Kind of evidence: _____

Limitation: _____

4. Sometimes, when people are sexually abused as children, they push the memory of the abuse outside of their awareness and can't remember the incident when they are adults. Then when they talk to a psychotherapist, the memory comes back. For example, my friend Linda was sexually abused by her stepfather when she was 4, but she couldn't remember it until she went to a psychologist at age 20.

Argument: _____

Kind of evidence: _____

Limitation: _____

Answers to Recognizing Kinds of Nonscientific Evidence

1. Argument: *We should not fight wars and waste lives.*

Kind of evidence: *authority*

Limitation: *Einstein was an expert in physics, not politics.*

2. Argument: *Human aggression is instinctive according to Freud.*

Kind of evidence: *authority*

Limitation: *Freud's ideas were speculative, not based on scientific research.*

3. Argument: *Mentally retarded people should not attend school with people of normal intelligence because the mentally retarded cannot learn how to read.*

Kind of evidence: *common sense*

Limitation: *This is based on unverified opinion and, in fact, is untrue.*

4. Argument: *People who are sexually abused as children cannot remember the experience later, because my friend Linda was sexually abused and she couldn't remember it.*

Kind of evidence: *anecdote*

Limitation: *This is only one case, which may be unique.*

Science as an Approach to Knowledge and Evidence

We have seen in our overview of nonscientific approaches to knowledge, summarized in Table 2.1, that none of these methods by itself provides a good way to correct mistaken ideas. Fortunately, there are approaches to knowledge that are **self-correcting**—namely, critical thinking and science. In both critical thinking and science, we examine the evidence relevant to some claim or hypothesis and then draw a sound conclusion from it. If we later discover that more or better evidence supports the other side of the argument, then we change our conclusion. Similarly, if we discover that our reasoning was faulty, then we also change our conclusion. Science is self-correcting because it combines rationality with an empirical approach to knowledge. A scientist makes observations under carefully controlled conditions and then reasons about the meaning of those observations. For the scientist, observation is the fundamental source of evidence; it is often through observation that faulty conclusions are corrected.

The scientist's goal in making observations and reasoning about their meaning is to find lawful relations among variables. A **variable** is a characteristic or event of interest that can take on different values. For example, a psychologist interested in selfish behavior may measure this by having a person rate herself on a selfishness scale ranging from 1, "not at all selfish," to 7, "extremely self-ish." Often, a scientist makes an educated guess about how one variable relates to another variable, called a hypothesis.

Hypotheses originate from different sources. As mentioned in Chapter 1, a hypothesis is often deduced from a theory in the form of a specific prediction: a claim about what will happen if we assume that some theory is true. For example, from the general theory that people are motivated by self-interest, we might predict that a person who has the opportunity to behave either selfishly or unselfishly in a new situation will behave selfishly. Hypotheses can also be formed through inductive reasoning from a set of observations, even if no the-ory has yet been proposed to explain the observations.

Regardless of its origins, a good hypothesis must be testable and falsifiable. For it to be **testable,** one must be able to make observations on the variables of interest. For example, if we could not find observable behaviors that reflected or indicated selfishness, then hypotheses about selfishness would be untestable. For a hypothesis to be **falsifiable,** it must be possible to make observations that would disconfirm it or show it to be wrong (Popper, 1961).

An interesting example of falsifiability comes from the study of ESP. Some parapsychologists have argued that the reason certain ESP experiments fail to show evidence for ESP is that interference from the skeptical observations of a nonbelieving scientist creates "negative vibrations." These disturb the subtle and fragile effects of ESP, so that it does not appear as long as the skeptical observer is present. Not only does this argument violate the principle of objec-tive observation that is so important to the conduct of science, but it also ren-ders the ESP hypothesis unfalsifiable. A failure to find evidence for ESP is not interpreted as disconfirming evidence for ESP, but as interference from the act of studying it. One could always raise this objection.

To test a hypothesis, a scientist must operationally define the variables under study. An **operational definition** involves the representation of variables in terms of methods, procedures, and measurements. For example, a psychologist testing a hypothesis about selfishness might operationally define a research par-ticipant as selfish when that person gets a certain score on a psychological inventory designed to measure the trait of selfishness. Similarly, selfish behav-ior might be operationally defined as unwillingness to help another person in need of help with homework. The specific hypothesis in this case predicts that a person with the selfishness trait would not likely help other people who need help with their homework.

In order to decide whether this hypothesis can be confirmed, a researcher would make systematic observations and measurements of the helping behavior of various individuals, quantifying these observations in the form of data to be analyzed and interpreted. Often, the researcher conducts statistical analyses of the data, using probability to estimate the likelihood of obtaining some research result by chance. **Probability** is "the likelihood that a particular event or rela-tion will occur" (Vogt, 1993, p. 178). Specifically, if a researcher found a very low probability that the observed difference between a selfish group and an unselfish group on helping was due simply to chance (for example, if fewer than 5 times out of 100, the difference was probably due to chance), then the researcher would conclude that the two groups do differ from what would be expected by chance. Such a difference is said to be **significant.** Researchers use probability to decide whether the observations they have made support particular hypotheses of interest. They base the decision on probability estimates of the likelihood of obtaining particular research results.

The significant results of one study are not enough to convince scientists to accept a particular hypothesis. Science assumes that observations made under the same or similar controlled conditions should be able to be **replicated,** or repeated. The results of a number of research studies in which the same or similar variables have been investigated then can be compared and offered as evidence in support of or against some theory. One way to examine the research evidence relevant to a question is to read a review of the literature. A **literature review** is a critical examination of the research and other evidence relevant to a particular hypothesis or theory. For example, a social psychologist might compare and evaluate the relevant research from the literature on selfish behavior to decide whether the claim that people are motivated primarily by their own self-interest is supported by the research.

When scientific research is used as evidence, consistency in the findings is sought. If most of the studies offer support for a hypothesis or theory and these studies have been done well, then by inductive reasoning we may tentatively conclude that the current evidence supports the theory. We would then accept the theory until more and better data come along. In this way, the quantity of evidence supporting one position versus another contributes to the inductive conclusion we draw. As we will see in the next section, however, the quality of the evidence is often an even more important factor in drawing inductive conclusions.

Causation and the Quality of Scientific Evidence

Like the nonscientific kinds of evidence we examined earlier, scientific research can also vary in quality. Because the methods of science involve using observation to test hypotheses and to evaluate theories, the quality of the evidence offered by scientific research depends on observations' being made with objectivity, without error, and under carefully controlled conditions.

The quality of the evidence provided by scientific research methods also depends on the degree to which a particular method is able to establish a causal relation between variables. Recall that as a science, the goals of psychology are to describe, predict, explain, and control or manipulate behavior. In order to reach the important goal of explaining behavior, we must be able to show the causes of behavior. When we speak of a cause, we are referring to something that has produced an effect, an event that led up to another event, or the reason something happened (Zechmeister & Johnson, 1992). To better understand how something might be the cause of a behavior, let's look closely at the **three criteria for establishing causation.** Note that a criterion is a standard that must be met or a condition that must be present in order to decide that something is true.

1. **Covariation: Two events must covary or change together.**
2. **Time order: One event must occur before the other.**
3. **Elimination of plausible alternative explanations: Other plausible explanations for the covariation must be eliminated.**

To illustrate the operation of each of these criteria in causation, let's return to the question of whether Lee Fried's ESP (precognition) caused his supposed correct prediction of the crash of the two 747s. First, to show that the covariation criterion was met, we would have to show that the operation of ESP varied with the event of the confirmed prediction. In other words, he had the premonition only with the event; when he did not make a prediction, there was no crash. Since the two events apparently occurred together in time, this suggests that covariation was present. Second, it initially appeared that the ESP did occur before the letter was delivered, although no other verification that ESP had occurred was demonstrated. Third, alternative explanations also appeared to be eliminated. A sealed letter, which would appear resistant to tampering, was sent to a public figure, lending credibility to the ESP explanation and dispelling the alternative explanation of cheating.

A closer examination of the events in this case, however, shows that none of the criteria was actually met. Two plausible alternatives were not checked. First, someone should have checked how many guesses of other events Fried had made. Frequently, fortunetellers guess a lot and so sometimes they are right, simply by chance. The second plausible explanation is that Fried engaged in trickery, which he eventually admitted. This potential explanation should have been checked before anyone concluded that ESP was the cause. For example, Fried might have had access to the letter after the crash had occurred—which apparently was the case. This fact suggests that he did not know about the crash until after it occurred, throwing time order into doubt. Only Fried's word supported the use of ESP, and he later recanted his claim that he used ESP.

Analysis of this example makes clear the virtual impossibility of demonstrating causation through an anecdote or a single case. Similarly, evidence based on a case study may be limited because a case study investigates the behavior of only a single individual; also the researcher often cannot control all the variables that may be having an effect on a subject. In general, case studies provide a detailed description of an individual life or problem. Although covariation of variables can sometimes be shown, it is much more difficult to show that one variable always goes before another. Frequently, it is even more difficult to eliminate other variables in the situation that could be having an effect besides the one that is supposed to be the cause. We call these other variables in the research situation that could provide alternative explanations extraneous variables.

Strengths and Weaknesses of Research Methods

Various research methods differ in the kind of information they can provide and in the quality of that information. In particular, the methods differ in the extent that extraneous variables are controlled and the degree to which causal inferences may be made using the methods. Table 2.2 shows the strengths and weaknesses of various commonly used research methods. One important idea in Table 2.2 is that only the experimental method allows the researcher to make a causal inference, because only in an experiment can all the criteria for causation be met. In the following, this and other strengths and limitations of each method will be briefly reviewed.

Survey research involves asking subjects questions. Surveys and questionnaires, while economical, are prone to a number of problems and limitations. For example, if researchers do not sample respondents in a way representative of the populations being studied, then it will be difficult to make a valid generalization from the respondents to the population. Also, respondents may not be honest in reporting their opinions or may not remember factual information accurately when asked. While covariation may be shown between one item and another, the other two criteria for causation may not be met. In particular, it is very difficult to control extraneous variables that could be affecting respondents' answers.

Field studies and naturalistic observation are methods that have the advantage of providing information collected in the natural environment and so avoid the artificiality of laboratory research. Since observed behaviors are simply part of a stream of behavior, however, it is difficult to establish the time order of behaviors and very difficult to eliminate other extraneous variables. Suppose you are observing a person for selfish behaviors in his natural environment. The person may be responding to a variety of situational variables, such as rewards for being generous, that are also affecting the apparently unselfish behavior.

Correlation allows one to find a quantitative relation between two or more variables. For example, a researcher might find a positive correlation between feelings of empathy and the willingness to help. In other words, as a person's feeling of empathy becomes stronger, so does a person's tendency to help. The example makes clear that empathy and the tendency to help are covarying; time order, however, is more difficult to establish. A person may first empathize with a person in need and then help; but the relation between the two variables may also be in the other direction. Helping other people may reinforce feelings of empathy, making helpers feel more connected to the suffering people they help. Other variables that cannot be controlled also may covary with variables in the correlation. For example, feelings of guilt may also covary with empathy and the tendency to help, so that the more a person helps, the less guilt he or she feels.

Correlation does allow one variable to be predicted from another and so has advantages over other evidence, like anecdotes, in which no prediction is possible. Correlation does not, however, allow us to make inferences about cause and effect. What we need is a method that allows us to manipulate one variable so that it comes before the other variable, allowing the time order criterion to be established.

TABLE 2.2

Comparison of potential strengths and weaknesses of some common scientific research methods

Method	Strengths	Weaknesses
Case study	Detailed description of individual; can be used to generate hypotheses	Based on only one subject; can't easily generalize to groups or all people; subjectivity, bias, error in observer's description; can't infer causation
Survey research	Economical method of gathering much information	Sampling and selection bias; problems of self-reporting, such as respondents' dishonesty or memory failure; can't infer causation
Field studies (naturalistic observation)	Observations made in natural environment; can be generalized to real world	Little control over extraneous variables; bias and differences in observers; can't infer cause and effect
Correlation	Allows for quantitative analysis of relations between variables	Can't control some extraneous variables; can't determine time order, so can't infer causation
Quasi-experiments	Allows comparison of groups; can control some extraneous variables	Can't truly manipulate independent variable and can't do random assignment; can't infer cause and effect
Experiment	Can control extraneous variables; can manipulate independent variable; can infer cause and effect	Conditions of observation are artificial; difficult to generalize to real-world situations

Experiments do allow us to make causal inferences because the manipulation and control of variables can allow the criteria of covariation and time order to be met. In an experiment, a researcher manipulates an **independent variable**—a variable that the researcher would like to be able to show has a causal effect on another variable, the dependent variable. The **dependent variable** is the measured variable; in psychological research, it is almost always some behavior. For example, in a true experiment one could create conditions that lead either to more helping or to less helping. Suppose a researcher wanted to test the hypothesis that people who think they alone are in a position to assist someone in need will be more likely to help than when they think other people also know about the person's need. An experimenter could quite easily vary the levels of the independent variable so that one group thought they alone knew about a person who was in need, such as someone having an epileptic seizure (Darley & Latané, 1968). Subjects in a second group would be led to believe that other people knew that the person was having a seizure. These two groups form the two levels of the independent variable. Having first manipulated this independent variable, the experimenter then looks to see the effect of this manipulation on the dependent variable. In this case, the dependent variable is the willingness to help the person in need. The independent variable has at least two levels, allowing us to observe a differential effect of it on the dependent variable. Because the two levels were presented before the dependent variable, the criterion of time order has been met. And because the independent variable was presented in association with the dependent variable and because the two groups differed significantly in their willingness to help, the criterion of covariation has been met.

Suppose that statistical comparison of the two treatments showed that subjects in the group who thought no other person knew of the person's problem tended to help more than those in the group who thought that other people knew about the problem. One might conclude that knowing that someone else was aware of a person's problem would make one less likely to help, through what Darley and Latané (1968) have called "diffusion of responsibility." The third criterion, the elimination of plausible alternatives, must also be met, however, before it can be shown that diffusion of responsibility caused people not to help.

The experimenter's goal is to show that the independent variable, and no other, had the effect on the dependent variable. When the experimenter has done so, the experiment is said to have **internal validity.** Experimental controls allow for the elimination of plausible alternative explanations other than the independent variable. It is assumed that good evidence for a claim comes from studies that control for or eliminate other competing explanations.

What if it was discovered, however, that the experimenter always tested members of the group who thought that other people were aware of the person's problem before testing members of the group who thought they alone were aware of the problem? Next, suppose that the participants in the study were volunteers, and those who signed up first for the experiment were the most eager to help. It might be concluded that they were already more likely to help because they were the first to volunteer for the study. In this case, the variable of time of volunteering is confounded with whether or not one was aware of the plight of the person needing help. A **confounding** variable is an extraneous variable that covaries with the independent variable and could also plausibly account for the changes in the dependent variable. Whenever an extraneous variable is confounded with the independent variable, the experiment's internal validity is threatened. In this case it becomes difficult for the experimenter to infer that it really was the independent variable—the number of people who were aware of the person' sproblem—and not the variable time of volunteering that was having the effect on the likelihood of helping. Therefore we cannot necessarily conclude that awareness that others know about a person's problem will lead to less helping. Fortunately, when experiments are designed well and set up correctly with appropriate controls, we are able to eliminate many, if not all, sources of confounding.

≈ PRACTICE YOUR THINKING 2.2

Identifying Variables in Experiments

In each of the following research examples, identify the independent variable and the dependent variable. Remember that an independent variable is the one manipulated by the experimenter. The dependent variable is a behavior that is free to vary and is measured by the experimenter.

1. An experimenter wanted to find out whether a study strategy involving putting list items into categories was more effective for learning a list of words than a strategy involving rote rehearsal. She had one group of randomly assigned subjects study words such as *chair, dog, rose, table, rabbit, carnation,* and *book* by putting the words into categories such as furniture and animals. The rote rehearsal group simply repeated the list words over and over to themselves. Both groups then recalled the words one week later.

Independent variable: _____

Dependent variable: _____

2. An experiment by Darley and Latané (1968) found that a person is more likely to help if alone than if part of a group. Suppose another experimenter wanted to replicate the study. She had an assistant drop a stack of books in the presence of individual students or in front of groups of students. Then, she kept track of whether or not a subject helped and whether that subject had been alone or in a group.

Independent variable: _____

Dependent variable: _____

Answers to Identifying Variables in Experiments

1. Independent variable: *kind of learning strategy*
   Dependent variable: *recall of list words*
2. Independent variable: *whether the subject was alone or in a group*
   Dependent variable: *whether or not someone helped pick up the books*

Quasi-experiments are similar to experiments, but unlike true experiments, do not allow the researcher to truly manipulate an independent variable. In quasi-experiments, subjects are not randomly assigned to conditions as in true experiments, but instead are selected, often on the basis of some preexisting characteristic. For example, using a quasi-experimental design, we might compare men and women on their willingness to help; however, by comparing men and women we have not truly manipulated an independent variable. We have simply selected male and female subjects to be in our conditions. The problem is that males and females might already differ from one another at the outset on a number of variables related to the willingness to help.

Because we cannot randomly assign subjects to treatment conditions in a quasi-experiment, we are unable to control some of the differences between subjects in our treatment groups the way we can in a true experiment. Moreover, without truly manipulating an independent variable, we cannot establish time order and so we are not able to draw causal inferences from quasi-experiments, as we can from true experiments. Like experiments, however, quasi-experiments can sometimes allow for control of extraneous variables. So, we could treat our two groups of subjects in an equivalent manner, testing them under similar conditions.

In summary, the manipulation of independent variables allows the experimenter to meet the criteria of covariation and time order, and the control of extraneous variables allows for meeting the criterion of the elimination of plausible alternatives. At least with regard to making a causal inference, therefore, the experimental method provides better-quality data than the case study, correlational study, or quasi-experimental study.

Note that a scientist, like a religious or other kind of authority, may make authoritative statements based on research findings that can be used as evidence in support of some claim. Just as a religious authority sometimes may be wrong, so may the scientist. The evidence offered by a scientific authority, however, may have more credibility, if indeed this evidence is based on repeated observations and sound reasoning about their meaning. If new research evidence does not support a claim, then a scientist may change his or her mind about the claim based on this new evidence. A scientific authority also may change his or her mind if there has been a mistake in the reasonable evaluation of the research evidence.

Nevertheless, the conclusions of scientific research are only as good as the quality of the evidence on which those conclusions are based. For example, if a scientist carrying out a research study was not really measuring what he or she intended or perhaps made errors in measurement, then conclusions based on that research data could be erroneous. Fortunately, science is self-correcting; the first scientist's errors can be discovered by other scientists seeking to replicate and make sense of the first scientist's observations.

≈ PRACTICE YOUR THINKING 2.3

Analyzing Research for Causal Relations

In the following examples, your task is to decide whether a conclusion based on the research results is warranted. To do so, you must evaluate the quality of the evidence based on the results presented and the research methods used. Only if all three criteria for causation are met should you conclude that a causal inference can be drawn from the example. To help you judge the quality of the evidence presented in each example, answer the following questions:

1. What kind of research methods were used? Ask yourself whether a variable has been manipulated. If comparisons are made between samples or subjects are randomly assigned to treatment groups, then the research probably is an experiment. If measures are simply taken on two variables, then the research is likely a correlational study.

2. What criteria for causation have been met?

3. How strong an inference can be made based on meeting these criteria? Also take into account other factors, such as sample size, that enhance or hinder this conclusion.

A. Do you like to take a break from your studying? If the answer is yes, then you may be doing something that actually makes your study time more efficient. Researchers examined the study habits of college students in an effort to investigate this question. In their study, they kept track of the learning of students who studied the same material over a one-week period. They also monitored the number of breaks that students scheduled and took for themselves. They found that students who took more scheduled breaks also tended to learn more, whereas students who had tended to take fewer scheduled breaks tended to have lower learning scores.

After hearing these results, Joe Student decided to take more study breaks the next time he studied for an exam. Is Joe's decision justified, based on the evidence presented in the preceding paragraph? Use the following questions to help you analyze and explain your answer.

A.1. What research method was used?_____

A.2. Which criteria were met?_____

A.3. How strong an inference can be made?_____

_____

_____

B. Recently, a research team claimed to have made a breakthrough in the nondrug treatment of children with attention deficit/hyperactivity disorder (ADHD). Previous treatment of such children often included administration of stimulant drugs such as Ritalin. Paradoxically, the drug treatment that stimulates the central nervous system of the ADHD children actually helps them to maintain focused attention on their schoolwork and other tasks and reduces some of their "hyperactive" symptoms. The treatment may have this effect because the ADHD children are underaroused; ordinarily, without medication, they seek to self-stimulate to maintain a higher level of arousal.

The new treatment involves teaching ADHD students how to arouse themselves with thoughts about how exciting their work is as they do schoolwork. The researcher randomly selected 60 students from a group of same-aged children diagnosed as having ADHD. She randomly assigned the subjects to two groups of 30 each, one that got the new concentration study procedure and another group that studied using their usual techniques. She pretested them on a learning task requiring sustained focused attention and then posttested them on the same task after treatment or after the same amount of time. All students were taught by the same teachers. In addition, the students were trained and tested during the summer because all the children were off their medication during the summer. The researcher found that the two groups did not differ significantly on the pretest, but the concentration group scored significantly higher on the learning test after treatment than the other group. She concluded that the treatment was effective.

Upon hearing these results, the school board concluded that the school district should implement the training program for all of its ADHD students of this age. Is their decision justified?

B.1.   What research method was used?_____

B.2.   Which criteria were met?_____

B.3.   How strong an inference can be made?_____

_____

_____

Answers to Analyzing Research for Causal Relations

A.1.   *Correlation between amount learned and number of study breaks.*

A.2.   *It meets only the covariation criterion.*

A.3.   *It would be a mistake for Joe to conclude that study breaks cause better learning. The relation may be in the other direction; students who learn well may tend to take more scheduled breaks, perhaps because they manage their study time better. If Joe is not already a good learner, then taking a break will not help.*

B.1.   *True experiment with the special treatment and usual study procedures as two levels of the independent variable. The dependent variable was performance on the learning test.*

B.2.   *The researchers have truly manipulated an independent variable. They controlled the students' level of functioning, and the same teachers taught the students—thus eliminating both these alternative explanations of the significant effect on the dependent variable.*

B.3.   *All three criteria for causation may have been met and so the school board may be justified in its action. While this treatment sounds effective, its positive effects should be replicated in another experiment before many resources are directed toward implementing the treatment.*

Quantity of Evidence

How strong an inductive inference can be made depends also on the **quantity** of evidence that supports or does not support a claim. The quantity of evidence is a factor in two ways. First, one must consider the number of studies supporting or not supporting a theory. Assuming that the quality of the studies is equal, if many more studies support a hypothesis or theory than do not, one is inclined to accept the hypothesis or theory until more or better evidence comes along that does not support it. In practice, however, quantity considerations can seldom be separated from considerations of quality. For example, if one well-done study that does not support a hypothesis can be shown to have better tested the hypothesis than a much larger number of studies that support the hypothesis, then that single study will call into question the evidence from the larger number supporting the hypothesis. Such a situation might occur if the single well-done study not supporting the theory either controlled or manipulated an important variable that the other studies failed to take into account. Also, as we have seen, some types of research evidence allow us to make stronger causal inferences than others. So, for example, a single, well-done experiment supporting a hypothesis would likely be weighed more heavily than three case studies against it.

A second quantity consideration involves taking into account the number of observations made on the variable, with more observations preferable to fewer observations. It is assumed that in the long run, data from a study with more observations are more reliable than data from a study with fewer observations. Practically speaking, it is often difficult to judge a study based on the number of observations it involved. Since literature reviews often do not mention the size of the samples in studies being reviewed, to find out how large the samples were, one must check the published research report itself.

You should also be aware that because researchers draw their conclusions based on samples, some uncertainty is always involved in interpreting researchers' results. When we use research results as evidence, therefore, we are using evidence that necessarily has uncertainty associated with it.

Hypothetico-Deductive Reasoning in Psychology and Everyday Life

This chapter has emphasized how much of scientific and everyday reasoning is inductive, in distinction to the deductive reasoning discussed in the last chapter. In fact, effective thinking about both everyday and scientific questions uses a combination of the two, called **hypothetico-deductive** reasoning. The prefix *hypothetico* refers to the way, in inductive reasoning, hypotheses and theories are generated from observations in order to account for those observations. The term *deductive* refers to deductive reasoning's process of making predictions about what ought to be observed if the theory or hypothesis is assumed to be true (Popper, 1961).

Before we examine how hypothetico-deductive reasoning is used in psychology, let's examine some everyday instances of it. You have been using a form of hypothetico-deductive reasoning since your childhood; for example, you have probably used it in trying to figure out why something wasn't working. As a child trying to find out why your electric-powered car was not working, for instance, you first might have hypothesized that the switch was not turned on. You then might have predicted that if you turned the switch on, the car would begin going. Suppose you tried the switch, and it didn't help. So you next hypothesized that the batteries were not in right. You then might have thought, "If I fiddle with the batteries, the car will go." Putting this hypothesis to the test, you might have pushed on the batteries, and if the car then worked, your hypothesis would have been confirmed.

Now, allow me to illustrate with an example from my own childhood. When I was 7 years old—long before I knew much about scientific or critical thinking—I used hypothetico-deductive reasoning to discover that Santa Claus is not real. As a child, I always went to my grandparents' home to celebrate Christmas Eve. Each year, about 10 P.M., Santa Claus would pay a visit. Something about Santa seemed vaguely familiar. I made a number of observations and generated the hypothesis that Santa was actually my grandfather. I probably used other evidence, such as the statements of my friends that Santa was not real, to help me come up with the hypothesis based on the more general theory that Santa is not real.

Next, using deductive reasoning, I predicted that if Grandpa was Santa Claus, then my grandfather would come up missing when Santa arrived. This is a plausible prediction based on the hypothesis that Grandpa was Santa and consistent with what I knew about physical reality—that no one can be in two places at once, Superman notwithstanding. However, if I observed that Grandpa was missing when Santa appeared, this would not necessarily mean that Grandpa was Santa. He could have left coincidentally (though why would anyone leave when Santa was coming?). I devised a further test that would nail it down. My grandfather always wore a silver initial ring with the letter P for Paulsen. I predicted that if my grandfather forgot to remove the ring, then Santa would be wearing an initial ring with the letter P. Indeed, when Santa came, my grandfather did disappear, and Santa was wearing the same initial ring, confirming my hypothesis. That Santa wore an initial ring with a P, not S or C, contributed to the internal validity of my little everyday experiment. In all honesty, I don't know whether I consciously thought of these predictions when I was 7—but I can say that I did conduct a test of the hypothesis that included these details.

Psychology makes extensive use of hypothetico-deductive reasoning. We have seen how a researcher in psychology may observe that people are more likely to help or cooperate if you give them a small gift. For example, a well-known fact in sales is that salespeople frequently give prospective customers small gifts to encourage their cooperation in a sale (Zimbardo & Leippe, 1991). From these observations you might form the hypothesis that people in a good mood are more likely to help. You could then derive a prediction like that of Isen and Levin (1972), who predicted that people who were given a cookie before being asked to help would be more likely to volunteer to help than people not given such a gift. Clinicians also use hypothetico-deductive reasoning in diagnosing their clients' problems. Clinicians often generate hypotheses about the nature of these problems and then make predictions consistent with the hypotheses. For example, if a client complains about feeling sad and defeated much of the time, then a clinical psychologist might hypothesize that the person is depressed. Consistent with the depression hypothesis, the psychologist might then predict that the depressed client should also show signs of sleep disturbance, fatigue, or some other symptoms of depression. These hypotheses can help the clinician to think critically about the client's problem.

Summary

In this chapter, we saw that through inductive reasoning, one may reason from observations, facts, and specific cases to a general rule or principle, such as a theory. To draw a sound conclusion in an inductive argument, the critical thinker must evaluate all the evidence relevant to all sides of a question in terms of the evidence's quantity and quality. The more evidence, and the higher its quality, in support of one side rather than another, the stronger the support for that side. The strength of the inductive conclusions we draw may vary from weak to strong, but, unlike deductive arguments, inductive arguments never lead to certainty. Consequently, critical thinkers and scientists are cautious about the inductive conclusions they draw.

The critical thinking task involves evaluating the evidence relevant to a claim, taking into account both the quantity and quality of the evidence, in order to draw a sound conclusion. The quality of evidence supporting a claim depends on the kind of nonscientific evidence and research methods used. As compared to nonscientific approaches to knowledge and evidence, the scientific approach has the advantage of being self-correcting. Some scientific methods, however, provide better evidence than others. In particular, only the experimental method provides the means for making a causal inference.

In addition to the quality of evidence, the strength of an inductive argument depends on the quantity of evidence. For example, a theory is more strongly supported when many studies support it rather than fewer, especially if the studies are of high quality. Similarly, a study with a larger sample size can more strongly support a theory than one of a smaller sample size.

Finally, scientific thinking and much critical thinking in everyday situations are a combination of deductive and inductive reasoning called hypothetico-deductive thinking.

Review Questions

How are theories developed?
What is inductive reasoning? Generalization?
   How do we evaluate an inductive argument?
      Quality of evidence
      Can you distinguish primary from secondary sources?
      Quantity of evidence
   Can critical thinking be taught?
   Why must we be careful in drawing inductive arguments?
What are the characteristics of inductive arguments, and how are they like and unlike deductive arguments?
   Why should we be cautious about personal, commonsense, or folk "theories"?
      What is the evidence for ESP?

What do we use the standard of plausibility for?

What is the critical thinking task?

What are some nonscientific sources of evidence?

What is common sense?

Anecdotal evidence?

Statements of authority?

What are the strengths and weaknesses of each?

What is science? What two approaches are combined to make it?

What are the advantages of science as an approach to knowledge?

What are the three criteria for causation?

How is the quality of scientific evidence related to causality?

What are extraneous variables?

Compare and contrast common research methods with respect to their strengths and weaknesses, especially with regard to demonstrating causation?

Survey research?

Field studies?

Correlation?

Experiments?

Quasi-experiments?

What is confounding and how does it relate to internal validity?

Can you identify independent, dependent, and extraneous variables?

Do you know how to evaluate a research study description to decide whether it allows for a causal inference?

What is hypothetico-deductive reasoning, and how is it used?

References

Bailey, J. F. (1979). The effects of an instructional paradigm on the development of critical thinking of college students in a introductory botany course (Doctoral dissertation, Purdue University). *Dissertation Abstracts International, 39*, 480A.

Beckman, V. E. (1956). An investigation of the contributions to critical thinking made by courses in argumentation and discussed in selected colleges (Doctoral dissertation, University of Minnesota). *Dissertation Abstracts International, 16*, 2551A.

Bem, D. J., & Honorton, C. (1994). Does psi exist? Evidence for an anomalous process of information transfer. *Psychological Bulletin, 115*, 4–18.

Bensley, D. A., Bolton, M., Palardy, B., Brooks, J., & Langan, D. (1995, April). *Assessing instruction with tests of scientific and critical thinking.* Paper presented at the 66th annual meeting of the Eastern Psychological Association, Boston.

Bensley, D. A., & Haynes, C. (1995). The acquisition of general purpose strategic knowledge for argumentation. *Teaching of Psychology, 22*, 41–45.

Blackmore, S. (1992). Psychic experiences: Psychic illusions. *Skeptical Inquirer, 16*, 367–376.

Coscarelli, W., & Schwen, T. (1979). Effects of three algorithmic representations on critical thinking, laboratory efficiency, and final grade. *Educational Communication and Technology, 27*, 58–64.

Dansereau, D., McDonald, B., Collins, K., Garland, J., Holley, C., Dickhoff, G., & Evans, S. (1979). Evaluation of a learning strategy system. In H. O'Neil & C. Spielberger, (Eds.), *Cognitive and affective learning strategies.* New York: Academic Press.

Darley, J., & Latané, B. (1968). Bystander intervention in emergencies. *Journal of Personality and Social Psychology, 8*, 377–383.

Fox, L., Marsh, G., & Crandall, J. (1983, April 30). *The effect of college classroom experiences on formal operational thinking.* Paper presented at the annual convention of the Western Psychological Association, San Francisco.

Gallup, G. H., & Newport, F. (1991). Belief in paranormal phenomena among adult Americans. *Skeptical Inquirer, 15*, 137–146.

Garnham, A., & Oakhill, J. (1994). *Thinking and reasoning*. Oxford, England: Blackwell.

Gendin, S. (1981). ESP: A conceptual analysis. *Skeptical Inquirer, 5*, 367–376.

Gilovich, T. (1991). *How we know what isn't so: The fallibility of human reason in everyday life*. New York: Free Press.

Halpern, D. F. (1993). Assessing the effectiveness of critical thinking instruction. *Journal of General Education, 42*, 238–254.

Halpern, D. F. (1996). *Thought and knowledge: An introduction to critical thinking* (3rd ed.). Hillsdale, NJ: Lawrence Erlbaum.

Herrnstein, R. J., Nickerson, R. S., de Sanchez, M., & Swets, J. A. (1986). Teaching thinking skills. *American Psychologist, 11*, 1279–1289.

Institute for the Advancement of Philosophy for Children (n.d.). *Research in philosophy for children*. Upper Montclair, NJ: Montclair.

Isen, A. M., & Levin, P. F. (1972). Effect of feeling good on helping: Cookies and kindness. *Journal of Personality and Social Psychology, 21*, 384–388.

Kolb, B., & Whishaw, I. Q. (1990). *Fundamentals of human neuropsychology* (3rd ed.). New York: W. H. Freeman.

Kuhn, D. (1993). Connecting scientific and informal reasoning. *Merrill-Palmer Quarterly, 39*, 74–103.

Mentkowski, M., & Strait, M. J. (1983). *A longitudinal study of student change in cognitive development, learning styles, and generic abilities in an outcome-centered liberal arts curriculum* (Final Report to the National Institute of Education: Research Rep. No. 6 [NIE-G-77-0058]. Milwaukee: Alverno College, Office of Research and Evaluation.

Myers, A., & Hansen, C. (1996). *Experimental Psychology* (4th ed.). Pacific Grove, CA: Brooks/Cole.

Popper, K. R. (1961). *The logic of scientific discovery*. New York: Basic Books.

Randi, J. (1977). The media and reports on the paranormal. *The Humanist, 37*, 45–47.

Stanovich, K. E. (1996). *How to think straight about psychology* (3rd ed.). New York: Harper-Collins.

Suksringarm, P. (1976). An experimental study comparing the effects of BSCS and the traditional biology on achievement understanding of science, critical thinking ability, and attitude towards science of first year students at the Sakon Nakorn Teachers College, Thailand. (Doctoral dissertation, Pennsylvania State University). *Dissertation Abstracts International, 37*, 2764A.

Tomlinson-Keasey, C., & Eisert, D. (1977). Second year evaluation of the ADAPT program. In *Multidisciplinary Piagetian-based programs for college freshmen: ADAPT*. Lincoln: University of Nebraska.

Tomlinson-Keasey, C., Williams, V., & Eisert, D. (1977). Evaluation Report of the first year of the ADAPT program. In *Multidisciplinary Piagetian-based programs for college freshmen: ADAPT*. Lincoln: University of Nebraska.

Tweeney, R. D. (1991). Informal reasoning in science. In J. Voss, D. Perkins, & J. Segal (Eds.), *Informal reasoning and education* (pp. 3–16). Hillsdale, NJ: Lawrence Erlbaum.

Vogt, W. P. (1993). *Dictionary of statistics and methodology*. Newbury Park, CA: Sage Publications.

Zechmeister, E. B., & Johnson, J. E. (1992). *Critical thinking: A functional approach*. Pacific Grove, CA: Brooks/Cole.

Zimbardo, P. G., & Leippe, M. R. (1991). *The psychology of attitude change and social influence*. New York: McGraw-Hill.

Analyzing Discussions of Psychological Questions

Learning Objectives

• To learn how to actively read a passage so that one can understand it and be prepared to critically analyze it.

• To learn how to identify the central question, organize the relevant evidence, and draw a sound conclusion from the information presented in a review of the literature in psychology.

• To think critically about a specific form of the nature versus nurture question and other important issues in social psychology, related to prosocial behavior and helping.

What Do You Think?

What do you think—are people basically selfish? You probably have an opinion on this important question. You have had experience with people doing nice things for you. Were they being selfless, or were they really doing it for some ulterior motive? In recent years, economists have revived the idea that people basically look out for their own interests and that this selfishness is virtuous as long as no harm is done to another. What do you think?

Whether people are basically selfish is a question fundamental to our view of human behavior and has intrigued philosophers, social psychologists, and other scientists for many years. In psychology, it is part of a larger discussion on the basis of **prosocial behavior,** or any behavior focused on benefiting others or society at large, such as helping behavior. In many discussions of whether people are selfish, the question is phrased in terms of whether people are altruistic. **Altruism** is helping or aiding another without the intention of receiving any benefit in return (Schroeder, Penner, Dovidio, & Piliavin, 1995). In this chapter we will examine part of the large body of literature on whether people are selfish or altruistic.

How to Critically Analyze a Psychological Discussion

Most of us have an opinion about whether people are basically selfish, but how do we know whether we are right? What do psychologists think about this question, and how do they decide? We would hope that a psychologist would use critical thinking to answer this question. Evaluating the relevant evidence is the first step. In Chapter 2, we discussed how a sound inductive argument depends on evaluating the quantity and quality of the evidence, and we compared various types of scientific and nonscientific evidence in terms of their quality. In this chapter you will have the opportunity to apply this knowledge in order to draw a conclusion from the evidence concerning people's selfishness. To help you learn how to critically analyze and evaluate this kind of discussion, you should use the following questions to organize your approach.

≋ PRACTICE YOUR THINKING 3.1

Critically Reading a Literature Review: Are People Basically Selfish?

The following questions are designed to help you check whether you are finding and understanding important parts of the arguments found in this passage discussing an important question in social psychology. They should help you to evaluate the evidence presented and to draw a sound conclusion as you read the passage.

Questions to Prepare You for Critical Reading

1. What is the central question? What claims are being made?

2. What evidence has been presented that is relevant to evaluating each side of the question? To answer this question, first organize the relevant evidence under one category for evidence supporting the claim, and other relevant evidence under evidence not supporting the claim. Then label each piece of evidence as to its kind—whether it is a nonscientific kind of evidence, such as an anecdote or authority; or scientific research evidence (see Tables 2.1 and 2.2 for help).

3. Evaluate the quality and quantity of the evidence so that you can draw a sound conclusion based on the evidence presented.

4. Do any assumptions create problems for this conclusion? If any assumptions you made were more carefully examined, might you come to a different conclusion?

5. What are some implications of this conclusion? **Implications** are related inferences that are suggested or implied by the initial conclusion one has drawn. For example, if you concluded that people are basically selfish, what does this conclusion suggest will happen when you ask strangers for charitable contributions?

You should read through each question again before you read the passage, trying to keep them in mind. Then, see whether you can answer each question after you read the passage. To do so, you need to read each passage actively. (See the form on pages 60–62 that you can use to answer the critical reading questions. You may wish to photocopy this form so that you can use it repeatedly throughout this book.)

Suggestions for Becoming an Active Reader

The following suggestions should help you get the most out of the critical reading passages presented in this book. Too often, we find that we are automatically saying the words while reading to ourselves without comprehending their meaning. This kind of reading is passive and leaves us saying to ourselves, "I just finished reading this but I don't know what it said." This passive kind of reading is ineffective and will not allow you to think critically about what you read.

To avoid passive reading, after you have read over the critical thinking questions, you should carefully read over the passage, checking yourself for your comprehension as you go along. As you read, ask yourself frequently, "Am I understanding the words I am reading? Am I following the arguments being made? Am I finding the information I need to answer the questions? Questioning yourself in this manner will ensure active reading. If you think that you understand the passage after you have read through it once, read through the questions again and try to answer them as you read through the passage a second time. Then try to write answers to the questions.

Appendix A will also help you identify the important parts of arguments. It provides a list of words and expressions that critical thinkers frequently use in presenting claims, evidence, and conclusions. For example, the expression *he proposed* would usually indicate that a claim was being introduced. The expressions *in fact* and *because* are usually followed by evidence. The term *found* suggests a particular kind of evidence, that is, that scientific research results are being used in supporting some position with respect to some claim or hypothesis. You can use the appendix as a heuristic, or "rule of thumb," for identifying the claims, evidence, and conclusions to help you to begin to analyze the arguments you read and hear.

Remember that, because critically reading the passages requires inductive reasoning, you must take into account the quality of the sources of evidence in your reading. In some cases, looking at the titles of the references in the reference section at the end of the chapter may help you to determine what kind of evidence is being used. For example, the word *effect* in the title may indicate that an experiment was conducted. Then, you may use Tables 2.1 and 2.2 to help you to evaluate how good are the kinds or sources of evidence you have identified from the discussion.

Are People Basically Selfish?

The question of whether people are basically selfish will be addressed in two ways. In one sense, this question may be restated as whether people are selfish by *nature*. As such, it is closely related to the broader "nature versus nurture" question. The nature side of this question asks whether people have innate tendencies to act to further their own self-interest. Similarly, we might also ask whether the trait of altruism is built into people—in other words, is there a biological basis for people to act to benefit others without any interest in how such actions will benefit themselves?

The nurture side of the question proposes that people develop the traits of selfishness or altruism through learning, experience, or the influence of their culture. In this view, altruism is not something basic to an individual that unfolds from built-in tendencies, but rather something acquired through learning and experience.

The second way of addressing the question whether people are basically selfish asks whether people, for the most part, behave or are motivated to behave to further their own self-interest. The discussion that follows will address these two approaches to the question of people's selfishness by selectively reviewing the literature. We will begin by discussing the biological basis for selfishness.

Charles Darwin's evolutionary theory has been used to argue both for and against the idea that people are by nature altruistic or unselfish (Rapoport, 1991). According to Darwin's theory, natural selection operates so that those organisms with a trait that helps them to survive and reproduce will tend to pass that trait along to their offspring. According to one view, a trait like altruism could be preserved in a species if it helped members of the group survive. Trivers (1985) argued that altruism may be preserved in a species along kinship lines. For example, an individual will sacrifice resources, even his or her life, for a close relative such as a brother or offspring, because the relative shares 50% of the same genes. This could tend to preserve the individual's own genes by helping these related individuals to survive long enough to breed and pass along the shared genes.

Other biologists and some psychologists have pointed out that this idea of group selection is a misunderstanding of natural selection and that natural selection actually only occurs at the individual level (Dawkins, 1989). According to this other view, there is no selective advantage for animals that sacrifice their own resources or threaten their own lives to help other, unrelated individuals. If the mechanism for passing along one's genes depends only on individual survival, then it makes no sense for an individual to help others if it does not promote the individual's own survival. Therefore, any individual with an altruistic gene that gives its food to another or risks its life for another is at a selective disadvantage. It may not live long enough to breed and as a result will not pass along its gene for altruism to its off-spring. Helping others, especially those outside of one's kinship group, is very costly and would likely be selected against.

Yet, many documented cases suggest that people are altruistic and may be willing to help, even risk their lives for other unrelated individuals, when they do not stand to gain from that help. For example, when a jet airliner crashed into the icy Potomac River one winter several years ago, a bystander named Lenny Skutnik imperiled his own life by repeatedly diving into the frigid waters to save some of the passengers. Another revealing example of altruism, however—a story told about Abraham Lincoln—casts some doubt on the selflessness behind altruism. Lincoln is said to have ordered the train he was riding to stop so that some drowning pigs he saw out the window could be saved. Lincoln reported that he had not done this out of an altruistic motive but rather to avoid having a guilty conscience over the matter (Batson, Bolen, Cross, Neuringer-Benefiel, 1986).

In addition, there are also many documented cases of people who have failed to help those in need. For example, in 1964 in New York City, a 28-year-old woman named Kitty Genovese was assaulted three different times over a 30-minute period and then killed while 38 different people in her neighborhood who were aware of her plight did nothing to intervene or help her—they did not even call the police.

This tragedy inspired John Darley and Bib Latané to investigate what factors would lead a person to help another person in an emergency. Darley and Latané (1968) staged a situation in which college students were randomly assigned to a group who heard over an intercom what sounded like a person having an epileptic seizure. When a second group of randomly assigned subjects thought they alone had overheard the seizure, 85% of them tried to get help for the victim, but when they thought that others had also overheard the seizure, only 30% sought help. Darley and Latané (1968) found that people were not simply apathetic about the plight of another, but less likely to intervene when they knew that other people were also aware of the person's plight. This effect has been called diffusion of responsibility.

Research like this raises the question whether altruistic persons actually may be helping others for a selfish motive such as avoiding distress or guilt. Alternatively, do some people engage in altruistic acts because they feel empathy for a suffering person—sympathy, compassion, or tenderness? To investigate that question, Coke, Batson, and McDavis (1978) conducted a study in which people heard a radio broadcast that requested participants to help a graduate student complete a study.

In responses to a questionnaire, they found that feelings of personal distress in subjects were only modestly related to willingness to participate while feelings of empathy were strongly related to willingness to participate. The study suggested that people may be altruistic primarily for unselfish, empathic reasons. Eisenberg and Fabes (1990) noted in a recent review that empathy—the vicarious response involving concern for someone else's distress or need—can result either in sympathy for the other person or in personal distress in response to the other's distress.

One psychologist, Hoffman (1981), argued that humans have a biologically based empathy mechanism that is automatically activated when a person in need is encountered. In a review of the literature, Hoffman found support for the idea that empathic responses may not be under voluntary control. He also cited research by MacLean showing that the visual processing part of the brain is connected to the emotional part of the brain. This connection may underlie people's ability to "see with feeling." In addition, developmental research has shown that infants only 1 or 2 days old cry in response to other infants' crying. This idea of an innate empathic mechanism is also consistent with adults' statements that they helped others in emergency situations automatically, without thinking.

Other developmental research suggests that the reasons a young person helps may be complex. For example, Kenrick (1989) found that by the age of about six, children will engage in helping behavior to punish themselves in order to make up for a bad deed they have done. Cialdini, Baumann, and Kenrick (1981) reported in a review of the literature that by the time people are in their late teens they will help others when no one is watching or even though no one will know they have helped.

While these results suggest that altruism develops by the late teens, the research on socialization—that is, how people acquire characteristics and values through their social groups—suggests that people do not start out as altruists but rather develop this trait after considerable practice, rewards, observation of altruistic models, and the internalization of altruistic values (Grusec, 1991). Based on another review of the research on the socialization of prosocial behavior, Kim and Stevens (1987) argued that parents exert considerable influence on the development of altruism and other prosocial characteristics when they communicate their expectations for prosocial behavior, reward young children for showing it, and punish them for failures to show it, and when they model prosocial behavior for their children to observe in various situations. The authors also pointed out that parents who use inductive reasoning with their children to justify the need for prosocial behavior will be more effective in helping their children to develop the disposition to behave prosocially than parents who simply request such behavior.

Whereas Cialdini et al. (1981) found that people in their late teens will help even when no one else is aware of it, research by Batson et al. (1986) found that helping occurred more when the failure to help was likely to be detected by someone else than when it was likely to be undetected. The pattern of correlations with empathy scores in this study was also consistent with the idea that people help others to avoid feeling guilt, rather than out of an unselfish, empathic concern for the person needing help.

Other studies have shown that empathy may lead to helping without egoistic motives. A study by Fultz, Batson, Fortenbach, McCarthy, and Varney (1986) found that subjects who felt more empathy offered to help regardless of whether they thought they were going to be evaluated on whether they helped or not, suggesting that empathy does not result in helping for the egoistic or selfish reason of avoiding social disapproval. In a study consistent with this last finding, Sibicky, Schroeder, and Dovidio (1995) randomly assigned their subjects into groups that were induced to be either high or low in empathy by having statements read to them suggesting that kind of mental set. They found that empathic subjects gave fewer hints to help other subjects when they were told that the hints could hurt the subjects later in the experiment. These results suggested that empathy increases sensitivity to others' needs.

Other research on empathy has produced negative results. Cialdini, Schaller, Houlihan, Arps, Fultz, and Beaman (1987) proposed that the reason empathic people help is to relieve their sadness in observing a sufferer in need. When they experimentally separated sadness and empathy, they found that sadness predicted subjects' levels of helping, but empathy did not. In a second experiment, they found that empathic subjects did not help much when they were led to believe that their moods would not be changed if they helped another person.

Another kind of research on personality difference in helping has shown that a person's individual tendency to be altruistic may differ. Romer, Gruder, and Lizardo (1986) conducted an experiment in which they had subjects complete personality tests and then classified the subjects as (1) altruistic, subjects who indicated that typically they were helpful to others with no expectation of something in return; (2) receptive-giving, subjects who would help others when they got something in return; or (3) selfish, subjects who wanted help from others but were not interested in giving any help. This initial testing suggested that not all people may be basically selfish, but some may be selfish and others may be altruistic.

In a second phase of the experiment, subjects were asked whether they would be willing to help a different, graduate student experimenter to complete her research project before the end of the semester. The subjects were then either promised course credit for participation or were not promised credit. Consistent with the initial personality test classification, the selfish students generally would not help regardless of whether or not they were promised a reward. The receptive-giving subjects volunteered more when they were promised course credit. Finally, the altruistic subjects volunteered more when they were not rewarded than when they were, resulting in what is called a person-by-situation interaction. The interaction shows that whether or not subjects volunteered depended on both their personality characteristic—whether they were altruistic, selfish, or receptive-giving—and on details of the situation (whether or not they were offered a reward). It may even be that the altruistic subjects tended to volunteer for selfish reasons such as the intrinsic reward of feeling good because they were helping someone.

Consistent with the results of the previous study by Romer et al. (1986), other situational and mood variables also seem to influence whether or not a person helps. For example, Isen and Levin (1972) found that subjects who were given a cookie beforehand were more likely to volunteer to help than those who did not receive a free cookie. In a second study they found that subjects who found a dime in a phone booth were more likely to help someone pick up some dropped papers than subjects who did not find a dime. Both experiments show that helping depends on a situational determinant—receiving a gift—and perhaps on the positive mood induced by the free gift. Consistent with the idea that mood influences helping, Batson (1990) reviewed a number of studies showing that people in a positive mood are more likely to help.

Still other research has shown that another detail of the situation—whether or not one has observed someone else helping—also affects a person's tendency to help. For example, Bryan and Test (1967) found that subjects were more likely to help a motorist with a flat tire if they had just observed someone else helping another motorist with a flat tire.

In conclusion, the question whether people are basically selfish at this point receives a complicated and mixed answer from a summary of the relevant evidence. Much anecdotal evidence, and statements of reputed authorities, support both sides of the question. Similarly, evaluation of higher-quality evidence from experimental research, some of which were true experiments, provides support for both the selfish and altruistic basis of behavior. While there is a strong biological argument against the selection of genes for altruism, there is some evidence for an innate mechanism for empathy that could promote helping. The research suggests that people often engage in altruistic behaviors to reduce personal distress, guilt, and other negative emotions, but they also may sometimes help because of empathy for another person without much concern for consequences to themselves. Also, although individuals appear to differ in terms of how selfish or how altruistic they are, some research suggests that their tendency to help another person depends on the situational details, especially whether or not they will be rewarded for their helping. Moreover, besides the influence of rewards, people are more likely to help after they have observed another person modeling helpful behavior. In addition to the evidence that helping is learned, there is evidence that rather than appearing early in the developmental sequence, altruism increases with socialization and development. Taken together, this evidence suggests that people are not by nature altruistic and that they acquire this trait over time and to different degrees.

You will find an additional copy of the following form in Appendix B. Copy this form—you will need it for other critical reading assignments.

Form for Answering Critical Reading Questions

Question 1:   What is the central question? What claim or claims are being made?

_____

_____

_____

_____

_____

_____

_____

Question 2:   What is the evidence relevant to evaluating the claim?

Evidence Supporting the Claim

1. _____

Kind of evidence: _____

2. _____

Kind of evidence: _____

3. _____

Kind of evidence: _____

4. _____

Kind of evidence: _____

5. _____

Kind of evidence: _____

6. _____

Kind of evidence:

7. _____

Kind of evidence: _____

8. _____

Kind of evidence: _____

Evidence Not Supporting the Claim

1. _____

Kind of evidence: _____

2. _____

Kind of evidence: _____

3. _____

Kind of evidence: _____

4. _____

Kind of evidence: _____

5. _____

Kind of evidence: _____

6. _____

Kind of evidence: _____

7. _____

Kind of evidence: _____

8. _____

Kind of evidence: _____

Evaluate the quality and quantity of the evidence presented so that you can draw a sound conclusion.

_____
_____
_____
_____
_____
_____
_____
_____
_____
_____
_____

Do any assumptions create problems for this conclusion?

_____
_____
_____
_____
_____
_____

What are some implications of this conclusion?

_____
_____
_____
_____
_____
_____

Answers to Critical Reading Questions

Question 1: What is the central question? What claims are being made? The claim being analyzed is that people are basically selfish or, on the contrary, that they are altruistic. Psychologists have studied this question by examining to what extent people will show helping behaviors and especially altruistic behaviors—truly selfless, helping behaviors in which the helping person neither receives a reward nor escapes negative consequences by helping. The assumption here is that engaging in helping behaviors without concern for personal reward or avoidance of negative consequences is unselfish.

Question 2: What evidence has been presented that is relevant to evaluating each side of the question, and what kind of evidence is it? A useful strategy for analyzing evidence in a passage like this is to organize and summarize the evidence into sets that correspond to all sides of the question. In this case, you organize the evidence under one heading for evidence supporting the claim and another heading for evidence not supporting the claim. Then you should classify the evidence as to what kind it is.

Evidence Supporting the Claim That People Are Selfish

1. Evolutionary theory correctly interpreted makes it difficult to explain the natural selection of altruism. (scientific authority)

2. Kitty Genovese was assualted, and her neighbors who were aware of her plight did nothing to help her. (anecdotal evidence)

3. Abraham Lincoln had a train stopped to help some drowning pigs, but he did this not for altruistic reasons but to avoid negative guilt feelings. (anecdotal evidence)

4. Batson et al. (1986) found that helping was more likely if a person was being evaluated, suggesting that avoidance of guilt, not true altruism, is the motive for helping. (experiment and correlation)

5. Cialdini et al. (1987) showed that empathic people help in order to relieve their sadness at observing a sufferer in need. They found that sadness predicted subjects' levels of helping, but their level of empathy did not, and that empathic subjects did not help much when they believed that their moods would not be changed if they helped another person. (experiment)

6. Darley and Latané (1968) found that while most people would help in a staged emergency, many wouldn't; whether or not someone helped depended on whether he or she thought someone else knew that help was needed. (experiment)

7. Kenrick (1989) found that by the age of about six, children will engage in helping behavior in order to punish themselves to make up for a bad deed they have done. (scientific case studies) (Compare this to the anecdote about Lincoln and guilt feelings.)

8. Romer et al. (1986) conducted an experiment in which they had subjects complete personality tests that suggested people differ in terms of how selfish and altruistic they are. The researchers found that whether or not subjects helped another person depended both on this individual difference and on characteristics of the situation—whether or not they were to receive a reward. (quasi-experiment)

9. Isen and Levin (1972) found that people helped when they received a gift even though the gift was not from the person needing the help; so helping could also be attributed to a positive mood. (experiment)

10. Bryan and Test (1967) found that people did not help no matter what but rather were more likely to help if they observed someone else helping first. (experiment)

Evidence Not Supporting the Claim That People Are Selfish

1. A bystander named Lenny Skutnik endangered himself by repeatedly diving into an icy river to save victims of an air crash, apparently without thought of reward. (anecdotal evidence)

2. Coke, Batson, and McDavis (1978) found that feelings of personal distress in subjects were only modestly related to willingness to participate while feelings of empathy were strongly related to willingness to participate. (scientific—questionnaire and correlation)

3. Hoffman (1981) reviewed research showing evidence for an innate mechanism for empathy. (scientific authority)

4. Fultz et al. (1986) found that subjects who felt more empathy offered to help whether or not they thought they were going to be evaluated, showing that empathy may exist independently of any avoidance of guilt. (scientific—experiment and correlation)

5. Cialdini et al. (1981) reported that by the time people are in their late teens they will help others even when no one will know they have helped. (scientific authority)

6. Sibicky et al. (1995) found that empathic subjects gave fewer hints to help other subjects when they were told that the hints could hurt the subjects later in the experiment, suggesting that empathy increases sensitivity to others' needs. (experiment)

Question 3: Evaluate the quality and quantity of the evidence so that you can draw a sound conclusion based on the evidence presented. You probably noticed as you tried to identify the various kinds of evidence that the critical reading passage described only some of the research evidence adequately to allow you to decide what kind of scientific evidence it was. When a study is simply cited, it is often difficult to identify the independent and dependent variables and hypotheses of the studies to decide whether the study was a true experiment. In such cases, you should go to the reference list and check the titles—better yet, read the original studies—to determine what kind of evidence is being cited. Other references should be treated as evidence from scientific authorities to be given cautious credence until that research and its interpretation can be more closely examined. In the study by Darley and Latané (1968), the independent variable was whether the subject thought he or she alone was overhearing the person having a seizure or instead thought other people had also overheard the seizure. The dependent variable was whether the subjects tried to get help for the supposed victim or not. The experimental hypothesis was that diffusion of responsibility would occur, resulting in less helping when more people were present in an emergency situation besides the potential helper, as opposed to when only the potential helper knew about the emergency. In the study by Romer et al. (1986), subjects were assigned to three different groups—altruistic, receptive-giving, and selfish—based on their responses to personality tests. This group assignment was one independent variable, although strictly speaking it was not a manipulated variable since subjects were not made to be altruistic or selfish but rather were selected based on their responses to the questionnaire. The second independent variable was whether or not subjects were promised course credit. The dependent variable was whether or not subjects volunteered to help with an experiment. The experimental hypothesis was that volunteering to help depends both on a person's personality type and on the situation (whether or not the reward of course credit was offered). It was predicted that a reward would not affect the volunteering of selfish people, but that receptive-giving people would tend to volunteer when they received a reward and that altruistic people would volunteer less when they received a reward.

Now that we have organized the evidence under the two positions discussed and have numbered and labeled the kinds of evidence, we can evaluate the quality and quantity of the evidence in order to draw a sound inductive conclusion. We can see that different kinds of evidence were offered in support of each side of the claim. Anecdotal evidence was offered to suggest that sometimes people help others in need with no apparent expectation of being rewarded or escaping negative feelings. Other anecdotal evidence suggested that sometimes people fail to help even though it would cost them little, or that people help to avoid feeling some negative emotion such as guilt. Anecdotal evidence is not scientific, since it is often based on a single observation of a real-world event that could not easily be repeated and in which many variables could have played a part and are not taken into account.

Other scientific research evidence was presented to show that all people are not strictly selfish. Some, identified by personality tests, at least appear to be altruistic. Also, people may be more likely to help when given an extrinsic reward (the receptive-giving) or alternatively when not given an extrinsic reward (the altruistic). The fact that altruists do not help when receiving an extrinsic reward does not mean that they do not reward themselves intrinsically for helping others. In fact, much research suggests that people do help to escape negative emotional consequences of not helping, such as guilt. Other research, however, suggests that a more important factor, such as empathy for the person in need of help, is the most important variable in helping behavior, consistent with the idea that people help for selfless reasons. This research is essentially correlational, however, and so it cannot be concluded that empathy caused the helping behaviors.

A summary of the evidence shows that it is mixed. The claim that people are basically selfish is contradicted by some of the evidence; the claim cannot simply be accepted. Some people are classified as altruistic, and sometimes people may be motivated to help for primarily nonselfish reasons. The evidence does suggest that there are individual differences in altruism and selfishness. Many people appear to be motivated for selfish reasons such as avoiding guilt, but some people may help out of compassion and concern for others. In general, whether or not someone helps depends on details of the situation such as the presence of a reward, one's mood, and whether or not one has observed a model helping. This research and research on the socialization of helping in children suggest that whether or not someone helps is at least partly learned. Indeed, Greene and Barash (1976) argued that it is not productive to view the development of learned aspects of altruistic behavior as separate from inherited tendencies, since all behaviors are a combination of both nature and nurture.

Question 4: Do any assumptions create problems for this conclusion? Might a more careful examination of any assumptions lead you to a different conclusion? At least two types of problems may be present in the critical reading passage reviewing the literature on altruism and helping behavior. First of all, the passage defined selfishness as an unwillingness to help another person. To test hypotheses and evaluate claims using the scientific approach requires that questions be quite specific and well defined. Unselfishness is operationally defined as the willingness to volunteer to help someone by being a subject in an experiment. This has the advantage of clarifying and revealing the complexity of questions such as whether people are basically selfish. If we use this limited definition, however, we also run the risk of creating a context so specific that it does not apply to the world at large—in other words, the breadth of the question is actually greater than our assumption. Could selfishness be defined in other ways that would be useful for us to examine? For example, could selfishness also be defined as greediness or as not paying attention to other people?

A second, related problem concerns the amount of evidence that has been presented. Leaving aside the issue of investigating other related questions, was the evidence presented all the important evidence relevant to the question at hand? There are many more studies on helping behavior—what do their results show?

Question 5: What are some implications of this conclusion? While it may not be concluded that all people are basically selfish, the research consistently supports the idea that some people are selfish and others will help only if they stand to gain from helping. This finding has a number of implications for those who seek others' help. For example, if you ask strangers for a contribution to a charity, expect that some will not give anything no matter what, whereas others will contribute if they get a tax write-off or if their contribution brings them social approval.

Your analysis of the critical reading passage gave you good practice in identifying different kinds of evidence. Other arguments you encounter can also be good opportunities for practice. Look for the kinds of evidence used in your textbooks and in conversations and newspaper and magazine articles about psychological questions. Listen for the arguments people make every day, and practice analyzing them.

Summary

This chapter covered how to critically read a passage that discusses a psychological question. Before we can critically read a prose passage, we must be able to understand it; active reading can help. Active reading involves making sure that you understand the words, ideas, and arguments of a passage as you read it. Monitor your own reading by asking yourself whether you understand, keeping your attention on your reading. You can improve your critical reading of a passage by asking yourself questions that will help you identify the main question and claims, identify and organize the relevant evidence, and label it as to kind so that you can evaluate it, drawing a sound conclusion based on the quality and quantity of the evidence.

The passage that you read addressed an important question in the study of prosocial behavior or behavior—that is focused toward benefiting others, and specifically whether people are basically selfish or instead unselfish, altruistically helping others without the intention of receiving any benefit in return. The question is related to the nature versus nurture question, and some biologists have questioned whether the genes for helping anyone except close relatives could be passed on to others through natural selection. Some people have helped others even at the risk of their own lives, whereas other cases show that people help for selfish reasons. Much research has focused on whether people help because of unselfish empathic concern or sympathy or because they want to avoid feeling personal distress that goes with not helping. Developmental research suggests that empathy may be innate, but helping behavior must be learned or socialized. Other research suggests that individuals differ in their tendency to help, with some people being selfish, others receptive-giving, and still others altruistic. Even so, whether or not someone helps often depends on situational variables such as whether or not they have been rewarded, what mood they are in, and whether or not they have recently observed someone else engaging in helping behavior. Evaluating the evidence on this question does not lead to a clear conclusion. It cannot be concluded, however, that even altruistic people help others for totally unselfish reasons.

Review Questions

What is active reading and how do you do it?

What is critical reading and how do you do it?

What is prosocial behavior?

What is altruism and how does it relate to selfishness?

What is the nature versus nurture question?

What is empathy?

What is a person-by-situation interaction?

How do rewards and the modeling of helping affect helping behavior?

References

Batson, C. D. (1990). Affect and altruism. In B. Moore & A. Isen (Eds.), *Affect and social behavior.* Cambridge, England: Cambridge University Press.

Batson, C. D., Bolen, M. H., Cross, J. A., & Neuringer-Benefiel, H. E. (1986). Where is the altruism in the altruistic personality? *Journal of Personality and Social Psychology, 50,* 212–220.

Bryan, J. H., & Test, M. A. (1967). Models and helping: Naturalistic studies in aiding behavior. *Journal of Personality and Social Psychology, 6,* 400–407.

Cialdini, R. B., Baumann, D. J., & Kenrick, D. T. (1981). Insights from sadness: A three-step model of the development of altruism as hedonism. *Developmental Review, 1,* 207–223.

Cialdini, R. B., Schaller, M., Houlihan, D., Arps, K., Fultz, J., & Beaman, A. (1987). Empathy-based helping: Is it selflessly or selfishly motivated? *Journal of Personality and Social Psychology, 52,* 749–758.

Coke, J. S., Batson, C. D., & McDavis, K. (1978). Empathic mediation of helping: A two-stage model. *Journal of Personality and Social Psychology, 36,* 752–766.

Darley, J., & Latané, B. (1968). Bystander intervention in emergencies. *Journal of Personality and Social Psychology, 8,* 377–383.

Dawkins, R. (1989). *The selfish gene* (2nd ed.). Oxford: Oxford University Press.

Eisenberg, N., & Fabes, R. A. (1990). Empathy: Conceptualization, measurement, and relation to prosocial behavior. *Motivation and Emotion, 14*, 131–149.

Fultz, J., Batson, C. D., Fortenbach, V., McCarthy, P., & Varney, L. (1986). Social evaluation and the empathy-altruism hypothesis. *Journal of Personality and Social Psychology, 50*, 761–769.

Greene, P. J., & Barash, D. P. (1976). Genetic basis of behavior—especially of altruism. *American Psychologist, 31*, 359–361.

Grusec, J. E. (1991). The socialization of altruism. In M. S. Clark (Ed.), *Review of personality and social psychology: Prosocial behavior* (Vol. 12, pp. 9–33). Newbury Park, CA: Sage.

Hoffman, M. L. (1981). Is altruism part of human nature? *Journal of Personality and Social Psychology, 40*, 121–137.

Isen, A. M., & Levin, P. F. (1972). Effect of feeling good on helping: Cookies and kindness. *Journal of Personality and Social Psychology, 21*, 384–388.

Kenrick, D. T. (1989). Selflessness examined: Is avoiding tar and feathers nonegoistic? *Behavioral and Brain Sciences, 12*, 711–712.

Kim, Y., & Stevens, J. H. (1987). The socialization of prosocial behavior in children. *Childhood Education, 63*, 200–206.

Rapoport, A. (1991). Ideological commitments in evolutionary theories. *Journal of Social Issues, 47*, 83–99.

Romer, D., Gruder, C. L., & Lizardo, T. (1986). A person-situation approach to altruistic behavior. *Journal of Personality and Social Psychology, 51*, 1001–1012.

Schroeder, D. A., Penner, L. A., Dovidio, J. F., & Piliavin, J. A. (1995). *The psychology of helping and altruism: Problems and puzzles.* New York: McGraw-Hill.

Sibicky, M. E., Schroeder, D. A., & Dovidio, J. F. (1995). Empathy and helping: Considering the consequences of intervention. *Basic and Applied Social Psychology, 16*, 435–453.

Trivers, R. (1985). *Social evolution.* Menlo Park, CA: Benjamin/Cummings.

The Mind, Brain, and Behavior: What's the Connection?

Learning Objectives

• To learn how our assumptions and beliefs affect the way we approach a question and the kinds of arguments we make.

• To critically read a discussion concerning the important psychological question of how the mind and body are related.

What Do You Think?

Have you ever been sick with a high fever, so that you felt spacey? Did it seem as if your mind was somehow disconnected from your body? Why do you think this occurred?

Imagine that your hair is naturally some other color, such as green or purple. How can your mind think of something that does not physically exist? Does your imagining this have some other sort of reality, perhaps a mental reality?

Some people apparently are able to walk across burning hot coals without experiencing pain or physical injury. Is this a case of mind over matter? What do you think?

When we examine these three examples, we see that the mental experience described in each seems to be different from what is apparently happening at the physical level of the body. In the first example, the effect of a fever suggests that people's mental experience can be affected, even distorted, by their physical condition. In the second example, the ability to imagine something that does not physically exist seems to suggest that the mind can go beyond the physical reality of the situation. Lastly, the example of walking on hot coals without pain suggests the possibility that the mind can control what we experience despite the physical reality of the situation. All three examples raise the question of how the mind is related to the body, a question philosophers have called the mind-body problem.

Philosophical Positions on the Mind-Body Problem

Philosophers and other thinkers have taken very different positions on the mind-body problem. Although you might take any of several positions, we will discuss the three basic positions people frequently take on this question. For example, some Western religions, like Christianity, view the body as material or physical and the soul or (mind) as immaterial or nonphysical (Robinson, 1981). This view, distinguishing the mind from the body as two separate and different entities, is called **dualism** (Hergenhahn, 1992). According to this view, while our bodies are limited by time and space, our minds or souls are able to go beyond these limitations—even to survive after our physical death. Traditional dualism holds that the nonphysical soul resides in the body during a person's lifetime but then leaves at the time of death.

Other philosophers have taken the very different position that the world is really all one thing. This view is called **monism.** According to monism, the mind and body only appear to be different, when actually they are one thing. Some monists, called **materialists,** believe the world is physical and governed by the influence of the environment on the physical body, with mental experience being just another aspect of the physical operation of the body. Others, called **idealists** or sometimes **mentalists,** believe the world is all mental and that we only can know the so-called physical world through our mental experience. Still others believe that the mind and body are actually one inseparable entity. These days, many brain scientists believe that if we knew enough, we would see that all behavior and mental processes could be reduced to the brain processes operating in the physical world.

Finally, the French philosopher Descartes offered a unique solution to the mind-body problem based on his unique background (Hothersall, 1984). This third position, called **interactionism,** assumes that the mind and body are separate entities but that they interact. Descartes, who said, "I think, therefore I am," did not doubt the reality of his mental experience; however, at the same time he was a scientist who made contributions to the study of bodily function. To resolve the conflict between these two approaches, he proposed that the nonphysical mind and the physical body were separate entities, but that they had a physical connection by means of a small gland near the center of the brain called the pineal gland. At this location the body could interact with the nonphysical mind, which could in turn affect the physical body.

≈ PRACTICE YOUR THINKING 4.1

Identifying Mind-Body Beliefs

In the following examples, see whether you can identify which philosophical position each person holds in the two examples that follow. After identifying these, decide which position is closest to your own; then think about why you take this position.

Example 1: Marla is a psychologist who works for the National Institute of Mental Health on a project involving the search for hormones that, when present in the brain, may determine the sex of an individual before birth. She thinks that a person's sexuality is determined by these hormones and that environmental influences have little impact. She hopes that her research on these biochemical mechanisms will explain the origins of sexual identity. Generally, when trying to explain some behavior, Marla avoids the term *mind* and confines her explanation to a discussion of brain mechanisms.

Marla is a _____

Example 2: Larry has been going to a Christian church since he was a small boy. He firmly believes that after he dies his soul will continue on even though his body will not. He believes that some sins are due to the desires of the physical body but that the soul is essentially incorruptible.

Larry is a _____

Which position is closest to your own? _____

Why do you take this position on the mind-body problem?

_____

_____

Answers to Identifying Mind-Body Beliefs

1. Marla is a *monist (physicalist)*.

2. Larry is a *dualist*.

3. You should examine your position carefully because some research suggests that students may endorse contradictory statements from different positions on the mind-body question. For example, Embree and Embree (1993) found that some students would agree to items stating that they both did not have a self and that they did not have a material body.

How Our Assumptions Affect Our Explanations of Behavior

The position one takes on the mind-body question can influence the kind of theories one believes, the approach one takes to investigating psychological questions, and even one's view of what is science. To illustrate, let's see what would happen to your views on these matters if you adopted one position versus another.

For example, suppose you were a monist. Many scientists who study the brain are monists. Often they believe that the mind and brain are one entity (Kalat, 1995). Other psychologists who are monists take a materialist position. They assume that only the physical or material world is real and that mental experience, such as thoughts and feelings, is simply a manifestation of the operation of the brain, which is a physical object. Therefore, the mind does not actually exist separately from the brain, but only appears to have a separate existence.

Two important influences of materialism have helped form the approach psychologists have taken to asking and answering their questions. For example, John Watson, the founder of behaviorism, was a materialist who argued that mental processes should not be studied by psychologists. One consequence of the influence of the behaviorists was that for many years, psychologists were discouraged from using mental events such as memories, mental imagery, and emotion in their causal explanations of behavior. Another example has been the influence of materialism on many psychologists who focus on nervous system issues. Many of these psychologists take a **reductionistic approach** to research. They assume that in order to understand mental experience we should study the nervous system and that when we finally understand it we will understand mental experience. In other words, they assume that the mind can be completely reduced to the brain activity occurring within the physical environment. Accordingly, this kind of materialist would pay almost exclusive attention to research evidence that investigates the nervous system as a basis for behavior, paying little attention to research investigating just mental processes. In addition, many materialists who take a reductionistic approach would argue that people do not have free will because their behavior is completely determined by the activity of their brains or by environmental forces acting upon their nervous systems.

On the other hand, if, as a monist, you took a mentalist position, then you might believe that only mental experience is real and that the brain is only known through our mental experience. For example, Kautz (1993), a critic of science, has argued that all knowledge already exists. He also questions the scientific assumption that there is an objective (physical) world outside of the self that can be studied through the scientific method.

As Kalat (1995) noted, people in general are often dualists, while brain scientists tend to be monists. In recent years, however, a new approach has become increasingly popular among scientists (Sperry, 1988). According to this view, mental states originate and depend upon brain activity, but when they emerge from brain activity they have somewhat different form. Just as oxygen and hydrogen may combine to form water—a substance with new and different properties that emerges from the combination of the original elements—so may mental states emerge from brain states and have different properties from the original brain states. Also, according to this view, the mind can control behavior, acting in a causal way upon the world, and allowing for some degree of free will (Sperry, 1988).

As you can see from this discussion, what position a person takes on the mind-body question can have important implications for one's approach to the study of human behavior. Also, Meier (1992) showed that clinical neuropsychologists who try to help people with problems related to their brain function have been greatly influenced by various views on the mind-body question over the years. It should be clear that a scientist's position on the mind-body problem is not just a matter of personal philosophy but can affect the scientist's approach to research on psychological questions.

The Mind-Body Problem as a Scientific Question

The mind-body problem itself can be investigated not just as a philosophical question, but also as a scientific question. To examine this question scientifically, one could make careful observations of behaviors that indicate underlying mental states or abilities and that correspond to specific changes in the brain.

For example, scientists who have studied the **physiology,** or functioning, of specific parts of the nervous system have sought to answer the mind-body question by asking where specific functions or abilities are located in the brain. This idea, called **localization of function,** assumes that particular behaviors, abilities, and dispositions are supported by specific areas of the brain.

Three methods of studying brain function have been used primarily to study localization of function. An older method developed by Broca, discussed in Chapters 1 and 2, involves relating a change in behavior or mental processes to damage that is identified as localized in one part of the brain. A second method called **ablation** involves making slices or cuts in the brain. A related method called **lesioning** involves destroying a specific area of the brain, sometimes by passing high levels of electricity to a confined area. A more recent method called **electrostimulation of the brain** involves sending minute amounts of electricity to specific cells or circuits in the brain. Cases in which damage to the brain occurs, such as brain damage, ablation, and lesioning, usually result in the loss of the function that the damaged area supported. In electrostimulation, stimulating an area of the brain usually produces the behavior supported by the area, but as in brain damage, electrostimulation can also result in a reduction of a specific behavior that is regulated by the area.

To better understand how psychologists and other brain scientists have addressed what is often termed the *mind-brain* question, we will critically examine a historical review of the literature on the question of where the mind is located. Perhaps, after evaluating the evidence in this discussion of the mind-body problem, you will reevaluate your own philosophical position on the question.

≋ PRACTICE YOUR THINKING 4.2

Critically Reading a Literature Review: Where Is the Mind Located?

To prepare you to read critically a discussion about the mind-body question in psychology, first read the questions below and then read the passage. Then answer the questions on a separate piece of paper following the form for answering the questions presented in Chapter 3.

Questions to Prepare You for Critical Reading

1.   What is the central question? What claims are being made?
2.   What is the evidence relevant to evaluating each side of the question? Organize the relevant evidence, with one category for evidence supporting the claim and the other for evidence not supporting the claim. Then label each piece of evidence as to kind.
3.   Evaluate the quality and quantity of the evidence and then draw a sound conclusion based on the evidence presented.
4.   Do any assumptions create problems for this conclusion?
5.   What are some implications of this conclusion?

Where Is the Mind Located?

The question of where in the body the mind is located is an old one. The concept of mind, however, is a relatively modern one; in the ancient world, this question was debated in terms of where the soul was located. For example, the ancient Sumerians thought the soul resided in the liver. Aristotle, the Greek philosopher, thought the heart was the most important organ and that the brain was part of a cooling mechanism. Even today, many people speak of the heart as if it were the place where love and emotion reside, as in many popular songs. Hippocrates, the ancient Greek physician, however, thought that the brain was where the mind resided. According to Kolb and Whishaw (1990), a controversy developed over whether the brain or the heart controlled the mind and behavior. Galen, surgeon to many gladiators in ancient Rome, witnessed the behavioral effects of head injuries. In experiments to test the heart versus brain hypothesis, Galen found that light pressure to the heart could cause pain but would not cause voluntary behavior to cease, whereas pressure on the brain could cause the cessation of voluntary behavior. The early philosophy and research, however, did not explain how the mind and body (brain) were related.

It was not until the 17th century that the French philosopher Descartes offered a unique solution to how the mind and body are related, called interactionism (Hothersall, 1984). He argued that the nonphysical mind and the physical body were separate entities, as the dualists claimed, but that the nonphysical mind could interact with the body at the location of a small gland near the center of the brain called the pineal gland. At this location the body could interact with the nonphysical mind which could, in turn, affect the physical body.

In the 19th century, many studies of clinical cases supported the idea that many behaviors and mental functions were based on brain activity. Primarily, these were studies of individuals with brain damage, whose behavior changed as a result. Some startling evidence for the notion that there is a physical basis for the mind came from the case of Phineas Gage, as reported by his doctor (Blakemore, 1977). Gage was foreman of a railroad crew, a responsible man liked by his fellow workers. In 1848 while tamping some gunpowder into a hole in a boulder to help clear an area for track, a spark ignited the gunpowder and sent the iron tamping rod through his left cheek and out the top front of his skull. Miraculously, he recovered physically, but his behavior and apparently his mind showed drastic changes. He became ornery, irresponsible, and subject to emotional outbursts. Though it is not certain what damage actually occurred, the tamping rod may have damaged forebrain areas responsible for emotional regulation.

Increasingly, in the 19th century, the study of the relation between the brain and mind focused on the question of localization of function. Researchers examined locations in the brain that control specific behaviors, abilities, and bodily functions. In the early 1800s, two anatomists, Franz Gall and Johan Spurzheim, argued that particular characteristics and abilities of individuals were due to the relatively larger size of specific brain areas. Gall had observed during his youth that students with large protruding eyes had good memories. He concluded that the brain areas for memory in the students with protruding eyes were more highly developed than those students with poorer memories who lacked the trait of protruding eyes. Even the tendency to steal corresponded to protuberance in the skull (Gall, 1966, originally published in 1825). Gall and Spurzheim went on to observe the skulls of a number of people and the traits that they thought went with particular bumps and protrusions. Phrenology was the name Gall and Spurzheim gave this study of the relation between the skull's surface features and mental and behavioral characteristics. The two anatomists created elaborate maps of the surface of the brain and the mental faculties and characteristics they thought went with the areas. Phrenology became quite popular, and many people went to exhibitions to have their "heads examined" by phrenologists who could supposedly tell them about their true natures.

Phrenology, however, had its critics, such as Magendie, the famous physiologist who, as the story goes, put Spurzheim to the test (Krech, 1960). Magendie had preserved the brain of the brilliant French philosopher and mathematician Laplace. He offered Spurzheim the opportunity to observe the pickled brain of this intellectual giant. Spurzheim, ever eager to examine brains and correspond them to traits, accepted the invitation. Unbeknownst to Spurzheim, Magendie had substituted the preserved brain of an imbecile for the test. Spurzheim is said to have admired the brain of the imbecile as if it were the brain of Laplace, thus calling phrenological theory into question.

Flourens (1960) and others developed more rigorous ways of studying localization of function. Flourens developed the technique of ablation, systematically destroying parts of the brain and observing the resulting changes in behavior. Based on destruction of various amounts and areas of the brain, he concluded that the brain was the seat of intelligence, and the cerebellum (a hindbrain structure) controlled movement, while the medulla oblongata (another hindbrain structure) controlled basic life functions. He concluded, however, that specific intelligent functions were not localized in the brain.

Paul Broca (1966) found that the ability to produce coherent speech was localized in the frontal region on the left side of the brain. Broca autopsied several patients who during their lives could not speak but, oddly enough, could understand speech. He observed that these patients showed damage in this same region. These cases showed that a specific function related to language was indeed localized.

Wernicke then discovered that language ability was localized in more than one specific brain area. In contrast to Broca's patients, who could understand but not speak, Wernicke's patients with damage to the left temporal region of the brain could speak but could not understand language. Wernicke argued that this was evidence that language abilities were not simply localized in one area of the brain, as localization of function theory might predict. Instead, components of complex abilities like language are localized to specific areas (Kolb & Whishaw, 1990).

Others also argued that the cortex or outer layer of the brain was not dedicated to specific functions. Goltz removed large portions of the brain, including all of the neocortex in dogs, and observed that they could still show coordinated movements and basic perceptual abilities. He interpreted his findings as indicating a general lowering of the will and impairment of the intellect that was proportional to the amount of brain tissue destroyed, findings that argued against localization of function (Goltz, 1960). Similarly, Lashley (1929) used the ablation technique on rats to determine whether the memory for how to run through a maze was stored in a specific place. He found that animals with large areas of their brains destroyed could still run the maze, results that suggested that long-term memory may be stored in a number of locations in the brain, rather than being localized. Note, however, that

Lashley may not have destroyed specific areas as precisely as he thought he did (Schneider & Tarshis, 1995).

Later, a case study of an unfortunate man called H. M. showed that some memory processes are indeed localized to specific areas of the brain (Millner, 1966). H. M. underwent surgery for his epilepsy, and doctors severed a small forebrain structure called the hippocampus. After his surgery, H. M. was unable to recall anything that happened to him since before he had his surgery. Each time his doctor would come to check on him he would have to be reintroduced!

Other attempts to control behavior problems with psychosurgery sometimes produced dramatic changes in the personalities of the individuals operated on. For example, some people who were considered impulsive troublemakers were turned into very lethargic, unemotional persons.

Fritsch and Hitzig in the late 1800s made another important discovery, that electrical stimulation of specific areas of the brain would produce particular behaviors, further supporting the idea of localization of function (Fritsch & Hitzig, 1960). Bartholow (1874) stimulated the left side of a patient's brain and observed muscular contractions in the opposite side of the body. Penfield (1975) stimulated the brains of patients undergoing brain surgery for epilepsy and observed that they frequently showed changes in mental experience. When stimulated they reported a variety of mental experiences that were as if they were reliving the experiences. One woman reported hearing a mother calling her son; and a man reported hearing an orchestra playing in a concert hall.

In addition, a large number of experiments have shown that electrostimulation of specific areas of the brain can produce motivated behaviors and emotional experience, such as aggressive behaviors and feelings of intense pleasure. Olds and Millner (1954) implanted tiny electrodes that could deliver a very small electrical pulse to a region called the septal area in rats. The researchers found that the rats would press a bar literally thousands of times just to deliver a minute electrical pulse to their brains after each press, suggesting that the animals found the self-stimulation very rewarding. Other research showed that stimulating a midbrain structure called the hippocampus in cats would help bring on a predatory attack behavior controlled by another structure, the hypothalamus (Siegel & Flynn, 1968). Results of these electrostimulation studies suggest that specific functions and behaviors may be localized in the brain but may not be regulated by a single structure.

≈ PRACTICE YOUR THINKING 4.3

Updating Your Beliefs

Answer the five critical thinking questions about the critical reading passage; after you have answered the questions, you can check your answers in Appendix C. Then think about how the conclusion drawn from the discussion relates to your own beliefs. People who are critical thinkers pay attention to and are persuaded by sound arguments—that is, conclusions that are supported by strong evidence. To help you reexamine your position on the mind-body question, answer the following questions.

1.   What was your initial belief about the connection between the mind and brain before reading the passage?

_____

2.   What conclusion did you draw from the critical reading passage about where the mind is located?

_____

3.   Now that you have read the passage, has your belief changed?

_____

Why or why not?

_____

_____

_____

Summary

This chapter discussed three basic positions on the important question of how the mind is related to the body. Dualists believe that the mind and body are two separate and distinct entities. Monists believe that mind and body are the same entity. Some monists, called materialists, believe that the world is actually all physical, whereas idealists believe that the reality of the world is based on subjective experience. A third position argues that the mind and body are separate entities but that they interact on some level.

One scientific approach to the mind-body problem involves investigating what parts of the brain support which behaviors and abilities—the question of localization of function. A survey of the research on this question shows that many specific functions, including what we might call mental abilities and experiences, have been found to depend on brain activity in specific areas. This supports the materialist conclusion that mental experience depends upon brain activity.

Review Questions

What is the mind-body problem?

What are the three positions on the mind-body question and how do they differ from each other?

Who were the behaviorists and what position did they take?

What is a reductionistic approach?

What is the difference between most people's position on this question and what many scientists believe?

What is physiology?

What is localization of function?

Describe three common physiological methods for studying brain processes.

What conclusion can be drawn from investigating the location of the mind or mental processes?

What conclusion can be drawn about localization of function?

References

Bartholow, R. (1874). Experimental investigation into the functions of the human brain. *American Journal of Medical Sciences, 67,* 305–313.

Blakemore, C. (1977). *Mechanics of the mind.* New York: Cambridge University Press.

Broca, P. (1966). Remarques sur le siege de la faculté du langage articulé, d'une observation d'aphemie. In R. Herrnstein & E. Boring (Eds.), *A sourcebook in the history of psychology.* Cambridge, MA: Harvard University Press.

Embree, R. A., & Embree, M. C. (1993). The personal scale as a measure of individual differences in commitment to the mind-body beliefs proposed by F. F. Centore. *Psychological Reports, 73,* 411–428.

Flourens, P. (1960). Investigations of the properties and functions of the various parts that compose the cerebral mass. In G. von Bonin (Ed.), *The cerebral cortex.* Springfield, IL: Charles C Thomas.

Fritsch, G., & Hitzig, G. (1960). On the electrical excitability of the cerebrum. In G. von Bonin (Ed.), *The cerebral cortex.* Springfield, IL: Charles C Thomas.

Gall, F. (1966). On the functions of the brain and each of its parts. In R. Herrnstein & E. Boring (Eds.), *A sourcebook in the history of psychology.* Cambridge, MA: Harvard University Press.

Goltz, F. (1960). On the functions of the hemispheres. In G. von Bonin (Ed.), *The cerebral cortex.* Springfield, IL: Charles C Thomas.

Hergenhahn, B. R. (1992). *An introduction to the history of psychology* (2nd ed.). Belmont, CA: Wadsworth.

Hothersall, D. (1984). *History of psychology.* New York: Random House.

Kalat, J. W. (1995). *Biological psychology* (5th ed.). Pacific Grove, CA: Brooks/Cole.

Kautz, W. H. (1993). Parapsychology, science, and intuition. In B. Kane, J. Millay, & D. Brown (Ed.), *Silver threads: 25 years of parapsychology research.* Westport, CT: Praeger.

Kolb, B., & Whishaw, I. Q. (1990). *Fundamentals of human neuropsychology.* New York: W. H. Freeman.

Krech, D. (1960). Cortical localization of function. In L. Postman (Ed.), *Psychology in the making.* New York: Knopf.

Lashley, K. S. (1929). *Brain mechanisms and intelligence: A quantitative study of injuries to the brain.* Chicago: University of Chicago Press.

Meier, M. J. (1992). Modern clinical neuropsychology in historical perspective. *American Psychologist, 47,* 550–558.

Millner, B. (1966). Amnesia following operation on the temporal lobes. In C. Whitty & O. Zangwill (Eds.), *Amnesia* (pp. 109–133). London: Butterworths.

Olds, J., & Millner, P. (1954). Positive reinforcement produced by electrical stimulation of the septal area and other regions of the rat brain. *Journal of Comparative and Physiological Psychology, 47,* 419–427.

Penfield, W. (1975). *The mystery of the mind.* Princeton, NJ: Princeton University Press.

Robinson, D. B. (1981). *An intellectual history of psychology* (Rev. ed.). New York: Macmillan.

Schneider, A. M., & Tarshis, B. (1995). *Elements of physiological psychology.* New York: McGraw-Hill.

Siegel, A., & Flynn, J. P. (1968). Differential effects of electrical stimulation and lesions of the hippocampus and adjacent regions upon attack behavior in cats. *Brain Research, 7,* 252–267.

Sperry, R. W. (1988). Psychology's mentalist paradigm and the religion/science tension. *American Psychologist, 43,* 607–613.

CHAPTER FIVE

Do We Perceive the World as It Is?

Learning Objectives

• To find out whether what we perceive is an accurate representation of the object world.

• To find out what visual illusions can tell us about perception.

• To examine how theories and hypotheses are used to account for phenomena such as visual illusions, and then are revised when shown to be insufficient.

What Do You Think?

Do we perceive what's really out there or not? To help you think about this important question, take a look at Figure 5.1 and describe what you see. Most people
report that they see a white triangle in the center of the figure that sometimes
appears brighter than the rest of the page. What do you see?

If you look closely at Figure 5.1 and think about what you are seeing, you will
realize that in fact there is no triangle. The triangle you see is defined by the
contours of the figures surrounding it: It is an illusion. This kind of illusion, for
obvious reasons, is called illusory contours.

What Are Illusions?

If the triangle is not physically there in the object world, then where is it? It
must be a product of our perceptual system.

Now take a close look at Figure 5.2. Do you notice something strange about
this figure? Figure 5.2 is interesting in two ways: First, we perceive a triangle
figure in three dimensions that is impossible in the real object world. Second,
we perceive this impossible figure in the same way that we take for granted in
our ordinary perception of many pictures; that is, we perceive this two-dimensional drawing in depth, as if it were in three dimensions. When artists and
photographers give us the illusion of depth in their two-dimensional representations of the world, they play a sort of trick upon us that goes unnoticed in our
ordinary perception.

Figure 5.1 Illusory
contours.

Figure 5.2 A paradoxical figure.

Despite the illusions we experience every day, most of the time we trust our perceptions. We behave as if we are perceiving objects exactly as they are in the world. People express this everyday approach to perception when they say that seeing is believing, or that they won't believe something until they see it with their own eyes. We often trust what we see or perceive as an accurate reflection of what is truly there—but should we? People also often say that things are not always as they appear to be. Is what you see what you get, or is what you see different from the actual objects of your perception? This question has important implications for critical thinking, because we often assume that what we have seen or perceived directly provides us with good evidence upon which to base a conclusion.

Like other important questions in psychology, this question has a long history. In the fifth century B.C., Epicurus proposed, in his "copy" theory of perception, that we do perceive the world as it is. According to Epicurus, objects send little copies of themselves to our eyes, which we then perceive (Epicurus, 1966). This view suggests that what we perceive, because it copies the object world, is therefore very much like the true world.

The Greek philosopher Plato took a very different view on this question, arguing that what we perceive is a rather crude reflection of the real world (Plato, 1956). Furthermore, Plato believed that we cannot trust the knowledge we get from our senses. In his famous cave analogy, he argued that our perception of objects is like that of a man chained to the wall of a cave who can see only the shadows of the objects behind him reflected on the wall of the cave in front of him. According to Plato, we do not perceive objects themselves, but rather shadows of the actual objects. We cannot perceive the actual forms of the objects through our senses; only through reason can we come to know the essence of the objects.

Whether we can know the world as it truly is through our senses is an important question because we constantly rely upon information from our senses to make judgments and to solve problems. Our senses are continuously presented with information. Through the processes of **perception,** this sensory information is organized and interpreted. If our perceptions are in error or misleading, then this can have disastrous effects on subsequent judgments. A driver might misjudge the distance between his car and another person's. A surgeon might apply her scalpel in the wrong place during surgery. Both scientific and critical thinking depend on observation as a source of evidence. If our perception is in error, then we may draw the wrong conclusion when we seek to evaluate evidence coming from observation, even if we followed the rules of logic and good thinking in coming to a conclusion.

One useful way to think about this question is to ask whether our perceptions faithfully correspond to the physical energy changes impinging on our senses. To answer this question, let's examine some visual illusions in more detail. If our perception can be tricked by these illusions, then this is evidence that our sensory-perceptual system is somehow transforming the physical stimulus into perceptual experience that is different from what is actually out there.

To investigate this question, let's begin by examining your own experience in observing the moon. Have you ever noticed how much larger the moon looks when it is near the horizon than when it is higher up in the night sky? Often, when the moon is full in autumn, it looks big and orange on the horizon, and people call it the harvest moon. In fact, people frequently report that the moon looks much larger near the horizon than when it is higher up in the sky, as shown in Figure 5.3.

≋ PRACTICE YOUR THINKING 5.1

Generating Hypotheses About Illusions

What's going on in this situation? Try to generate your own hypotheses to explain this phenomenon. Think of a plausible explanation: in other words, one that is con-

Figure 5.3 A comparison of how the moon often appears on the horizon versus higher in the sky (*from Goldstein, 1996*).

sistent with the facts and with your observations. The usual experience with the moon illusion is that the moon looks larger on the horizon than when farther up in the sky. What could be influencing your judgment of the moon's size? It might help to think about what kinds of things influence your judgment of the size of other objects; you might try picking up an object, moving it around, and comparing it to the size of another object.

Hypothesis 1: _____

Hypothesis 2: _____

Hypothesis 3: _____

Answers to Generating Hypotheses About Experiences

People often offer the following hypotheses to account for the moon illusion. Perhaps you thought of one of these.

Hypothesis 1: The moon looks larger on the horizon because it is closer in distance to the earth when it is near the horizon than when it is higher up in the sky.

First of all, it can be easily demonstrated that the moon is not getting smaller as it moves up in the sky. The earth and moon are maintaining a relatively constant distance from each other. The moon simply appears to rise as the earth rotates and the moon maintains a relatively constant orbit around the earth. You can demonstrate to yourself that the moon is not getting smaller as it rises by holding a notecard a constant four inches from one eye (keep the other eye closed). When the moon is just above the horizon, hold the notecard so that its edge crosses the central, horizontal diameter of the moon, and mark the distance across it on your notecard. Then about an hour later, when the moon has risen and appears smaller to you, repeat your measurement procedure, comparing the size of the risen moon to the previous measurement taken on the horizon. If you have not made a measurement error, the two measurements should show that the moon is the same size in both locations.

Hypothesis 2: Dust in the atmosphere that is close to the horizon makes the moon look more orange and larger than it actually is.

Particles in the air do differentially reflect some wavelengths of light coming from the moon more than other wavelengths and so may affect the color of the moon we perceive; but these reflections do not magnify the size of the moon.

Hypothesis 3: The moon does not actually change its physical size as it changes position. Instead, our perception of the moon's apparent size changes. In fact, this last hypothesis is the most correct. The incorrect estimation of the moon's size relative to its position in the sky is called the moon illusion. This hypothesis, however, mostly describes the effect; it does little to explain how it is occurring.

To better understand this illusory effect, let's first examine some other pictures and then try to explain the effects with these pictures. Take a look at the two figures

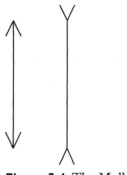

Figure 5.4 The Muller-Lyer
Illusion (*from Goldstein, 1996*).

in Figure 5.4. Compare the length of the two central lines in the figures. Does one seem longer than the other?

People usually report that the central line in the figure on the right appears longer than the central line in the figure on the left. Measure them and demonstrate to yourself that they are the same length.

Now inspect Figure 5.5 and compare the length of the two horizontal white lines in the picture. Does one seem longer than the other?

People usually report that the horizontal white line on the top looks longer than the lower white line. As before, if you measure the length of the two lines, you will see that they are actually the same length.

Just as in Figures 5.3 and 5.4, our perceptions seem to have differed from physical reality—that is, to have been in error. What is going on? Why would we have a perceptual system that provides us with erroneous information, when judgments based on such erroneous perceptions could also be in error, with disastrous results?

Examining a Theory of Size Illusions

Gregory (1966) offered one explanation of these illusions based on our experience with objects in depth. According to Gregory, the left-hand figure in Figure 5.6 (on page 88) reminds us of the outside contours of a building projecting toward us, while the right-hand figure in Figure 5.6 reminds us of inside contours of the corner of a building projecting away from us.

Stop for a moment and look at the corners of the walls in the room you are in. Walls that project toward you, as in the left-hand side of Figure 5.6, tend to be closer to you, whereas receding corners, as in the right-hand side of the figure, tend to be farther away from you. Through repeated experience with these kinds of stimuli, information about the position of one object relative to another in the environment comes to signal depth. Information in the retinal image that, correlated with the relative position of objects in the world, comes to sig-

Figure 5.5 The Ponzo illusion (*courtesy of E. Bruce Goldstein, from* Sensation and Perception, *4th ed., 1996*).

nal depth is called a **depth cue** (Goldstein, 1996). Even if we are not aware of the presence of these depth cues, they have an automatic effect on our perception of depth. So, for example, the corner projecting away from us in the right-hand side of Figure 5.6 would automatically signal depth information.

Not only do depth cues contribute to our judgments about the relative position of one object in the environment with respect to another, they also influence our judgments of size. For example, suppose you were looking up a suburban street at a row of tract houses all of the same size. The ones in your foreground would appear both larger and closer to you while the ones in the background would appear both smaller and farther away.

Our perceptual system also uses depth information to tell us that an object is not changing its size as it changes its position. An object closer to us will take up more area on our retinas than when that object is farther away. But it would not be helpful for you to change your judgment of an object's size every time its position changed. For example, it would not be useful for you to judge my height to be 5´ 8´´ when I am standing two yards away from you, and only 2´ 10´´ (half as tall) when I am 4 yards or twice the distance from you. Instead, you would most likely judge me to be about 5´ 8´´ at both distances. When your size estimate does not change even though the stimulus condition of distance has changed, your perception is showing constancy. In particular, your perception is showing **size constancy**: the tendency to perceive an object to be the same size even when its distance varies.

Figure 5.6 The Muller-Lyer figures as they may appear in the inside and outside corners of buildings (*courtesy of E. Bruce Goldstein, from* Sensation and Perception, *4th ed., 1996*).

Besides depth information, another factor important in judgments of size is an object's physical size as indicated by the size of its image on the retina, or what is called the **visual angle** of the stimulus. Holway and Boring (1941) conducted an experiment in which they showed that subjects' size judgments depended more and more on visual angle when information about depth was eliminated. When information about the depth of the objects being judged was present, subjects' judgments showed size constancy. But when depth information was eliminated, subjects' judgments were consistent with the object's visual angle or its actual size on the retina. According to Gregory (1963), our perceptual system has a size-distance scaling mechanism that takes into account a person's perceived distance when calculating a person's size. This mechanism also accounts for size constancy in our perceptions. The size-distance scaling mechanism is applied automatically and unconsciously when cues about depth like those found in the contour of a corner are present in a situation, even when those cues are not related to a contour, as in the Muller-Lyer illusion (Figure 5.4). This misapplication of size constancy then leads to our mistaken perception of the length of the lines in the Muller-Lyer illusion. When we look at the line on the right in Figure 5.4, depth cues that signal a corner projecting away from us (as in the right-hand side of Figure 5.6) automatically come into play. In Figure 5.6, the depth cue signals that the central line or shaft is relatively farther away in the right-hand part of the figure, as compared to the corner projecting toward us in the left-hand part of the figure, which signals that the central line is relatively closer. When our perceptual system compares the two central lines, which are actually equal in length, it takes into account this depth information and contributes to the inference that the central shaft on the right must be father away and therefore larger than the central shaft on the left.

A similar kind of explanation involving depth cues can be given for the Ponzo illusion (Figure 5.5). We have much experience with converging parallel lines suggesting depth in our viewing of everyday scenes. For example, notice how the parallel lines in ceiling or floor tiles appear to come closer together as they get farther away from us in our view of a room. Our repeated experience with parallel lines converging as they recede into the distance makes them become a depth cue. Artists use parallel lines converging toward a vanishing point in the distance to create the impression of depth as part of a technique called **linear perspective.** We can also use information from this depth cue to help us make judgments about the size of objects in the environment. In the case of the Ponzo illusion depicted in Figure 5.5, the upper horizontal white line is perceived as relatively larger than it actually is because the converging parallel lines of the train tracks suggest that it is farther away than the lower horizontal white line.

The influence of depth cues may also help explain the moon illusion. When the moon is on the horizon, many more depth cues could signal the relative distance of the moon. Some examples of these cues are the converging parallel lines of buildings or roads, the decreasing size of trees as they approach the horizon, or the fact that objects in the environment appear to cover up or to be in front of the moon. All of these may contribute to the perception that the moon is farther away than it actually is. On the other hand, when the moon is higher up in the sky, fewer if any cues are present that could signal depth and the relative position of the moon. Consequently, our judgment of the size of the moon is less affected by depth cues so that we rely more on the actual size of the moon's image as it falls on our retina.

Problems with the Theory

You might conclude from this discussion that misapplied size constancy and the use of depth cues to make size judgments could account for how our perceptual system comes to be tricked by illusions such as the Muller-Lyer illusion in Figure 5.4. This theory, however, although it can explain some of these size illusions, cannot explain some other relevant examples. In Figure 5.7 you can see that the same illusory effect occurs with line length as in the Muller-Lyer illusion, but this new figure has circles on the ends of the lines instead of inward and outward projecting rays. Ask yourself why the misapplied size constancy theory cannot account for the illusory effect with the similar figure in Figure 5.7. Take a moment and try to answer the question. Ask yourself what the theory assumes and how it accounts for the other illusions discussed. Then look at the new figure and ask yourself how it is like the Muller-Lyer and how it is different in important ways. How does the result from this illusion cause problems for misapplied size constancy?

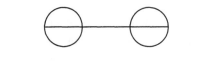

Figure 5.7 The Muller-Lyer effect in very different figures (*from Goldstein, 1996*).

You should have noticed that the ends in the new figure are very different from the receding and abutting edges of the corners of architectural structures that form our common experience with objects in depth. Nevertheless, the illusion persists without these cues; so this bit of evidence poses problems for the theory that are not readily resolved. Similarly, other research suggests that the Muller-Lyer illusion occurs in three-dimensional forms of the illusion (Delucia & Hochberg, 1991; Nijhawan, 1991). Also, an early study by Waite and Massaro (1970) failed to support Gregory's (1963) size constancy theory. Still other research suggests that eye movements may account for the effect of the Muller-Lyer illusion (Virsu, 1971). Perhaps when subjects scan the length of the wings-out part of the Muller-Lyer figure, their eye movements may be overshooting the extent of the shaft or central line of the illusion and may be continuing along the wings-out rays. When subjects are trained to be more accurate in scanning the length of the shaft, then the illusion should decrease, with subjects estimating the length of the shaft more accurately.

Handling Problems with a Theory

Recall from Chapters 1 and 2 that a theory is a rule or principle that is consistent with and is used to explain a set of observations. While Gregory's theory that depth cues arising from regularities found in our experience of the environment could explain how we come to use this information to misjudge the length of the central shaft of the Muller-Lyer illusion, this theory has difficulty explaining why we experience the illusion in objects that are not like the environment or in three-dimensional forms of the illusion. When a theory is no longer consistent with a set of relevant observations, then typically two things happen. First, the scientist checks the methods used to obtain the finding and then examines the reasoning behind the inconsistent observations. If these are not in error, then the scientist reexamines the theory. Gregory's (1963) theory, therefore, must be either modified to account for the discrepant data or else discarded. One way to save part of the theory is by incorporating it into the eye movement theory mentioned before. Depth cues that are acquired by repeated observation of the corners of rooms, for example, may lead people to develop sloppy eye movements as they scan the corners of rooms. This sloppiness may cause them, when they look at the Muller-Lyer illusion, to overshoot past the central line into the wings-out portion of the figure. If they are using their eye movements to judge the length of the central shaft, then this may cause them to overestimate the length of the central shaft in the figure.

What Do Illusions Tell Us About Perception?

So how should we think about the effects of illusions on our perceptions? One useful approach is to think of illusions as failed hypotheses (Gregory, 1980). More than a century ago, the great German physicist and physiologist Herman von Helmholtz proposed that our perception is like a conclusion we draw about the sensory data that we take in. We make an unconscious inference based on the information available to us; this inference is more or less likely to be correct. Sometimes, however, in attempting to interpret this information, our perceptual system applies rules in a way that causes us to accept an incorrect hypothesis, so that we experience an illusion. This view suggests that the perceiver is like a hypothesis tester.

This view is consistent with much of the research on illusions and theories, especially those that emphasize the influence of cues on depth perception. We have seen, though, that our theories cannot yet explain even a seemingly simple illusion like the Muller-Lyer. Further research is needed; perhaps more important is the need for new ways of thinking about illusions, or theories that can account for more of the research observations.

≈ PRACTICE YOUR THINKING 5.2

Questioning Observations as Evidence

Use what you have learned about illusions, their effects on perception, and the role of theory in studying them to answer the following questions.

1. What would you say to someone who said that seeing is believing?

2. Because our perceptions are sometimes susceptible to error and distortion, should we not trust observations made through our senses?

3. Think of two examples of how visual illusions might interfere with your critical thinking or judgment.

4. What might be done to get around or to minimize the impact of perceptual errors and distortions on our thinking?

5. What would you say to someone who said, "I think Gregory's theory of the influence of depth information on size estimation is correct?"

Summary

Do we perceive the object world as it really is? Epicurus's copy theory holds that what we perceive is a copy of what is there, whereas Plato argued that our perception gives us incorrect information about the world. Visual illusions demonstrate that our perception is sometimes different from the object world. We may think of our perception as similar to hypothesis testing in which we draw an inference based on our best guess as to the source of the sensory stimulation. Sometimes, as in our perceptions of illusions, our inference is wrong and we misperceive.

People use information about depth and about visual angle, or an image's size on the retina, to make size judgments. These factors can affect both size illusions and size constancy. If little depth information is present, then a person will make size judgments based on visual angle. When depth information is present, size judgments may show size constancy; that is, with the help of depth cues an observer will tend to judge the object as the same size even when its distance from the observer is changing. Gregory proposed that we have a size-distance scaling mechanism that we use to make judgments of size. According to this theory, we use information about depth to judge the position of objects in the environment. Then we automatically scale our judgment of size, given the assumption about object's distance. Size-distance scaling has not been supported by some of the research; illusions like the Muller-Lyer illusion can be produced with stimuli that do not resemble our experience with the environment. When theories like size-distance scaling are inconsistent with observations, then the scientist first looks to see whether there was any error in observation or problems with the methods used. Then the scientist examines the theory's reasoning to see whether some mistaken assumption has been overlooked. Finally, the theory is either expanded, adding an assumption as needed, or the theory is discarded completely.

Review Questions

What is perception?

What is an illusion?

What does copy theory propose?

How is copy theory different from Plato's ideas about perception?

What is a depth cue and where does it come from?

What is linear perspective?

What is perceptual constancy? Size constancy?

Why do we have them?

How does size distance scaling explain size constancy?

How does misapplied size constancy explain illusions of size?

What's wrong with the theory of size distance scaling and misapplied size constancy?

Can we trust the information and evidence we get through our perception?

References

Delucia, P. R., & Hochberg, J. (1991). Geometrical illusions in solid objects under ordinary viewing conditions. *Perception and Psychophysics, 50,* 547–554.

Epicurus. (1966). On perception of objects as mediated by the images that emanate from the objects. In R. Herrnstein & E. Boring (Eds.), *A sourcebook in the history of psychology.* Cambridge, MA: Harvard University Press.

Erlebacher, A., & Sekuler, R. (1969). Explanation of the Muller-Lyer illusion: Confusion theory explained. *Journal of Experimental Psychology, 80,* 462–467.

Goldstein, E. B. (1996). *Sensation and perception* (4th ed.). Pacific Grove, CA: Brooks/Cole.

Gregory, R. L. (1963). Distortion of visual space as inappropriate constancy scaling. *Nature, 199,* 678–680.

Gregory, R. L. (1966). *Eye and brain.* New York: McGraw-Hill.

Gregory, R. L. (1980). In R. L. Gregory & E. H. Gombrich (Eds.), *Illusions in nature and art.* New York: Charles Scribner's Sons.

Holway, A. H., & Boring, E. G. (1941). Determinants of apparent visual angle size with distance variant. *American Journal of Psychology, 54,* 21–37.

Nijhawan, R. (1991). Three-dimensional Muller-Lyer illusion. *Perception and Psychophysics, 49,* 333–341.

Plato. (1956). *Great dialogues of Plato* (W. H. Rouse, Trans.). New York: New American Library.

Virsu, V. (1971). Tendencies to eye movement, and misperception of curvature, direction, and length. *Perception and Psychophysics, 9,* 65–72.

Waite, H., & Massaro, D. W. (1970). Test of Gregory's constancy scaling explanation of the Muller-Lyer illusion. *Nature, 227,* 733–734.

The Extraordinary Claims Made About Hypnosis

Learning Objectives

• To find out whether some of the extraordinary claims about hypnosis are true and to reflect upon our own beliefs about such claims.

• To critically read a review of the psychological literature about whether or not hypnosis can improve memory.

What Do You Think?

We have all heard extraordinary claims about people who have shown supernormal abilities under hypnosis. Many stories on television and in novels suggest that a person can be made to commit a crime or be controlled by another person through hypnosis. Perhaps you have heard that people can undergo major surgery or extensive dental work with only hypnosis as a painkiller. Or you may have heard that criminal investigators use hypnosis to help witnesses recall details of crimes that they could not at first recall. Are these extraordinary claims true? What do you think?

What Is Hypnosis?

Many psychologists agree that hypnosis is similar to other ordinary states involving relaxation, concentration, and suggestion. Under hypnosis, a person may experience "changes in perception, thinking, memory, and behavior" including temporary paralysis, hallucinations, and forgetting "in response to suggestions by the hypnotist" (Farthing, 1992, p. 337). In fact, susceptibility to hypnosis, or hypnotizability, is often measured by the number of suggestions to engage in certain behaviors or to have certain experiences that a subject successfully carries out. Common hypnotic suggestions include the suggestion that one's arm held straight out for several seconds is becoming too heavy to hold up, the suggestion that a fly is buzzing around one's face, and the suggestion to forget the events that occurred during the hypnotic procedure. Some subjects are found to pass very few of these items and so are classified as low hypnotizables, whereas others pass most of them and so are classified as high hypnotizables.

While it may seem convenient to define hypnosis as an altered state of consciousness or awareness, much debate has taken place over this proposition. As Farthing (1992) noted, many hypnosis researchers would agree that hypnosis produces subjective experiences that are dramatically altered from normal waking awareness. But when the attempt is made to define hypnosis as a particular state of consciousness, with its own specific pattern of behaviors and physiological changes differentiating it from other states of consciousness, hypnosis does not seem so clearly distinct. While sleep has been shown to have particular brainwave patterns that accompany it (Rechtschaffen & Kales, 1968), and some emotional states have been differentiated by heart rate and skin temperature (Ekman, Levinson, & Friesen, 1983), physiological signs accompanying hypnosis have been less reliably produced.

Also, psychologists often do not agree on whether hypnosis gives people special abilities, such as the ability to ward off severe pain. Since Esdaile's pioneering work in the 1800s, hypnosis has been successfully used as the only anesthetic in some major surgeries (Orne & Dinges, 1989). While hypnosis is effective in thwarting pain, it is not clear whether it is more effective than other nonhypnotic strategies that involve distraction and reinterpretation of pain (Spanos, Radtke-Bodorik, Ferguson, & Jones, 1979; Devine & Spanos, 1990). The degree to which pain reduction is possible may depend on a person's hypnotic susceptibility.

Sometimes, people's commonsense "theories" about hypnosis may lead to unfounded fears about its dangers. For example, a common idea is that hypnosis can be used to make people do harmful or immoral acts that they would not otherwise do. Farthing (1992) cited cases in which hypnotists have seduced their subjects and have tricked subjects into physical violence. Except for those subjects who believe that they lose control during hypnosis or those who are motivated to resign control to the hypnotist, though, subjects ordinarily can refuse to comply with hypnotic suggestions if they want to. An interesting experiment by Orne and Evans (1965) investigated this question of whether instructions provided to hypnotized people would induce them to commit a harmful and immoral act. Orne and Evans compared the effects of instructions to handle a venomous snake, to immerse one's hands in strong nitric acid, and to throw the nitric acid in the experimenter's face on five different groups of subjects—one group who were unhypnotized, a second group who pretended to be hypnotized, a third group who were hypnotized but pressed to comply with the instructions, a fourth group who were unhypnotized but not pressed to comply, and a fifth group who were simply given the instructions outside the context of the experiment. Surprisingly, they found that subjects from all of the groups except the nonexperimental control group were willing to do all three acts. Note that some subjects said they did not believe that the experimenter would ask them to do anything harmful; indeed, the experimenter had substituted a harmless liquid for the acid prior to instructing subjects to throw the acid. It may be that both hypnotized and unhypnotized subjects will comply with instructions to do something harmful and immoral within certain social contexts.

We now turn to a discussion of another controversial claim made for hypnosis—that is, that it can help people to remember things not previously remembered. We will examine this claim in detail; but first, let's examine your opinion about this question more closely.

≋ PRACTICE YOUR THINKING 6.1

Assessing Your Beliefs About Hypnosis

Part of critical thinking involves reflecting on your own beliefs and assumptions, evaluating the evidence relevant to the claims to decide what to believe. You probably have your own beliefs about hypnosis and memory. For example, you may have heard that police sometimes use hypnosis to help a witness recall previously unremembered details of a crime. You may have heard that therapists sometimes use hypnosis to help their clients recall buried memories of sexual abuse. Think about your own beliefs regarding hypnosis and memory, and then answer the following questions. Next read the critical reading passage on hypnosis and memory in the next section and observe whether any of your beliefs change.

1. Can people better recall details of a crime after being hypnotized? _____

2. Can people accurately recall the details of a time early in their lives or even from a former life through age regression, a hypnotic procedure in which the person is asked to "go back" to an earlier time? _____

3. Can hypnosis be used to help a person reliably recall details of their experience of having been abducted by aliens? _____

≈ PRACTICE YOUR THINKING 6.2

Critically Reading a Literature Review: Does Hypnosis Improve Memory?

The following critical reading passage examines a question related to hypnosis and memory. In the process described in Chapter 3, read through the following critical reading questions first, then read the passage, and then try to answer the questions. It may help you to analyze the passage if you underline words from the language of argumentation, found in Appendix A, as they appear in the passage. Then, think about what part of an argument each word signals and how the basic question is being clarified and made more specific as it is discussed. Tables 2.1 and 2.2 should also help you to identify the kinds of evidence used in the passage.

Questions to Prepare You for Critical Reading

1. What is the central question? What claims are being made?

2. What evidence has been presented that is relevant to evaluating each side of the question? Organize the evidence under one category for evidence supporting the claim and another for relevant evidence not supporting the claim. Then label each piece of evidence as to its kind.

3. Evaluate the quality and quantity of the evidence so that you can draw a sound conclusion based on the evidence presented.

4. Do any assumptions create problems for this conclusion?

5. What are some implications of this conclusion?

Does Hypnosis Improve Memory?

A popular view is that individuals have extraordinary abilities while under hypnosis, such as supernormal memory. When hypnosis helps a person to recall information that he or she did not previously recall, this is termed 'hypnotic hypermnesia'. Many clinicians and their clients also believe that hypnosis can improve memory (e. g. Wolberg, 1982).

The notion that hypnosis can improve recall has received support from documented cases in which law enforcement agents have obtained useful evidence from eyewitnesses who, prior to hypnosis, had difficulty recalling details of the crimes they witnessed. One example of the success of hypnosis in refreshing the memory of a crime comes from the case of *People vs. Woods et al.* (cited in Smith, 1983), better known as the Chowchilla kidnapping case. In Chowchilla, California, kidnappers abducted 26 children and their bus driver and secluded them in an underground, rectangular enclosure. The bus driver and two of the older children were able to escape by digging through to the surface and then contacted the police. Although the bus driver had tried to memorize the license plate numbers of the abductors' vehicles at the time of the abduction, he was unable to recall the plate numbers to police. The police gave him hypnotic instructions that he should imagine sitting in his favorite easy chair to watch the crime unfold on television. He then recalled two license plate numbers, one of which turned out to be off by only one number. His testimony enabled police to speed up their investigation and apprehend the kidnappers. In a review of the literature, Smith (1983) cited other cases in which hypnosis has later improved memory of events and crimes that were observed under unhypnotized (awake) conditions but were not well remembered prior to hypnosis.

Hypnosis has been used since the time of Freud as a method for helping people with psychological problems to recall traumatic or anxiety-provoking events from their pasts, especially from their childhood. Similarly, it has long been thought that through hypnosis subjects could regress to an earlier age when given a suggestion to imagine that they were back at an earlier time. In many examples from stage and laboratory, hypnotized adults who are given suggestions to return to an earlier age have shown changes in their speech and facial expressions appropriate to that younger age. When researchers have checked such people's memories of events from previous times, they found that age-regressed subjects did not accurately remember details (Nash, Drake, Wiley, Khalsa, & Lynn, 1986). In a review of the literature on hypnotic age regression, Nash (1987) concluded that there was little evidence that hypnotically age-regressed subjects actually returned to a mental state like their original state or that their recall improved. In fact, through hypnotic age regression, subjects may recall incidents, even former lives, that they actually may have constructed based on other experiences. Spanos, Menary, Gabora, Dubreuil, and Dewhirst (1991) found that subjects who were hypnotized, age-regressed, and given suggestions to recall former lives often did so; however, the lives they recalled were frequently based on historical figures with whom they were familiar. Nevertheless, the subjects often recalled these lives inaccurately.

Some early research showed that hypnosis did enhance memory for information from a person's past. According to a literature review by Relinger (1984), however, later psychological laboratory experiments concerning people's memory for nonsense syllables and other items of low meaningfulness failed to show any benefits from hypnosis.

After some of these successes in refreshing memory with hypnosis, police departments began to use hypnosis as an investigative tool in the 1960s. One result was a renewed interest among psychologists in researching hynotic hypermnesia. In order to explain inconsistent findings concerning hypnosis and recall, psychologists began to investigate conditions that might produce hypnotic hypermnesia. Relinger (1984), in the same review of the literature on hypnotic hypermnesia, argued that hypnotic hypermnesia tended to occur in studies of memory for meaningful material but not for material of low meaningfulness. A review by Erdelyi (1994) also observed this trend; however, an experiment by Mingay (1985) found that hypnotized subjects were not more accurate than unhypnotized subjects in recalling meaningful visual material.

Other studies tried to make the laboratory situation more like the setting of a crime and its investigation. Because crimes are often witnessed during states of heightened arousal, subjects' arousal was heightened to make the experiment more like the natural situation. Subjects were sometimes also deceived into believing that actual crimes had been committed. In general, these experiments have not resulted in subjects' showing better memory than non-hypnotized subjects, according to Smith's (1983) review of these studies.

Other research has shown that what looks like a hypermnesic effect in fact may not be due to hypnosis. Erdelyi and Becker (1974) showed that with repeated attempts at recall, even without hypnosis, subjects remember things that they did not previously recall. Because many early studies examined memory initially without hypnosis and then under hypnosis, improved recall attributed to hypnosis actually may have been due simply to repeated attempts at recall. Repeated attempts at recall thus may explain situations in which a witness first unsuccessfully attempts to recall details of a crime and then is later able to recall the details after being hypnotized. In a recent review of the literature, Erdelyi (1994) concluded that the repeated attempts to recall initially unrecalled information account for any increase in recall after hypnosis, rather than hypnosis per se being responsible.

Some well-controlled studies, however, have shown that hypnosis improves recall. For example, Dhanens and Lundy (1975) conducted an experiment in which they compared different groups of subjects who were all highly susceptible to hypnosis. These different treatment groups were tested under various memory testing conditions on their ability to recall a prose passage immediately after learning it and then a week later. Any gain in their recall was thought to indicate a hypermnesia effect. Unhypnotized subjects were asked to recall the prose passage after receiving no additional instructions, after instructions to relax, after hypnotic regression instructions, or after motivational instructions. Still other treatment groups were hypnotized and then asked to recall the prose passage after receiving either the same regression or the same motivational instructions as their unhypnotized counterparts. In the most important results of the experiment, the researchers found that the hypnotized groups, who also got motivational instructions, showed the most gain in their recall of the passage, suggesting a hypnotic hypermnesia effect.

Two other problems have been found with the use of hypnosis to refresh memory. First, some researchers, like Laurence and Perry (1983), have shown experimentally that a hypnotized person may be given a false suggestion while trying to recall some event and will incorporate this false suggestion into memory, thus creating a pseudomemory. Then, outside of hypnosis, these subjects will recall these pseudomemories as if they were true. Sheehan, Statham, and Jamieson (1991) created pseudomemories about events viewed in videotapes and found that these events persisted at least two weeks after the viewing. It is not clear what caused the pseudomemories. Spanos and McLean (1985) produced pseudomemories in all 11 highly hypnotizable subjects they tested, but under special reporting conditions almost all subjects acknowledged the memories were imagined; these results suggested that the failure to recall was due to bias from the reporting procedure, not actual distortion of the memories. According to a literature review by Spanos, Burgess, and Burgess (1994), people who form pseudomemories of being abducted by aliens often do so within the context of hypnotic and structured interviews that create demands for the reporting of such experiences, which people then come to interpret as actual memories of abduction.

The formation of pseudomemories can create problems for those using hypnosis to obtain information. Coons (1988) studied the case of a woman interviewed by police who used a particularly suggestive interrogative technique. This led to the woman's confessing to a crime she did not commit and developing symptoms of multiple personality disorder created by the suggestions.

A second problem with using hypnosis to help recall memories is hypnotized subjects' overconfidence in their memories. Although subjects in the Sheehan et al. (1991) study who recalled pseudomemories were not more confident of their memories than were those who did not recall pseudomemories, subjects in other studies often have been more confident of pseudomemories formed during hypnosis. For a review, see the Council on Scientific Affairs, American Medical Association (1985).

In summary, hypnosis has sometimes been found to be effective in helping police to solve crimes by helping witnesses to recall more information. Although hypnotically age-regressed individuals appear to return to an earlier time, their recall of details from that time has been found to be inaccurate. Studies that have shown hypnosis to improve recall have examined the recall of meaningful information. Most studies seeking to simulate realistic natural conditions have failed to show hypnotic hypermnesia. Other studies have suggested that improvement in recall may have been due to repeated attempts at recall rather than to hypnosis per se. Finally, false memories have been created within the context of hypnosis; moreover, subjects often report that they are confident of the accuracy of false or inaccurate memories. In an extensive review of the literature, a panel of experts on hypnosis and memory concluded that hypnosis does not improve recall of meaningless information and when hypnosis does affect recall of meaningful information it may increase the recall of both accurate and inaccurate information (Council on Scientific Affairs, American Medical Association, 1985).

After you have answered the critical reading questions in Practice Your Thinking 6.2, you can compare your answers to those in Appendix B.

≈ PRACTICE YOUR THINKING 6.3

Reassessing Your Beliefs About Hypnosis

After reading the literature review, did any of your beliefs about hypnosis and memory change? Evaluate your present beliefs by answering the questions from Practice Your Thinking 6.1 again and then compare them to your previous answers. You may also compare your new answers to the ones provided at the end of this section.

1. Can people better recall details of a crime after being hypnotized? _____

2. Can people accurately recall the details of a time early in their lives or even from a former life through age regression, a hypnotic procedure in which the person is asked to go back to an earlier time? _____

3. Can hypnosis be used to help people reliably recall details of their experience of having been abducted by aliens? _____

Answers to Reassessing Your Beliefs About Hypnosis

1. From the evidence presented in the literature review, there is little reason to believe that using hypnosis to help a person recall details of a crime will greatly improve recall, especially as compared to simply having someone recall a second time. In fact, if not used correctly, hypnosis may lead to less accurate memory.

2. The research on age regression suggests that people may even recall the details of an earlier time in their lives less accurately after hypnotic age regression. As far as recalling events from former lives is concerned, there is no evidence that the implausible claim of reincarnation is correct. Even if reincarnation does occur, the research reviewed suggests that people can be led to report such memories through hypnotic recall suggestions, but these memories are often historically inaccurate.

3. Similarly, very little evidence other than anecdotes supports the claim that alien abduction does indeed occur. If it did, however, recovering such memories through hypnosis could lead to pseudomemories if the hypnotic interview were improperly conducted.

Summary

Hypnosis is a very controversial phenomenon in psychology. Hypnosis involves a hypnotist's imparting suggestions to a subject to have certain experiences and to behave in certain ways. For example, hypnotized subjects frequently experience changes in their memory, thinking, behavior, and awareness in general. Psychologists do not agree about whether hypnosis is a separate state of consciousness distinct from other states.

Claims about people's abilities under hypnosis are also controversial. For example, the claim that hypnosis can lead to the experience of less pain has been generally supported, but it is not clear whether or not hypnosis leads to greater pain reduction than the use of cognitive strategies such as distraction and reinterpretation. Similarly, the claim that hypnotized people can be made to do harmful and immoral acts is supported by some anecdotes and research; however, other research suggests that unhypnotized subjects in the appropriate social context will do the same acts.

The claim that hypnosis could help people to recall previously unrecalled information was examined in detail. People have recalled more details of crimes after being hypnotized than they did before hypnosis, and early research showed that hypnosis helped subjects recall more. Later research, with better controls and using more realistic testing situations, generally failed to show improvement in recall due to hypnosis. Research on hypnotic age regression showed that people often do not accurately recall information from their pasts after being hypnotized. Furthermore, memory under hypnosis is often less reliable than ordinary recall because false memories or pseudomemories can be easily suggested. Sometimes, too, people are more confident of memories recalled under hypnosis than of other memories. In general, the research evidence does not support the claim that hypnosis can help people to recover previously unrecalled information accurately. An implication of this conclusion is that law enforcement investigators and others must be very cautious in interpreting memories obtained through hypnosis.

Review Questions

What is hypnosis? Is it a separate state of consciousness? How is it measured?

Can hypnosis help a person ward off pain?

Can a hypnotized person be made to commit harmful and immoral acts?

What are some claims made about the effects of hypnosis on memory?

What is hypnotic hypermnesia versus ordinary hypermnesia?

What is age regression? Does it lead to accurate memories?

What is a pseudomemory? How is it created?

How confident are hypnotized subjects about their memory?

References

Coons, P. M. (1988). Misuse of forensic hypnosis: A hypnotically elicited false confession with the apparent creation of a multiple personality. *International Journal of Clinical and Experimental Hypnosis, 36*, 1–11.

Council on Scientific Affairs, American Medical Association (1985). Scientific status of refreshing recollection by the use of hypnosis. *Journal of the American Medical Association, 253*, 1918–1923.

Devine, D. P., & Spanos, N. P. (1990). Effectiveness of maximally different cognitive strategies and expectancy in attenuation of reported pain. *Journal of Personality and Social Psychology, 58*, 672–678.

Dhanens, T. P., & Lundy, R. M. (1975). Hypnotic and waking suggestions and recall. *International Journal of Clinical and Experimental Hypnosis, 23*, 68–79.

Ekman, P., Levinson, R., & Friesen, W. (1983). Autonomic nervous system activity distinguishes among emotion. *Science, 221*, 1208–1210.

Erdelyi, M. H. (1994). Hypnotic hypermnesia: The empty set of hypermnesia. *International Journal of Clinical and Experimental Hypnosis, 42*, 379–390.

Erdelyi, M. H., & Becker, J. (1974). Hypermnesia for pictures: Incremental memory for pictures but not words in multiple recall trials. *Cognitive Psychology, 6*, 159–171.

Farthing, G. W. (1992). *The psychology of consciousness.* Englewood Cliffs, NJ: Prentice-Hall.

Laurence, J. R., & Perry, C. W. (1983). Hypnotically created memories among highly hypnotizable subjects. *Science, 222*, 523–524.

Mingay, D. L. (1985). Hypnosis and memory for incidentally learned scenes. *British Journal of Experimental and Clinical Hypnosis, 3*, 173–183.

Nash, M. (1987). What, if anything, is regressed about hypnotic age regression? A review of the empirical literature. *Psychological Bulletin, 102*, 42–52.

Nash, M., Drake, S., Wiley, S., Khalsa, S., & Lynn, S. (1986). Accuracy of recall by hypnotically age-regressed subjects. *Journal of Abnormal Psychology, 95*, 298–300.

Orne, M. T., & Dinges, D. F. (1989). Hypnosis. In P. Wall & R. Melzack (Eds.), *Textbook of pain* (2nd ed.). Edinburgh: Churchill Livingstone.

Orne, M. T., & Evans, F. J. (1965). Social control in the psychological experiment: Antisocial behavior and hypnosis. *Journal of Personality and Social Psychology, 1,* 189–200.

Rechtschaffen, A., & Kales, A. (1968). A manual of standardized terminology, techniques and scoring systems for sleep stages of human subjects. (National Institute of Health Publication No. 204.) Washington, DC: United States Government Printing Office.

Relinger, H. (1984). Hypnotic hypermnesia: A critical review. *American Journal of Clinical Hypnosis, 26,* 212–225.

Sheehan, P. W., Statham, D., & Jamieson, G. (1991). Pseudomemory effects over time in the hypnotic setting. *Journal of Abnormal Psychology, 100,* 39–44.

Smith, M. C. (1983). Hypnotic enhancement of witnesses: Does it work? *Psychological Bulletin, 94,* 387–407.

Spanos, N. P., Burgess, C. A., & Burgess, M. F. (1994). Past-life identities, UFO abductions, and satanic ritual abuse: The social construction of memories. *International Journal of Clinical and Experimental Hypnosis, 42,* 433–446.

Spanos, N. P., & McLean, J. (1985). Hypnotically created pseudomemories: Memory distortions or reporting biases. *British Journal of Experimental and Clinical Hypnosis, 3,* 155–159.

Spanos, N. P., Menary, E., Gabora, N. J., Dubreuil, S. C., & Dewhirst, B. (1991). Secondary identity enactments during hypnotic past-life regression: A sociocognitive perspective. *Journal of Personality and Social Psychology, 61,* 308–320.

Spanos, N. P., Radtke-Bodorik, H. L., Ferguson, J. D., & Jones, B. (1979). The effects of hypnotic susceptibility, suggestions for analgesia, and the utilization of cognitive strategies on the reduction of pain. *Journal of Abnormal Psychology, 88,* 282–292.

Wolberg, L. R. (1982). *Hypnosis: Is it for you?* (2nd ed.). New York: Dembner Books.

Critical Thinking and Learning: Making Predictions and Reasoning from Definitions

Learning Objectives

• To learn how to use deductive reasoning to make predictions from theories—in particular, theories of learning.

• To learn to reason from a definition to a specific experience from your own life and to write about it.

What Do You Think?

Can people acquire mental disorders through learning? For example, can a person become depressed through learning? What do you think? More generally, what role does learning play in determining who we are as individuals?

In this chapter, we examine these important questions as we learn how to think critically about learning. In particular, we focus on two important applications of deductive reasoning: using deductive reasoning to make predictions from theories of learning and reasoning from definitions of learning. Recall from Chapter 2 that much of our best thinking in everyday situations and in psychology is hypothetico-deductive. The research psychologist generates a hypothesis or theory that is consistent with observation, makes a prediction based on the hypothesis, and then tests the prediction. In this example, the scientist has used deductive reasoning to make a prediction by reasoning from a general principle to a specific case—that is, the expected outcome of a research study. We will examine how research psychologists and clinical psychologists can use deductive reasoning to make predictions, and in a second important application, we will reason from a definition to an example.

Using Deductive Reasoning to Make Predictions

Recall from Chapter 1 that an important use of deductive reasoning in science is to make predictions from theories, so that the implications of the theory or hypothesis can be tested. For example, Seligman (1975) proposed a psychological theory of depression called learned helplessness. According to this theory, a person learns to be helpless after encountering negative, uncontrollable life events. Using this theory, we could generate the hypothesis that subjects who experience tragic events that they are unable to control will tend to become depressed. In particular, we might predict that nondepressed subjects made helpless by being presented with inescapable noise would behave more like depressed subjects than would nondepressed subjects who were not made helpless. This result is in fact what Klein and Seligman (1976) found.

A prediction based on a theory can also be made about a specific person. In this case, one might predict that a person showing helpless behavior would be depressed. This prediction is a deductive inference, because it involves reasoning from the theory to the specific case. Let's examine how an argument might be put into the form of a conditional deductive argument as discussed in Chapter 1.

> Premise 1: If people learn to be helpless by encountering negative, uncontrollable life events (**antecedent**), then they will become depressed (**consequent**).
>
> Premise 2: John's mother died and he lost his job, and he didn't feel like trying.
>
> Conclusion: Therefore, John became depressed.

Now, let's analyze this argument. Recall from Chapter 1 that a valid deductive argument must first be valid or have correct logical form and then have all true premises leading to a true conclusion. The argument presented here does have valid form: It is an example of asserting the antecedent. Second, if we assume that the premises are true—and in this case we can—then the conclusion that John is depressed necessarily follows from the premises. To summarize, we first decided that this deductive argument was valid, and then, after applying the rule that if all of the premises are true, then the conclusion must necessarily be true, we concluded that this argument is sound.

A clinician might use learned helplessness theory and the fact that John had these disheartening and unavoidable life events to predict that John is depressed. Also, if John is supposed to be depressed, then other symptoms of depression should also be present; the clinician can look for these. Making predictions based on a theory or hypothesis in this way is the deductive part of hypothetico-deductive reasoning. Clinicians engage in deductive reasoning when trying to diagnose or understand a client's problem. They also use inductive reasoning to come up with their hypotheses—the *hypothetico* part. In actual mental status examinations, clinicians collect a variety of kinds of evidence from interviews, behavioral observations, and psychological tests to generate hypotheses about what disorder a person may have and then whether these different sources of evidence support one diagnosis more than another. (See Chapter 12 for more on diagnosing mental disorders.)

In summary, both research and clinical psychologists use deductive reasoning to generate predictions. Research scientists use deductive reasoning to form hypotheses, making predictions from theories about the outcomes of experiments and other research. Clinicians use deductive reasoning to make predictions about specific cases or clients they derive from hypotheses or theories. To better understand how this is done, each of the following problems asks you to use deductive reasoning to try to generate your own prediction about either a case or experimental result from two important learning theories.

≈ PRACTICE YOUR THINKING 7.1

Making Predictions

Each of the following problems presents the description of a theory. Read the description through and try to understand the theory. Identify the basic assumptions or premises of the theory. Then, use the "if…then" format of a conditional deductive argument to construct an argument that makes a prediction about the specific problem example. Put your conditional argument in the form of three statements that do each of the following, in order:

1. Restate the theory in the form of a conditional premise that makes a true general statement about the condition for learning to occur.

2. Put the specific example into a statement using the valid form of asserting the antecedent.

    3. Put the specific example into a statement in which the consequent follows as a true conclusion from the first two premises.

If you do not remember how conditional arguments are analyzed, review that section of Chapter 1.

    A. Elaborating on the ideas of Thorndike, B. F. Skinner proposed that the occurrence of a particular behavior depends on the consequences of that behavior (Skinner, 1938). The idea that the rate of performing a behavior depends on the stimulus consequences of the behavior is called **contingency.** In one type of contingency Skinner called **positive reinforcement,** a behavior increases in frequency when followed by a positive stimulus consequence such as a reward. For example, suppose a teacher wanted to increase class attendance, and so put the following contingency in place: each day that a student attended, the teacher gave the student a point toward his or her final grade. After putting this contingency in place, the teacher observed that attendance increased.

    Now, use the following specific example to make a prediction from Skinner's theory to an experimental result. Suppose a psychologist puts the following contingency in place. One group of rats is rewarded with a food pellet every time they walk into a certain area of their cages. A second group is given the same number of food pellets no matter how they move.

A.1. General statement in "if … then" form:_____

_____

A.2. Assertion of specific antecedent: _____

_____

A.3. True consequent statement follows: _____

_____

    B. Bandura argued that people learn not simply through reinforcement of behaviors that they have actually engaged in but also by observing the consequences of other people's behaviors. This kind of learning is called **observational learning.** According to Bandura's social learning theory, people frequently learn how to behave and react by observing how other people who model certain behaviors respond in particular situations. A famous experiment by Bandura, Ross, and Ross (1963) illustrates how observational learning can influence the rate of aggressive behavior in young children. The researchers had two groups of nursery school children observe one of two different adult models playing with a clown punching bag doll in another room. One group observed the adult assaulting the doll and engaging in some unique aggressive behaviors. The other group observed the model playing in a nonaggressive fashion with the doll. Later, when each group was let into the room to play, the group who watched the aggressive model engaged in many more of the same unique aggressive behaviors than the group who observed the nonaggressive model. This and many other studies suggested that people, especially children, would increase their frequency of aggressive behaviors after viewing an aggressive model, even when they observed the model on film.

Now, let's examine a second example, and this time make a prediction based on Bandura's theory of aggression and the following description of a young boy. A mother was concerned about her young son who watched some of the more violent cartoon shows on Saturday morning television. In many of these cartoons, the characters fought and physically injured each other as part of the stories.

B.1.　General statement in "if … then" form:_____

_____

B.2.　Assertion of specific antecedent:_____

_____

B.3.　True consequent statement follows:_____

_____

Answers to Making Predictions

A.1.　General statement in "if … then" form: *If a behavior is followed by a positive stimulus consequence, then it will increase in frequency.*

A.2.　Assertion of specific antecedent: *One group of rats receives food when they walk to a certain area of their cages.*

A.3.　True consequent statement follows: *The behavior of walking to a certain area of the cage in the group that was rewarded for this behavior will increase in frequency.*

B.1.　General statement in "if … then" form: *If a person observes a model engaging in aggression, then that person is later more likely to engage in aggressive behavior.*

B.2.　Assertion of specific antecedent: *The young boy is watching a lot of aggressive behaviors modeled on television.*

B.3.　True consequent statement follows: *The boy will be expected to increase the number of aggressive behaviors he engages in.*

Reasoning from a Definition to an Example

The second important use of deductive reasoning in psychology that we will examine involves reasoning from a definition to an example. We will examine how you can reason from two different definitions of learning, one behavioral and one cognitive. Suppose you were trying to decide whether an example from your own life experience is a case of learning.

Reasoning from a Behavioral Definition of Learning

To reason from a behavioral definition properly, we should use deductive reasoning to see whether the example from your life fits the definition of learning. To decide whether your experience is an example of learning, we could compare the experience with the following commonly used **behavioral definition of learning:** Learning is a relatively permanent change in behavior that is due to practice or experience.

Reasoning from a psychological definition like this one to a real-life example is often a complex task, because frequently both definitions and examples have multiple parts. Fortunately, there are strategies to simplify this task and to draw a sound conclusion about whether a particular case is an example of a general principle. The strategy for reasoning from a definition to an example has three steps.

1. Identify and break down the various parts of the definition so that they can be stated as a set of conditions in the general premise.
2. Identify and break down the parts of the example that seem relevant to the definition and then assert them as specific cases of the antecedent to make a valid argument.
3. Decide whether each of the statements is true. If they are all true, then the conclusion must follow that your example is a true example of learning.

Breaking down the learning definition into parts or separate conditions, we can say that leaning is: (1) a change in behavior (2) that is relatively permanent (3) due to practice or experience. In order for an example to fit this definition, it must have all the features of the definition, and these features must be true. Let's assume someone thought of the following example as an experience that she thinks fits the definition of learning. Read over the example and follow the three-step strategy set out in the preceding paragraph to decide whether this example fits the definition.

> When I was five years old, I wanted to be able to ride a bicycle like the older kids. At first I tried, and I couldn't do it. I kept getting up back onto the bike when I fell down, and I got so that I could go farther and farther without falling down. Finally, after doing this every day for about a week, I got so I could ride down the sidewalk without falling off my bike. After that, I seldom fell off, and even when I didn't ride my bike sometimes for several days at a time, the next time I got on it I didn't fall off.

What were the results of your analysis? Does this example fit the definition of learning? Using the three steps, we first see that the person in the example showed a change in behavior: Initially she did not know how to ride a bike and then she acquired this behavior, getting to the point of not falling down at all. Second, this new behavior was relatively permanent: Even when she didn't ride her bike for several days, she still did not fall off when she rode it. Third, the acquisition of the response was due to experience or practice: She practiced, repeatedly trying to ride the bicycle. Since the example shows true instances of all three of the parts of the definition, we can reasonably conclude that the example is an example of learning.

It is also possible to reason deductively from a definition and instead show that an example is not a true case of a definition. In this use of deductive reasoning, it is helpful to remember the rule that if any of the premises is false, then a conclusion based on those premises must be false. Consider the following observation of an experience, and then analyze deductively whether the example does or does not fit the definition. Recall that in deductive reasoning all the premises, or conditions, must be true for the conclusion to be true. If in the following example any of the three parts of the definition of learning does not occur, then it must be concluded that the example is not a case of this definition of learning. Read the following description of the experience of a college freshman, and then decide whether it fits the definition of learning.

> When I was in grade school, I really was not interested in girls. In fact, my friends and I used to tease them, and I seldom talked to any of the girls in my class. Then, when I got to junior high, I started talking to the girls more and more, sometimes walking them home, and I seldom teased them in a mean way. In fact, I started to call them up and go to movies with them. I'm 19 now, and I talk to women even more; I go out on dates, and probably have more friends who are women than men.

First of all, this example shows a change in behavior: At first, he teased the girls and did not talk to them; then he started talking to them and did not tease them. Second, the change was relatively permanent: He continued much later to engage in the new behaviors he acquired, talking to women and engaging in friendly activities. Third, it is true that his behavior with respect to girls did change, but it is difficult to identify an experience that was related to the change in behavior. In fact, we can think of other changes besides experience or practice that might have caused the change in behavior: for example, sexual maturation. Thus what looks like the change in behavior coincided with and was due to a change in sexual motivation resulting from maturation. So, the conclusion that the example fits the definition of learning cannot be true because one of its conditions, that the change in behavior be due to experience, is not true.

≈ PRACTICE YOUR THINKING 7.2

Reasoning from Your Own Life Experience

Now, you try to think of one of your own experiences that would fit the definition of learning provided. Pick an experience that does not have strong emotional associations for you, but rather is simply an ordinary experience you have had. You may also pick an example of a situation from your own experience in which you have observed someone else's or a pet's behavior. Then, inspect this example to see whether it has all the features of the definition of learning. Once you think you have found a good example, complete the next two steps.

1. As in the examples presented in the preceding section, write a description of a situation from your experience that fits the definition. Make sure that you include any details that are necessary for justifying that your example does indeed fit all parts of the definition.

2. Then, in a second paragraph, provide justification that your example fits the definition. Go through your example, part by part, and see whether the three features of the definition of learning all apply, so that you can come to the sound conclusion that you have a good example of learning. This is an opportunity for you to use the language of argumentation found in Appendix A. For example, you might say: "I *conclude* that my experience is a good example of learning *because....*"

Now, try it again. This time you should think of an example that does *not* fit the definition. Think of another example from your own experience that fits part of the definition, but not all of it, so it would not actually be an example of learning even though it might at first look like one. As before, pick an experience that does not have strong emotional associations, just an ordinary experience—something that happened to you or a situation or behavior you observed. Then, inspect this example to see whether it has all three features of the definition of learning. One part of your example should not fit the definition. When you think you have found an example like this, complete the next two steps.

1. In a paragraph, write a description of an example from your experience that does *not* fit the definition. Make sure that you include all the details necessary for justifying that your example does appear to fit the definition, but that one condition of the definition is not satisfied, that is, does not fit.

2. Then, in a second paragraph, provide justification that your example only partly fits the definition and therefore is not a good example of learning. Go through your example part by part, and check it for the three features of the definition of learning, showing that a reasonable conclusion is that the example is not a good example of learning. Again, you may wish to use the language of argumentation found in Appendix A.

Reasoning from a Cognitive Definition of Learning

We have examined how to reason from one definition of learning, focused on behavior. It is also useful to learn how to reason from a definition focused more on cognitive aspects of learning. Examine the following **cognitive definition of learning:** Learning is a relatively permanent change in knowledge due to practice or experience.

If we break down this definition, we see that it is nearly identical to the behavioral definition of learning, except for one important condition. Learning is (1) a change in knowledge (2) that is relatively permanent (3) due to practice or experience. The difference, of course, is that the cognitive definition emphasizes that the knowledge of the learner is changing, rather than the behavior. For practice, use the methods we described before to reason from the cognitive definition to analyze whether the following example fits the cognitive definition of learning.

> I went to the party hoping to see Jill there. We had not been going together for two months, but I still missed her and hoped that we could get back together somehow. When I got to the party, I saw a friend of mine. He told me that he thought Jill was with somebody at the party. I told him that she wasn't. I had asked her out the week before, and although she said no, she had told me that she wasn't seeing anyone. Then, I saw her holding hands with this other guy. My heart sank. Although I pretended not to be upset by the news, I left the party as soon as I could.

All three conditions seem to be met by this example. At first, he does not know that Jill is seeing someone else, and then his knowledge state changes as he sees her with someone else. This new knowledge should be relatively permanent. It is not the kind of thing one soon forgets. This change in his knowledge occurred as a result of the experience of seeing Jill holding hands. Because all three conditions have been met, we can deduce that learning has taken place.

Finally, it should be noted that this example illustrates an important fact about our use of the cognitive definition of learning in practice. Even though we are requiring that a change in knowledge be met as a condition for concluding that learning has taken place, we nevertheless make this inference based on behavior. We conclude that his knowledge state has changed by what he has told us (a verbal behavior) and the behavior he described, leaving the party early. Cognitive psychologists, too, infer changes in knowledge from observed changes in behavior.

Summary

This chapter discussed how we reason from theories to examples. Scientists use deductive reasoning to make predictions from theories to test hypotheses, and clinical psychologists also use deductive reasoning to make hypotheses concerning the nature of their clients' problems. For example, based on learned helplessness theory, we could predict that someone who experiences traumatic events out of his or her control will become depressed.

We can also use deductive reasoning to reason from a definition of learning to an example from our experience to see whether the example fits the definition. To do this we must break down each definition and each example into their respective component parts and then compare them to see whether the example has the same parts as the definition. When we compare the cognitive and behavioral definitions of learning, we see that they are very similar except that the cognitive definition emphasizes changes in knowledge, not behavior.

Review Questions

How do researchers and clinical psychologists use deductive reasoning to make predictions from their theories?

What might we predict from learned helplessness theory about a person who suffers traumatic life events that are uncontrollable?

What is positive reinforcement?

How do we go about reasoning from a definition of learning to an example of behavior?

Compare and contrast the behavioral and the cognitive definitions of learning.

What is observational learning? What prediction could we make from it about a child who watches violent television?

References

Bandura, A., Ross, D., & Ross, S. A. (1963). Imitation of film-mediated aggressive models. *Journal of Abnormal and Social Psychology, 66,* 3–11.

Klein, D. C., & Seligman, M. E. (1976). Reversal of performance deficits and perceptual deficits in learned helplessness and depression. *Journal of Abnormal Psychology, 85,* 11–26.

Seligman, M. E. (1975). *Helplessness: On depression, helplessness, and death.* New York: W. H. Freeman.

Skinner, B. F. (1938). *The behavior of organisms: An experimental analysis.* New York: Appleton-Century-Crofts.

Memory and Critical Thinking

Learning Objectives

• To learn about the accuracy of memory.

• To learn how to critically read a psychological discussion—that is, how to identify the central question and claims, organize the evidence on all sides of the question, and evaluate the quality and quantity of the evidence so that you can draw a sound conclusion.

What Do You Think?

Perhaps you have heard it said that everything you ever have seen is still in your memory somewhere, but you just cannot access it all. Is this true? What do you think? Perhaps you have seen a memory expert on television who could remember exactly the names of 30 people he had just met. Is what we store in memory quite accurate, perhaps even an exact replica of what we have experienced? Then again, have you ever played the party game in which one person tells a story to another person and then the story is retold from person to person? When the story is retold to the last person, it is often quite different from the original. This last example suggests that memory may sometimes be quite inaccurate. What do you think?

Critical Thinking and Accuracy of Memory

The issue of the accuracy of memory is of special importance to critical thinking. During our lives, we make an enormous number of decisions based on our memories of facts and events. The clinical psychologist bases her diagnosis of a client's mental disorder on the psychologist's memory of symptoms and disorders. A juror decides about a defendant's guilt based on the memory of an eyewitness who testified about the crime. A research scientist remembers the results of previous studies and other relevant information in order to develop and test a theory. Even your own understanding of what you are reading right now depends on your ability to remember the meaning of words. In each case, if the person does not accurately remember, then he or she may make a faulty inference. The clinician may misdiagnose a person's psychological status; the juror may vote to wrongly convict the defendant; the scientist may develop an incorrect theory; the reader may misunderstand what was read and draw a wrong conclusion.

These examples suggest that the accuracy of memory is also fundamental to critical thinking. Recall that critical thinking involves the evaluation of evidence relevant to a claim so that a sound conclusion can be drawn about the claim. Whenever remembered facts or events are used as evidence in support of some claim, the quality of the conclusion drawn depends on the accuracy of the memory for the fact or event.

≋ PRACTICE YOUR THINKING 8.1

Critically Reading a Literature Review: Is Human Memory Accurate?

The critical reading passage that follows will examine this important question of how accurate human memory is. To prepare you to read this discussion in a critical fashion, first read over the questions that follow.

Questions to Prepare You for Critical Reading

1. What is the central question? What claims are being made?

2. What evidence has been presented relevant to evaluating each side of the question? Organize relevant evidence under the headings evidence supporting the claim and evidence not supporting the claim. Then label each piece of evidence as to its kind. Use Tables 2.1 and 2.2 to help you.

3. Evaluate the quality and quantity of the evidence so that you can draw a sound conclusion based on the evidence presented.

4. Do any assumptions create problems for the conclusion you have drawn?

5. What are some implications of this conclusion? Does the conclusion affect how we should approach the evidence we gather through eyewitness testimony? Can you think of other implications?

After you have answered the critical reading questions, check your answers against those in Appendix C. You will find a copy of these questions in the critical reading form in Appendix B. Copy the form—you will need it for other critical reading assignments. After completing the critical reading questions, answers are in Appendix C.

Is Human Memory Accurate?

It is commonly thought that what we remember is a copy of what we have experienced. According to this view, memory is "reproductive," and we may recall quite accurately. The pioneering work of Frederick Bartlett, however, showed that it may be more accurate to describe memory as "reconstructive" (Bartlett, 1932). In other words, what people recall is changed or reconstructed from the original inputs.

Bartlett (1932) demonstrated this reconstruction in experiments in which he presented subjects with story-like passages and then tested their recall of the passage, sometimes weeks later. One of Bartlett's most famous stimulus stories was *The War of the Ghosts,* a Native American story from the Northwest. The passage was a story of two young Native Americans who, while hunting seals, hear what they think is a war party. Then, five other men coming up to them in a canoe ask them to go with them to make war. One of the young men went, and the other did not. A fierce battle ensues and the one young man is hit by an arrow, but he does not think he is hit. Those he is with say he is hit, and he then realizes that they are ghosts. They take him back to his village, and he tells his people the story of the encounter with the war party, that he had been in a battle in which many people were killed, and that they said he was hit, but he thought he was not. The next morning the young man fell over, "something black came out of his mouth," and he died (Bartlett, 1932, p. 65).

After analyzing subjects' successive attempts to recall the passage, Bartlett noticed that what subjects recalled of the passage was changed in several important ways from the original passage. In general, they tended to recall the gist of the passage, not the verbatim or word-for-word text of the story. Also, subjects made several kinds of errors. Many of the errors could be classified as **omissions.** Subjects shortened the passage and often completely left out some details, especially unfamiliar ones like the names of the villages. Other errors, **intrusions,** involved subjects' mistakenly interjecting information into their recall of the story. Although the dominant detail of "something black" coming out of the young man's mouth tended to be recalled, sometimes such a fact was reinterpreted, as when one subject recalled that "he foamed at the mouth" (Baddeley, 1976). Bartlett also found that subjects' recall was consistent with their knowledge and attitudes; subjects would tend to distort their recall to fit these attitudes.

Most important, though, Bartlett argued that changes in subjects' recall of the passage were systematic, not just random errors. Bartlett argued that knowledge is organized into a knowledge structure called a schema. A schema can relate a number of kinds of different information into a single organized structure. For example, one's knowledge of Native American traditions may include such disparate information as the fact that Indians traveled on horseback or in boats such as birchbark canoes or dugouts. Also included in one's schema may be information about traditional Native American clothing, such as beaded clothing, feathered headdresses, or buffalo robes. In addition, the schema may contain knowledge about Native American homes such as tepees, wigwams, and lodges.

According to Bartlett, when encountering a story like *The War of the Ghosts,* subjects use their schema for Native American traditions to help them understand and remember the new information. The schema is used to fill in the gaps in the new information subjects encounter in the unfamiliar story. The schema helps integrate the new information, and subjects may recall the passage based on their schema. As time passes, subjects' recall becomes more and more consistent with the schema. In other words, subjects tend to reconstruct their recall of the story based on their schema.

Reconstruction of the original passage based on these schema can account for the various errors that subjects make in recalling the story. Schema effects could also account for cultural biases and stereotypes. For example, if a British subject had a schema that did not include knowledge of canoes, this might explain why the subject might recall a boat in place of a canoe. In this way subjects would reinterpret the passage so that it was consistent with their experience. Schema theory might also explain how a person who knows little about Native Americans might assume that they all live in tepees. People may omit information that is unfamiliar and not part of their schema. As time passes and the original details from the story fall from memory, subjects may also intrude more and more details consistent with their schema into their recalls of the story in order to fill in the gaps made by this missing information. Often, subjects then recall details consistent with their attitudes and cultural background because these details are also consistent with one's schema.

A number of other studies support the notion that people may use prior knowledge to reconstruct their memory of some event. Loftus and Palmer (1974) conducted an experiment showing that a leading question may cause subjects to reconstruct their memory of an automobile accident. Loftus and Palmer showed all subjects the same films of automobile accidents. Then, before the subjects were asked to estimate the speed of the vehicles, one group of subjects were asked about how fast the cars were going when they *smashed* into each other. Other groups of subjects were asked the same question, but the words *hit* and *contacted* were substituted for the word *smashed.*

The results showed that those asked the question with *smashed* estimated the cars' speed as 40.8 mph, whereas those asked the question with *hit* estimated the speed at 34 mph, and those with *contacted* estimated only 31.8 mph. This result suggests that subjects may have reconstructed their memories of the accident and their estimates based on the leading questions. But an alternative explanation is also possible: It may have been that the subjects' responses were simply biased by the words in the leading questions. To further investigate this question, Loftus and Palmer conducted a second experiment in which they again showed films of automobile accidents and then asked leading questions using the words *smashed* and *hit*. This time, however, a week after they received the leading questions, subjects were asked whether they had seen any broken glass. The results showed that subjects whose leading question contained the word *smashed* were more likely to have reported that they saw broken glass than those whose word was *hit*. This result suggests that subjects were indeed reconstructing their memory of the accidents based on the leading question information.

Another experiment by Sulin and Dooling (1974) showed that subjects' knowledge of famous individuals could lead them to make errors in recognition memory. Sulin and Dooling presented their subjects with brief descriptions of individuals, varying the titles of the descriptions. For example, one description was entitled *Helen Keller's Need for Professional Help*; it went on: "Helen Keller was a problem child from birth. She was wild, stubborn, and violent..." (Sulin & Dooling, 1974, p. 256). Other subjects received the same description, but the name Carol Harris was substituted for Helen Keller. In a recognition test one week later, subjects who read the Helen Keller description as opposed to the Carol Harris description were more likely to report and more confident that they had seen in the description the sentence "She was deaf, dumb, and blind." Presumably, subjects were using their knowledge of Helen Keller to reconstruct their memory of the description.

Other research suggests that a schema may be used to reconstruct our memory of places, not just our memory of stories and events. Brewer and Treyens (1981) brought student subjects to a professor's office and asked them to wait briefly for the experiment to begin. After 35 seconds, subjects were removed from the office, told that the experiment was actually about their memories of the office, and then asked to recall as many details about the office they had just visited as they could. Brewer and Treyens found that subjects' schema for an office helped them to recall accurately objects that were in the office and that were consistent with their expectations about such offices, such as that the office had a chair and a desk. But their schema apparently also led them to inaccurately recall objects they expected to see in the professor's office, such as books, which were not present.

In a recent study, Kidder, LaFleur, and Wells (1995) found that subjects may later recall as incidents of sexual harassment events that they did that not originally recall as such. Interviews revealed that originally subjects recalled certain incidents in which they were bothered by other individuals but, after time, came to reconceptualize the incidents as sexual harassment.

Other evidence from everyday experiences suggests that memory is inaccurate. Most people are familiar with stories that circulate about someone that totally distort the truth about that person. To some extent, these distortions may be due to people's reconstructing what they have heard about someone to make it consistent with their expectations about the person. Also, sometimes eyewitnesses inaccurately remember the details of crimes. For example, an eyewitness to a crime accused and identified a Catholic priest, Father Pagano, of committing a robbery. Father Pagano, who at the time was bald except for hair on the sides of his head, was mistaken for Ronald Clauser, a man with nearly a full head of hair, who later confessed to the crime (Wortman, Loftus, & Marshall, 1992).

In summary, schema theory, as Bartlett and others have conceived it, suggests that memory is reconstructive. Although a schema may help us to acquire new knowledge in memory, the schema also intrudes its already existing information—perhaps about boats instead of canoes, or about Helen Keller instead of Carol Harris. This knowledge from the schema becomes integrated with the new information that a person experiences and is more enduring than the new information. As a result, more and more schema-based information may be left as new information falls away, leaving a reconstructed memory that may be quite inaccurate (Brewer & Nakamura, 1984).

Although considerable evidence shows that people remember inaccurately, often reconstructing their memory based on their schema, other evidence suggests just the contrary. For example, actors sometimes remember hundreds of lines of script verbatim. Another example is Rajan Mahadevan, an Indian student who gave a public demonstration of his phenomenal memory in which he recalled the exact sequence of digits in pi out to the 31,812th digit before making an error (Plotnik, 1993). The feats of Rajan and other memory experts who use **mnemonics**—deliberate strategies for remembering new information—suggest that memory need not be inaccurate.

Another person with a phenomenally accurate memory, known simply as S., was studied extensively by the Russian psychologist Luria. For example, S. was able to learn a long series of nonsense syllables such as *ma va na sa na va,* with dozens of these syllables alternating in no particular order (Luria, 1968, p. 51). Not only was S. able to learn this long series and recall it accurately at a public performance, but when tested four years later he was still able to recall it accurately.

Another case study of someone supposed to have an extremely accurate memory, however, revealed that the subject's memory was not completely accurate. Neisser (1981) studied the memory of John Dean, former counsel to Richard Nixon who was forced to resign his post as a result of involvement in Watergate, a scandal that involved Republican Party workers' breaking into Democratic National Committee headquarters. Dean testified before the Senate Watergate Committee recalling details of conversations relevant to whether Nixon or other White House officials had knowledge of the break-in beforehand and whether a coverup was under way. Dean's testimony suggested both that he had a phenomenal memory for details of conversations that had occurred months before and that the President himself may have known about the break-in beforehand. Dean was hailed by some as "the human tape recorder." After Dean testified, it was discovered that the White House had made tape recordings of conversations—providing an excellent opportunity to verify Dean's recollections. An examination of Dean's testimony and the transcripts showed that Dean did accurately recall the gist of important meetings and what had transpired but that his memory of specific details of one meeting versus another tended to blur together.

Other physiological evidence suggests that information is stored as an accurate record of experience in memory. Penfield (1975), a brain surgeon who operated on many patients with epilepsy, would routinely test for normal brain tissue by electrically stimulating parts of his patients' brains before removing damaged areas. He reported that sometimes when he would stimulate a particular area a patient would describe a vivid memory of a prior experience. When he stimulated one patient, the patient reported hearing an orchestra playing a melody. Each time he restimulated the same area the patient would report hearing the melody again. Another patient reported hearing a conversation from his past. Electrostimulation appears to aid in retrieving a vivid memory of an event, but the memory may not necessarily be accurate. Such a memory should be compared to the original event before that conclusion can be drawn. Memories that people experience as accurate and believe to be accurate have been shown to be inaccurate when compared to the original experience, as was demonstrated in a study of memories retrieved through hypnotic age regression (Nash, Drake, Wiley, Khalsa, & Lynn, 1986).

At the same time, some evidence does show that hypnosis leads to accurate memory. In the Chowchilla kidnapping case in California, the bus driver who had witnessed the abduction of the children on his bus could not at first recall the license plate number from the kidnappers' vehicle. After being hypnotized, he could remember all but one of the digits in the license plate number. A review of the research evidence by Erdelyi (1994), however, suggests that hypnosis does not cause improvements in recall for previously unrecalled information over and above the improvements caused by simply repeating the attempt to recall the information. (See Chapter 6 for a discussion of whether hypnosis improves memory.)

Other research evidence suggests that memory is not purely reconstructive and that an accurate trace of the information may endure for a while. To investigate, Alba, Alexander, Hasher, and Caniglia (1981) used a recognition test, in which subjects typically are given more cues or hints than in a recall test, often receiving a copy of the original information as in a multiple-choice test (in contrast, in a recall test, like an essay exam, few cues are provided). The researchers found that when subjects were tested with a recognition test instead of the usual recall test, the subjects could remember the exact wording of the statements they had seen, not just the gist of the statements. Subjects accurately remembered the statements when given copies of them to recognize. Bates, Masling, and Kintch (1978) obtained similar results: Subjects were able to recognize a large percentage of the original sentences they heard from a soap opera as compared to close paraphrases of the actual sentences when tested soon after they first saw them.

In an experiment to investigate the conditions under which people reconstruct, Hasher and Griffin (1978) presented a story to subjects about a man walking through the woods. All subjects were given the title *Going Hunting* when they read the story; the title was expected to cause subjects to reconstruct their memory around their knowledge about hunting. At the time of recall, however, subjects were given two different titles. One group were given the same title as before; a second group were told that they had been mistakenly given the wrong title for the passage and should have been given the title *An Escaped Convict*—a title more consistent with the content of the story. The results showed that the first group, who got the wrong title, did reconstruct their memories around the theme of going hunting. The group who were told they had been given the wrong title did not necessarily reconstruct their memory around the title they had seen first. Instead they recalled the story's contents accurately.

In a review of the literature, Alba and Hasher (1983) cited a number of studies in which results showing schema-type reconstructive effects in memory depended on the kind of memory test used. The authors also argued that Bartlett's earlier findings supporting reconstruction in memory may have been a result of his experimental methods, not of the reconstructive effects of schema on memory.

Summary

An important question for critical thinking is whether memory is reproductive, so that it produces an accurate copy of events, or reconstructive, so that it is constructed from prior experience, cues in the recall system, and other information. If memory is inaccurate, then evidence based on memory reports is less reliable.

Early research by Bartlett showed that recall is often reconstructive. Tested on their recall of a passage, people made omissions or left out material. They also made errors of intrusion, adding to what they were asked to recall, sometimes intruding information and reinterpreting information based on their own experience. Their recall, while not accurate verbatim, was often accurate about the gist or basic sense of the material. Bartlett interpreted his results in terms of schema theory. He concluded that subjects reconstructed their recall using knowledge structures called schema that represent and organize the memory of our prior experience.

Considerable other research has shown reconstruction and schema-based effects on memory. Leading questions have been shown to cause subjects to reconstruct in recall. Subjects have been shown to integrate detail consistent with their prior knowledge that produces false recognitions. Subjects in one study used their knowledge of places to reconstruct their memories of a brief visit to an office; other research has shown that over time people reconstruct their memories around themes such as sexual harassment.

Still other evidence, however, suggests that memory need not be inaccurate. Actors and mnemonists can recall accurately, often word for word, when they deliberately study material. Research suggests that, at least for a brief period of time immediately after the material is presented, information may be available to support accurate recognition before memory becomes more based on the basic sense of the material. Some scientific authorities have argued that schema effects and reconstruction are related to the method used to test memory, and reconstruction is much more likely to be found on recall tests and with the passage of more time.

Based on a summary and evaluation of the evidence, one may conclude that recall is often schema-based and reconstructive. If a person is not a memory expert, does not deliberately try to learn material verbatim, or is not tested with a recognition test very soon after being presented with material to learn, the person's memory is likely to be less than completely accurate.

Review Questions

How does critical thinking depend on accurate memory? Explain.

What is reproductive versus reconstructive memory?

What kinds of errors did Bartlett find people make in recall?

What are omissions?

What are intrusions?

Did Bartlett find that his subjects remembered verbatim or for gist? Explain your answer.

What is schema theory, and how does it account for recall?

How might leading questions affect memory?

What are mnemonics? Who are mnemonists?

What does their ability to recall suggest?

Compare and contrast recognition memory and recall memory.

Is memory reproductive or reconstructive—accurate or inaccurate?

What are the implications of this conclusion for eyewitness testimony?

References

Alba, J. W., Alexander, S. G., Hasher, L., & Caniglia, K. (1981). The role of context in encoding information. *Journal of Experimental Psychology: Human Learning and Memory, 7,* 283–292.

Alba, J. W., & Hasher, L. (1983). Is memory schematic? *Psychological Bulletin, 93,* 203–231.

Baddeley, A. D. (1976). *The psychology of memory.* New York: Basic Books.

Bartlett, F. C. (1932). *Remembering: A study in experimental and social psychology.* Cambridge, England: Cambridge University Press.

Bates, E., Masling, M., & Kintch, W. (1978). Recognition memory for aspects of dialogue. *Journal of Experimental Psychology: Human Learning and Memory, 4,* 187–197.

Brewer, W. F., & Nakamura, G. V. (1984). The nature and functions of schemas. In R. Wyer & T. Srull (Eds.), *Handbook of social cognition.* Hillsdale, NJ: Lawrence Erlbaum.

Brewer, W. F., & Treyens, J. C. (1981). Role of schemata in memory for places. *Cognitive Psychology, 13,* 207–230.

Erdelyi, M. (1994). Hypnotic hypermnesia: The empty set of hypermnesia. *The International Journal of Clinical and Experimental Hypnosis, 42,* 379–390.

Hasher, L., & Griffin, M. (1978). Reconstructive and reproductive processes in memory. *Journal of Experimental Psychology: Human Learning and Memory, 4,* 318–330.

Kidder, L., LaFleur, R., & Wells, C. (1995). Recalling harassment, reconstructing experience. *Journal of Social Issues, 51,* 53–57.

Loftus, E. F., & Palmer, J. C. (1974). Reconstruction of automobile destruction: An interaction of language and memory. *Journal of Verbal Learning and Verbal Behavior, 13,* 585–589.

Luria, A. R. (1968). *The mind of a mnemonist.* New York: Avon Books.

Nash, M., Drake, S., Wiley, S., Khalsa, S., and Lynn, S. (1986). Accuracy of recall by hypnotic age-regressed subjects. *Journal of Abnormal Psychology, 95,* 298–300.

Neisser, U. (1981). John Dean's memory: A case study. *Cognition, 9,* 1–22.

Penfield, W. (1975). *The mystery of the mind.* Princeton, NJ: Princeton University Press.

Plotnik, R. (1993). *Introduction to psychology* (3rd ed.). Pacific Grove, CA: Brooks/Cole.

Sulin, R. A., & Dooling, D. J. (1974). Intrusion of a thematic idea in the retention of prose. *Journal of Experimental Psychology, 103,* 255–262.

Wortman, C. B., Loftus, E. F., & Marshall, M. E. (1992). *Psychology* (4th ed.). New York: Knopf.

Critical Thinking and Decision Making

Learning Objectives

• To learn about decision-making processes that go on in people's everyday and professional lives.

• To learn about decision-making strategies people use and decision errors they make.

• To learn how to make good judgments and effective decisions.

What Do You Think?

What do you think you will do after you graduate? Have you decided yet? If you have not decided, how will you come to a good decision? If you have decided, how do you know that you have made a good decision? In this chapter we will examine how you think when you make such decisions and how to improve this kind of decision.

The Consequences of Decisions

Deciding what you will do with your life is an example of a personal decision with far-reaching consequences. This decision could affect where you live, how much money you make, who your friends are, even how satisfied you are with your life in general. Little wonder that big decisions like this one often create anxiety and stress in decision makers. The stress and anxiety of decision making are due to an important characteristic of decisions—that is, that decisions involve uncertainty. That our personal decisions have important consequences for us also contributes to the stress of making decisions. When you stop to think about it, our world is the way it is because of people's decisions. Not only our decisions affect our lives; other people's do too. To illustrate the far-reaching consequences of other peoples' decisions on our lives, allow me to recount a story from my childhood.

When I was in the seventh grade, I remember sitting with my classmates waiting to find out whether the world was going to come to an end. At that time, the end of the world by nuclear annihilation was a distinct possibility. The United States and the then Soviet Union were as close to having a nuclear war as they had ever been due to decisions made by the leaders of the two countries. In 1962, during the Cold War, our government learned that the Soviet Union had secretly begun building a nuclear missile base in Cuba, just 90 miles off the coast of Florida (Bransford & Stein, 1993). President Kennedy, along with his advisers, judged that completion of the new base posed too great a threat to U.S. security to tolerate. Kennedy and his advisers decided to issue an ultimatum that the Soviet Union remove the base, and they sent U.S. warships to prevent the Soviets from delivering any more supplies to Cuba. During this era, there was already great fear that the Soviet Union would initiate a nuclear attack: Many people built fallout shelters to prepare for that possibility, and at school I remember practicing crouching under my desk covering my head during "duck and cover" drills designed to protect us from flying debris in the event of nuclear attack. In addition, Nikita Krustchev, the leader of the Soviet Union at the time, had a reputation for volatility. So, understandably, many feared the Soviet Union would respond to the U.S. warships with nuclear weapons. That day, my friends and I wondered whether World War III was about to begin, and our fates depended on decisions by the two most powerful men in the world. Would they make the right decisions, or would the world suffer the awful consequences?

Given the far-reaching consequences—our own and other people's decisions—can have on our lives, would it not seem wise to learn how to improve our decision making? To better understand how people make decisions, let's examine some important characteristics of the decision-making process.

Overview of the Decision-Making Process

To illustrate how a person goes through the decision-making process, we will discuss how a person might go about deciding what to do after graduation from college. First, we need to go over some basic terms psychologists use to discuss decision making.

Basic Terminology

Medin and Ross defined **decision making** as "generating, evaluating, and selecting among a set of relevant choices" (Medin & Ross, 1992, p. 395). If we had only one option or course of action, rather than a set of choices, we would feel no uncertainty, since no decision would be necessary. Similarly, if we did not care about the outcome of a decision, that decision would cause little anxiety; but Yates (1990, p. 3) defined a **decision** as "an action taken with the intention of producing a favorable outcome." Because we desire a favorable outcome and because we cannot immediately discern from the alternatives our best course of action, our decisions necessarily involve some risk and may lead to some stress and anxiety.

For example, if you have not already decided what you will do after college, you may be considering several options—such as going to graduate school, getting a job for a period of time to pay off your college debts, or traveling. It is not clear beforehand which option is best or even whether a better alternative course of action exists that you have not even considered. Decision making is a mental process leading to an outcome that is typically uncertain. Perhaps, a better understanding of the decision-making process and where decisions can go wrong would help you to make more effective decisions.

Although there are different ways to analyze the decision-making process, the discussion that follows divides the decision making process into six components. These components are similar to some of the parts found in Beyth-Marom, Novik, and Sloan (1987); Halpern (1996); and Zechmeister and Johnson (1992). These six components of the decision-making process are as follows.

1. Recognizing the need to make a decision
2. Thinking about your objectives and what a good decision would look like—defining the problem
3. Generating alternative courses of action or options

4. Listing the relevant dimensions for evaluating alternatives
5. Evaluating the alternatives or options
6. Selecting an option or deciding

You should think of these steps as occurring roughly in the order presented; however, sometimes the second step of thinking about objectives and defining the problem may have to be repeated after the options one has generated for alternative courses of action seem inadequate. Often, the decision maker must seek additional information to better define a problem. More information may help the decision maker generate other alternatives. We will discuss each of the six components in order, while acknowledging that real decisions do not always follow such a scheme.

Step 1: Recognizing the Need to Make a Decision

An important first step in making a decision is to realize that a decision needs to be made. Sometimes, people fail to realize that they have the opportunity to choose between two courses of action—one alternative that would further their personal or professional objectives and another that would help them little or even hurt them. One common approach to making decisions is **optimization,** or choosing an option that is most likely to help you reach your objectives. Returning to the question of what to do after graduation, suppose that you simply ignored the need to make this decision. In such a case, you might say to yourself, "I'm not worried, something will work out—it always does." While you will likely get some kind of job, will it be a job that you like or that is in your area of interest and uses your experience? Taking this strategy, you might end up with a job you could have obtained without a college education, doing little to optimize your chances of reaching goals you developed during college.

Step 2: Identifying Your Objectives and Defining the Problem

The real reason for difficulty in making this decision may be a need for **goals clarification.** Optimizing your chances of success is difficult unless you have well-formed objectives for making a decision or solving a problem in the first place. One way to help clarify your goals is to ask yourself what is important to you, overall, ignoring the details of specific problems and decisions that presently confront you. It may also help you to write down the things you like to do the best and classify them as to type (Zechmeister & Johnson, 1992). For example, perhaps one of the things you like to do best is to converse with people. You might classify this kind of activity as communication with people. Suppose that your favorite courses in psychology have been courses about adjustment, abnormal psychology, and the helping professions. You classify these interests under the category of helping people with their problems. Suppose, further, that your all-time favorite summer job was as a camp counselor two years ago. Perhaps you have a good relationship with a younger brother or sister who seems to enjoy playing with you. These latter examples you classify as being good with children. From these categories, you might extract the objectives of finding a job in which you could (1) talk to people, (2) help people with their problems, and (3) be around children.

As part of clarifying your objectives and defining the problem a decision calls for, you should think first about the quality of the decision that you need to make: What would a good decision look like? How good does your decision have to be? Although people often optimize and seek the best possible decision, sometimes they must make decisions rapidly. In these and other cases, the important thing may be to simply make a satisfactory decision. In this decision-making strategy, called **satisficing,** the decision maker selects an alternative that is good enough (Simon, 1957). Knowing how much time you have to make a decision is important to take into account when thinking about your objectives and how to make your decision. For example, if you have only 2 months to decide what you will do after you graduate because you have not thought about it much before, then you may wish to adopt a satisficing strategy, accepting a merely satisfactory alternative at least for the time being.

Step 3: Generating Alternative Courses of Action

Once you have thought about your objectives and defined the problem, then you need to proceed to the next step, generating alternative courses of action. Keeping your objectives in mind, you should generate as many alternative courses of action as possible that could help you meet your objectives. It is better to generate many relevant options than to consider too few, especially true if your aim is optimization.

Keeping in mind your objectives of finding a job where you can talk to people, help them with personal problems, and be around children, you might generate several options. For example, you might think of being a camp counselor, elementary school teacher, or child psychologist.

Step 4: Listing the Relevant Dimensions to Evaluate Alternatives

Decisions are often complex with many options and aspects, so a systematic approach to evaluating the alternatives is important. Recording your evaluation will help prevent your forgetting important information related to the decision and reduce bias in evaluation of the options. You may already be familiar with a method developed by Benjamin Franklin that involves systematically recording the pros and cons of a decision (Franklin, 1887). Under each alternative Franklin would list a positive or negative feature (pro or con) of that option. He would also give each feature a separate weight, taking into account that some features were more important and should be given some greater value than others. Then, he would add up the weights for each option and choose the one

TABLE 9.1

A balance sheet to decide what to do after graduation

	Pros	**Cons**
Camp Counselor	fun (+1) no pressure (+1)	low paying (−2) little advancement (−1)
Counselor/Clinical	interesting (+1) high prestige (+1) good pay (+2)	legally responsible (−1) on call often (−1) lots of school (−1)
Social Worker	only 9 to 5 (+1)	bureaucratic job (−3)
Psychiatrist	interesting (+1) good pay (+2) high prestige (+1)	legally responsible (−1) on call often (−1) lots of school (−1)
Pediatrician	good pay (+2) high prestige (+1)	legally responsible (−1) on call often (−1) lots of school (−1) not interesting (−1)
Guidance Counselor	only 9 to 5 (+1)	job is boring (−1)
Salesperson	no more school (+1) only 9 to 5 (+1) no legal responsibility (+1)	little advancement (−1) low pay (−2) low prestige (−1)

with the highest sum. For obvious reasons, this is often called a balance sheet approach.

Let's see how we might apply this system to the question of deciding what to do after graduation. The results of this method are shown in Table 9.1. You can see that the features or attributes are both positive and negative.

Add up the weights and see what you come up with. After doing this, you may have noticed that in this case the method offers little discrimination among the options. The best options are counselor/clinician and psychiatrist, which have totals of +1. Another problem with this method is that it may lead to nonequivalent comparisons of options because all options are not analyzed using the same dimensions.

We can improve upon this method if we group some of the features into more inclusive categories or dimensions and then rate each option on every dimension or aspect. See Table 9.2 for an example of this method. For example, we could combine the attributes from Table 9.1—"interesting," "not interesting," and "fun"—into one dimension simply called "interest level" that we could use to evaluate all the alternatives as seen in Table 9.2. Similarly, "9 to 5" and "on call often" from Table 9.1 become the more general category "hours" in Table 9.2.

TABLE 9.2

A multidimensional balance sheet to decide what to do after graduation

Weight	Interest Level (4)	Money (3)	Prestige (2)	Hours (2)	Legal Responsibility (1)	Totals
Camp Counselor	X			X	X	7
Counselor/Clinician	X	X	X			9
Social Worker	X		X	X		8
Psychiatrist		X	X			5
Pediatrician		X	X			5
Guidance Counselor	X			X	X	7
Salesperson				X	X	3

Step 5: Evaluating the Alternatives

The decision maker must find a way to evaluate the options so that they might be compared. The balance sheet methods we have examined allow you to evaluate options by assigning weights to each attribute or dimension and then summing these weights. When we add up the scores from Table 9.2, we see that counselor/clinician is the favorite. Rating each option on every dimension allows us to decide knowing that we have made somewhat equivalent comparisons. Research shows that people use multiple attributes in making complex decisions (Ranyard & Abdel-Nabi, 1993), and experts recommend using multidimensional balance sheets to support complex decision making (Beyth-Marom, Novik, & Sloan, 1987; Laskey & Campbell, 1991). Hogarth (1987) pointed out that choices are difficult partly because people have limited resources for processing all the relevant information. Writing down your choices and the relevant attributes may help you remember important information necessary for an effective decision.

Step 6: Selecting an Alternative

Once the options are assigned weights or some other values, then it is possible to make a decision. Using the balance sheet method, the option with the greatest summed weights should be selected. Like a sound conclusion, a good decision is consistent with the results of evaluating options.

As you probably noticed from examining the balance sheets, complex decisions also involve making many judgments. "A **judgment** is an opinion about what is or will be the status of some aspect of the world" (Yates, 1990, p. 6). We make judgments about many aspects of situations. We may judge the likelihood that some favorable outcome will result or the risk associated with taking a particular course of action. We may estimate the probability that someone is part of one group or another. Or we may rate our feelings toward one option versus another. Whatever the kind of judgment made, if it is faulty, any decision based on it will also be faulty. For example, if you are trying to decide what to do after college, and graduate school is one of your options, your decision may be partly based on judgments of the likelihood that you will get into the school you prefer. Suppose that you want to be a clinical psychologist and you judge that it is likely—a probability of .80—that you will get into a clinical psychology graduate program with a grade point average of 2.80. Because clinical psychology programs are some of the most competitive graduate programs, it is actually unlikely that you would get into one with a 2.80 GPA, and a decision to become a clinical psychologist based on your erroneous judgment would be unwise. Just as an incorrect assumption can lead to an unsound conclusion, as we saw in Chapter 2, so an incorrect judgment leads to a bad decision. Other similarities between decision making and critical thinking are worth noting, and we now turn to those similarities.

The Relationship Between Decision Making and Critical Thinking

While psychologists sometimes make distinctions between decision making and critical thinking, there are actually many similarities. Recall our working definition of critical thinking, as involving the evaluation of evidence relevant to some claim so that a sound conclusion about the claim can be drawn. Decision making also involves evaluating alternative courses of action and reflecting upon the evidence supporting one course of action versus another. Ennis's (1987) definition of critical thinking—as "reasonable, reflective thinking focused on *deciding* what to believe or do"—emphasizes the similarity between critical thinking and decision making. Before you decide on one course of action instead of another, you should examine the relevant evidence to determine which course of action is best.

Both critical thinking and decision making are purposeful activities. We usually assume that the choices that we make in decisions are conscious. An important aspect of critical thinking is its deliberate nature—we spend time and mental effort in evaluating evidence and alternatives. Much research shows that hasty decisions and premature conclusions lead to ineffective thinking and action. All the alternatives and evidence should be considered before committing yourself to a decision or a conclusion. In addition to this conscious, deliberate, and purposeful nature of both critical thinking and decision making, both processes also share the assumption that people should be rational.

Another important similarity between critical thinking and decision making is that both are done under conditions of uncertainty. Just as we are unsure of an outcome of a decision we make, so too we are frequently unsure of a conclusion or inference we make using critical thinking. Both involve generalizing beyond the available evidence and beyond what we know. Because we are uncertain about the outcome, decisions also usually involve some degree of risk.

Probability and Rational Decision Making

Because decision making always involves uncertainty, we use probability to estimate the risks associated with a particular decision or judgment. Recall that probability is the number of times a particular event of interest occurs out of the total number of ways that event can occur. We often think of probabilities in terms of the odds that something will happen. For example, the odds of getting heads on a particular coin toss with a fair coin is one out of two, because out of the two possible outcomes on a coin toss, heads or tails, there is only one way to get heads.

Probabilities are typically expressed in three different ways. We may express 1 out of 2 as a fraction, 1/2. This can also be expressed as a percentage or proportion, such as the probability of getting heads is .50 or 50%. Probabilities range from 0 to 1.00, with 0 representing a state in which the event does not occur and 1.00 representing the state in which the event always occurs. Probability is an expression of our degree of certainty; therefore it also tells us about our uncertainty that a particular event will occur. In tossing a fair coin we are only 50% certain that a particular toss will be heads, and necessarily we are 50% uncertain of this outcome. As you might expect, measuring uncertainty is a very important use of probability in evaluating judgments and decisions.

In psychology we often use the frequencies of observed events to estimate the probability of their occurring in the future. Another common use of probability in behavioral sciences such as psychology is statistical decision making to test hypotheses, as we discussed in Chapter 2. In fact, some psychologists who study decision making view the decision maker as a hypothesis tester, someone who evaluates the probabilities of options and hypotheses. Dawes (1988) connected the evaluation of probability with rational decision making. The rational decision maker pays attention to the probabilities of events. Unfortunately, the evidence that most people are not skilled at estimating probabilities is abundant (Kahneman & Tversky, 1973). This lack of skill may even account for some people's beliefs in paranormal events: Since people tend to overestimate the probability of coincidental events, they may attribute the lucky coincidence of a psychic's prediction coming true by chance to factors other than chance, such as precognition (Blackmore, 1992).

Using Heuristics

After realizing that a decision is needed, the next step is to generate options that will likely lead to reaching your goal. Psychologists have done extensive research on strategies people use to solve problems and make decisions and have found that people frequently use heuristics.

Heuristics are rules of thumb that are often helpful in solving a problem or making a decision. They are ways around more difficult and time-consuming methods of arriving at a conclusion. For example, suppose you are talking with a friend about the need for more diversity at your university, and she asks you what percentage of your school's psychology majors are members of an ethnic minority. One way to answer this question would be to get a list of all psychology majors from the registrar's office, identify and count the members of different groups, and then calculate the percentage. This kind of strategy, in which following the prescribed procedure always leads to a solution, is an **algorithm.** Although exhaustively searching the list and counting heads would always lead to a correct answer, using an algorithm can be very time-consuming.

Instead, most people would likely apply a heuristic in trying to answer this question. To illustrate, you might recall that of about 20 people in your last psychology class, 2 students were African American, 1 was Hispanic, and 1 was Asian American. You might then estimate that about 20% of the psychology majors are members of an ethnic minority. This estimate is a form of the **representativeness heuristic**. Your class is a small sample, though, and it may not be representative of the entire population of psychology majors at your school. When a sample is not representative, estimates based on it will be erroneous.

Another heuristic you might use in answering this question is **availability**. What if you have lots of friends who are members of minorities? What if you happen to sit next to African American students in three of your four classes? Your experience might inflate your estimates because it would be easy for you to think of such students. When we use the ease with which we retrieve information from memory to judge the frequency of an instance, then we are using the availability heuristic.

Errors and Other Problems in Decision Making

This section examines three kinds of problems people frequently have when making judgments and decisions that can present obstacles to effective thinking. One type of error may result from the incorrect application of a heuristic. Although heuristics frequently are useful in making judgments and decisions, sometimes they may not be used effectively as procedures. These errors in decision making are called **fallacies.** For example, the failure to take the base rate of some event into account may cause judgments based on representativeness to be in error.

A second kind of problem is the result of bias in judgment or decision making. For our purposes, **bias** is the systematic distortion of thinking in judgment and decision making. Sometimes knowledge we have may systematically distort our judgment. For example, in hindsight bias, knowledge gained after a decision was made makes it seem that the particular decision or decision error was understandable, even inevitable. Another example of the influence of bias is the tendency to seek evidence that confirms our beliefs and hypotheses—the confirmation bias.

A third kind of error in decision making and judgment may be viewed as a **metacognitive error,** or a discrepancy between the actual quality of people's decisions and their judgments of that quality. People are often found to be overconfident of their judgments and decisions.

Representativeness Errors

The representativeness heuristic is less likely to be a problem when the sample on which we are basing an inference really represents the relevant population. In the previous example, our judgment of the percentage of psychology majors who are members of ethnic minorities will tend to be more accurate if we are recalling the number of minority persons in a large class as opposed to a small class. This rule is called the law of large numbers. Unfortunately, people often behave as if the size of the sample they are generalizing from does not matter. As Matlin (1994) noted, people behave as if there were a law of small numbers. Recall from Chapter 2 that sound inductive inferences depend in part on the quantity of evidence supporting a claim. The strength of an inductive inference based on a sample depends in part on the size of the sample. An experiment with a larger sample will lead to a stronger inference than an experiment with a smaller sample that is otherwise identical to the first experiment.

Judgments based on representativeness usually involve the probability that an individual or small group is from a larger group. The simple probability that an individual randomly sampled from a population is a member of a particular group is equal to the number of individuals in that group divided by the total number of individuals. So if 38% of all psychologists are in clinical psychology, the most common field of specialization for psychologists, then the probability that an individual drawn randomly from the population of all psychologists will be a clinical psychologist is .38 (Stapp, Tucker, & VandenBos, 1985). This known probability is often referred to as the **base rate.** On the other hand, the base rate for experimental psychologists is 12%. Unfortunately, in making probability estimates people often commit an error called **failure to take into account base rate.** They tend to err by basing their judgments on the details of an example and the expectations the example creates.

Read the following description of a psychologist. Assume that in a sample of 100 psychologists, 76 are clinical psychologists and 24 are experimental psychologists. Then, on a scale from 0 to 100, judge how likely it is that the person in the following description is an experimental psychologist.

Bill has always liked solving mysteries and figuring out why people do the things they do. He is very exacting in measurement procedures he uses and very careful in his observations of people. He enjoys mathematics, statistics, and doing puzzles by himself.

If you rated the likelihood that Bill is an experimental psychologist as higher than 24, then you are failing to take base rate into account. Although the description of Bill may better fit your stereotype of a researcher than a clinician, your best guess of the probability that Bill is an experimental psychologist is the base rate. Many clinicians could also fit Bill's description. Since it is not known how these characteristics relate to clinical and experimental psychologists, we should go with the probability that is known (p = .24).

Another kind of error in using the representativeness heuristic to make probability judgments is called the **conjunction fallacy.** You can calculate the simple probability that an individual belongs to some category by dividing the number of individuals in the category by the total number of the group. Sometimes, we are interested in finding out the probability that two events will occur together—the probability of joint events. For example, we may be interested in the probability that someone belongs to a complex category with two features, such as the probability that a person is both a clinical psychologist and a woman. The probability that two events will occur together is the probability of the first event multiplied by the probability of the second event. The probability that a person is both a clinical psychologist and a woman equals the probability that a person is a clinical psychologist (p = .38) multiplied by the probability that a person is a woman (p = .55), which equals .21.

Now read the description of the person in question and make the judgment requested in the following example.

The subject is a 33-year-old person who loves to read. The person's hobbies are cooking and watercolor painting. This person is especially interested in how children think, has taken many classes in this area, and likes to talk to children about their problems.

Now, rank each of the following options on a scale of 1 to 6 according to the likelihood that each represents the person described (1 = most likely, 6 = least likely)

_____ The person is an experimental psychologist.

_____ The person is a male experimental psychologist.

_____ The person is a female experimental psychologist.

_____ The person is a clinical psychologist.

_____ The person is a female clinical psychologist.

_____ The person is a male clinical psychologist.

Often, people rank "female clinical psychologist" as a more likely option than just "clinical psychologist." The person in this example may have stereotypically feminine characteristics; but if we use probability to make the judgment, as we should, we realize that the person's being a clinical psychologist is more likely than the joint probability of the person's being both female and a clinical psychologist. Another way to look at this issue is to realize that the category of clinical psychologist is larger than the category of female clinical psychologist, so it is more likely that someone is from the larger category.

Availability Errors

Which do you think is the most likely cause of death, tornadoes or asthma? A study by Slovic, Fischoff, and Lichtenstein (1976) asked subjects this question and found that 58% of them thought that tornadoes were the more likely cause of death. In fact, however, 920 times as many people die from asthma than die from tornadoes. If you answered tornadoes, then you may have been influenced by the availability heuristic. We often use availability—or how easily we can bring related information to mind—to help us estimate the frequency of events. If the frequency of events we are trying to estimate is not correlated with our memory of related events, as in the case of the relative incidence of tornadoes versus asthma, then our estimate based on the availability heuristic will be in error.

Why do people tend to overestimate tornadoes as a cause of death as compared to asthma? Availability is a good explanation. Memories of killer tornadoes may be very vivid; tornadoes are covered more extensively by the media than are fatal cases of asthma. It is easier for most people to access memories of tornadoes than of asthma. Similarly, people often overestimate the number of deaths due to air travel as compared to automobile accidents. Actually, you are much safer flying than riding in a car, but media coverage of dramatic air crashes with many fatalities makes them memorable.

Availability also affects thinking and practice in psychology. When you are discussing something and trying to make an argument, you present evidence that is available—that you can easily retrieve from memory. Often the other person in the discussion thinks of some evidence that is unfamiliar to you. This new evidence could affect your judgment or decision if you considered it, but you are not likely to consider it on your own because it does not readily come to mind.

An example of availability in the practice of psychology concerns the diagnosis of mental disorders by clinicians. Dumont and Lecomte (1987) suggested that clinicians are more likely to diagnose a mental disorder if the symptoms for that disorder are vivid or if the clinician has recently had experience with a similar case.

Confirmation Bias

As you may recall from Chapter 1, confirmation bias is a pervasive tendency in thinking in which a person selects evidence that supports or confirms a favored hypothesis, theory, belief, choice, or option while ignoring disconfirming evidence. Confirmation bias can affect inductive reasoning, judgment, and decision making about scientific and everyday questions.

Before we examine the influence of this tendency on judgment and decision making, let's review how confirmation bias may affect the testing of an hypothesis. Wason (1960) provided a good demonstration of confirmation bias that you can try yourself. Your task is to discover the general rule that explains the organization of a particular series of numbers. If you think you know the rule, test your hypothesis by providing a different series that you think also conforms to the rule. In Wason's experiment subjects were then told whether or not the series they generated did fit the rule. Let's suppose you are given this series: 2, 4, 6, 8. Think for a moment and see if you can discover the rule underlying this series.

If you are like most people, and like the subjects in Wason's experiment, you came up with the rule that numbers in the series increase by 2, and you generated a series like this one: 12, 14, 16, 18. You would be told that the series was consistent with the rule. To further test your hypothesis, you might try another similar series (such as 200, 202, 204, 206) and again be told that the series fits the rule. At this point, you might guess that the rule is "any series of even numbers increasing by 2"; but the experimenter would tell you that is not the rule. Puzzled, you might try a different series and rule—such as the series 100, 200, 300, 400, an example of the rule that the series has an equal interval increase between each of the numbers. After being told that the series fits the rule, you might guess that the rule is that the series has increases of equal intervals; you would again be told that you have not found the rule. Wason found that this sort of testing would go on and on with subjects only sometimes discovering the rule. Have you figured it out yet? The rule is "any ascending whole number." A series such as 1, 4, 37, 430 would also be a positive instance and fit the rule.

If we examine the testing strategy that most people employ, we see that they tend to look for examples that are consistent with and confirm the rule they are entertaining while very infrequently testing a series that could disconfirm their favored hypothesis, such as 8, 6, 4, 2.

The confirmation bias has important implications for the conduct of science. First of all, bad theories get eliminated more quickly and good theories get strengthened the most when they are tested in situations in which they could be disconfirmed. The moral to the story is that the person seeking to improve his or her theory should make a special effort to look for evidence and conduct tests that could disconfirm it. A second implication of confirmation bias for the conduct of science is that scientists are also susceptible to this problem. Mahoney (1977) conducted an experiment in which editors of psychology journals were presented with articles for review that were either consistent with their own favored theories or inconsistent with them. Editors gave significantly better reviews to articles consistent with their favored theories than to those that disagreed with them. If people supposed to be objective and trained in critical evaluation are susceptible to the confirmation bias, people in general clearly need to become conscious of this bias and deliberately seek and fairly consider evidence that may disagree with their pet theories.

The confirmation bias can also influence clinical decision making. To help us better understand this, let's examine Table 9.3 a decision/evidence matrix for deciding whether a person has a mental disorder. Look at the data in Table 9.3.

TABLE 9.3

Matrix of symptoms and frequencies of occurrence of mental disorder

	Has Disorder		No Disorder
Has Symptoms	37		33
No Symptoms	17		13

Take a moment to think about it, and then decide whether the mental disorder goes with the symptoms.

The data in Table 9.3 were made up, but the idea is based on an actual study (Smedslund, 1963) of student nurses and their judgments of the relationship between symptoms and disease. Did you decide that there was a relationship between the symptoms and the presence of the mental disorder? If you did, you are in agreement with the nurses in the Smedslund study, but like them you are also being influenced by the confirmation bias.

People generally pay attention primarily to the upper left-hand quadrant of the matrix, which represents the presence of symptoms with the presence of the disorder. They also pay attention to the lower right-hand quadrant, or the absence of symptoms with the absence of a disorder. Notice, however, that in the other parts of the matrix are many instances of people who have the disorder with no symptoms and people who have the symptoms without the disorder. These provide disconfirming evidence for the hypothesis that these symptoms go with this disorder. This evidence should not be simply ignored or disregarded. In diagnosing mental disorders, clinicians often pay attention to only two or three of the symptoms that are prototypical of a disorder and may ignore other symptoms present (Gambrill, 1990). Clinicians should not entertain just one hypothesis or causal explanation that is consistent with part of a client's symptoms; rather, they should explore other explanations consistent with other symptoms. For further discussion of critical thinking and decision making in the diagnosis of mental disorders, see Chapter 12.

Illusory Correlation

As noted in Chapter 2, finding the covariation between variables—whether and how the values of variables change together—is an important part of making sense of the world. That information provides the basis for predicting how people will behave and finding causes of behavior. Both everyday and scientific theories make assumptions that certain variables relate to one another whether they actually do or not. For example, many people believe that having narrow, shifty eyes tends to go with criminal behavior. In fact, there is no good evidence that criminals tend to have narrow, shifty eyes; these variables do not correlate, in spite of many people's belief to the contrary. Such a belief is called an illusory correlation.

Unfortunately, illusory correlation is a thinking error that affects not only individuals' everyday thinking and judgments, but also the professional judgments of highly trained people such as clinical psychologists and research scientists. To illustrate this, let's examine the pseudoscientific approach of phrenology in the 19th century. The phrenologists believed that physical characteristics and behavioral tendencies or traits are correlated. As we saw in Chapter 4, this illusory correlation may have begun when Franz Gall noticed that one of his classmates with protruding eyes also had a superior verbal memory. Gall, Spurzheim, and other scientists then sought other examples of traits and abilities that corresponded to particular bumps and indentations in the skulls of individuals with various traits. From their observations they developed the theory that a specific trait corresponded to a bump or indentation in a particular place on the skull. Gall's original idea may have been influenced by the popular old notion that people with certain personality traits often have particular appearance characteristics. People's everyday theories, and even scientific theories, often begin with an idea shared by others in their group. Although the phrenologists found many cases that supposedly supported their notion, no rigorous scientific evidence supports the theory. By continuing to believe in a theory consistent with their expectations but unsupported by good evidence, Gall and Spurzheim were influenced by illusory correlation.

Halo Effect

Sometimes, when we evaluate someone or something, our positive evaluation concerning one dimension spills over and affects our evaluation on another dimension, making it more positive. This kind of bias, called the halo effect, is likely to occur when we have given a favorable rating to someone on a central trait so that our general mental attitude about the person affects our opinion about the person's specific characteristics (Rosenthal & Rosnow, 1991). The halo effect is a kind of response set, in that the person responds to the meaning behind the question with respect to their general positive attitude and does not respond to the specific content of the question.

Students and teachers are frequently called upon to evaluate one another (although students might argue that the number of opportunities for teachers to do so makes the evaluation a little one-sided). To illustrate the potential dangers of the halo effect, suppose that you were asked to judge your instructor's overall teaching ability on a course evaluation questionnaire. Further suppose that overall you like your instructor and the course, and so you evaluate the instructor quite favorably. Nothing is wrong with that, of course. But suppose that your overall evaluation and positive attitude made you respond more favorably to another item, such as how much the instructor stimulated your learning, than you otherwise would have if you had thought more about the item. Perhaps, although you generally like your instructor's teaching, you already knew a great deal about the subject going into the course and have not learned many new things. Nevertheless, your favorable attitude toward your instructor in general spills over to your evaluation of her on the specific characteristic that she stimulated your learning.

Teachers' evaluations of students are probably also subject to the halo effect (Matlin, 1994). Suppose a professor is filling out an evaluation of a student for the student's application to graduate school. If the teacher judges the student favorably on intelligence, then he or she may also tend to judge the student favorably on creativity, even though that professor had little opportunity to examine the student on that score. In this regard, the halo effect is like illusory correlation—that is, people may use their commonsense or implicit "theories" of personality to assume that two traits like intelligence and creativity go together.

Unfortunately, correcting or checking the influence of the halo effect on our judgments may not be easy. Research shows that sometimes when people are warned about the halo effect, they overcompensate in their ratings and evaluate someone more negatively than an accurate judgment warrants. It may help for the judge to treat each separate item in such a questionnaire as distinct. It may also help to combine the ratings of several trained judges using the same and different methods of rating (Rosenthal & Rosnow, 1991). Some evidence shows that people can be trained to be better judges, given information about different errors, practice sessions, and feedback and discussion about how to evaluate more precisely and objectively (Cooper, 1981).

Overconfidence

Much evidence shows that people often make judgment and decision errors. While errors certainly can be a problem, they would be less of one if people were aware that they were making an inferior judgment or decision. Unfortunately, though, people are often not very aware of their decision-making difficulties; in fact, people are often overconfident of their decisions' quality. Even decisions based on very little information or evidence are often the objects of this overconfidence. For example, in 1988, the captain of a U.S. Navy ship mistakenly judged an Iranian commercial airplane to be a military aircraft flying toward his ship intending to attack it. The captain made this decision primarily based on information from his radar; he did not seek to verify what the plane was doing. As a result, he decided to launch two missiles at the plane. All 290 civilian passengers on board the commercial aircraft were killed (Matlin, 1994).

Now that we have discussed some decision and judgment errors, the following practice problems will help you review and learn to apply these concepts to your everyday and psychological thinking. (Try to find examples in your own life and reading as well.)

≋ PRACTICE YOUR THINKING 9.1

Recognizing Decision and Judgment Errors

For each of the following situations, read through the situation and find the error or bias in judgment and decision making that best accounts for the example. Write what this error is and how it might have been avoided in the spaces below the example.

1. Cesár thought that Julie was romantically interested in him, but he was reluctant to ask her out until he was more sure. So he gathered some more information. First, he smiled at her, and she smiled back. Then he talked to her after class one day, and she was friendly. Another day, he asked her if she liked sports, and he found out they both liked tennis. Encouraged, he asked her out, but she said no, that she was already going with someone. Cesár felt bad.

What kind of error or bias is shown? _____

_____

What could have been done to avoid it? _____

_____

2. A clinical psychologist was discussing the problem of sexual abuse with a client. The therapist told her client that the sexual abuse of women was very prevalent. When her client asked her how common, the psychologist thought for a moment recalling several women she had seen recently whom she thought had been sexually abused. Based on the many that came to mind, the psychologist estimated that more than half of all women had been sexually abused.

What kind of error or bias is shown? _____

_____

What could have been done to avoid it? _____

_____

3. A psychologist sent out a questionnaire to a randomly selected group of individuals to find out their opinions about important people in their lives. She noticed that after an item in which respondents were asked to identify any-one who was their hero, respondents evaluated the people identified as their heroes more positively on traits for which these people were not generally known.

What kind of error or bias is shown? _____

What could have been done to avoid it? _____

Answers to Recognizing Decision and Judgment Errors

1. What kind of error or bias is shown? *Confirmation bias*

What could have been done to avoid it? *Cesár should have asked Julie or some-one who knew her for potentially disconfirming evidence.*

2.   What kind of error or bias is shown? *Availability*

What could have been done to avoid it? *The psychologist should not have relied upon this heuristic and instead should have consulted the psychological research to get a more accurate base rate.*

3.   What kind of error or bias is shown? *Halo effect*

What could have been done to avoid it? *The psychologist could have instructed respondents that even people whom we admire a lot may not have all positive characteristics and those whom we dislike may not have all negative characteristics. It might also help to think of each item as separate and distinct.*

Becoming Aware of How You Make Decisions

While an ability to recognize errors and biases in decision making and judgment is important, you also need to become aware of your own thinking as you make judgments and decisions. In the next two sections, you will be presented with two decision problems. What would you decide to do in each of these two decision cases? More important, how would you make your decision in each case? Recall that becoming aware of your own thought processes and how to control your thinking—or metacognition—is important to effective thinking. To help you promote your own metacognition while you make the following decisions, keep track of your thoughts as you make each decision so that you can reflect upon and analyze your own thought processes.

Psychologists know that people often have difficulty reporting the thought processes that go on while they solve a problem, make a judgment, or make a decision. Sometimes, people forget the thoughts they have as they occur during the decision making process. To minimize this forgetting, it is a good idea for people solving a problem or making a decision to report their thoughts as these thoughts occur during the problem-solving or decision-making process (Ericcson & Simon, 1984). To investigate ongoing thought processes occurring during the performance of some cognitive task, cognitive and other psychologists use method called the **think aloud procedure.** In this procedure, the researcher records the ongoing thoughts of a person who says his or her thoughts out loud as they occur during the process of coming to a solution or making a decision; the record is called a **think aloud protocol.**

≈ PRACTICE YOUR THINKING 9.2

Thinking Aloud as You Make Decisions

Use the think aloud procedure with a partner from your class or a friend to examine your thought processes as you make each decision. Just say your thoughts out loud as they occur to you in making your decision, and have another person write down these thoughts for later examination, in a think aloud protocol. Then trade places with the other person; and as he or she makes a decision in the second case, write down his or her thoughts. If no other person is available to record your thoughts for each case decision, then simply write down your own thoughts. This is called a retrospective report. You will forget a certain amount of information, but at least you will be able to examine some of your thoughts.

1.   Think aloud as you go through the process of deciding on a major. If you have already declared a major, then go through the decision process again as if you had not already decided (or allow your think aloud partner to make this decision).

2.   Imagine that on Thursday you have an important test in a difficult psychology course needed for your major. You would really like to get a B in the class, but so far you have a C average. Let's also assume that you have an opportunity to go to a party with someone to whom you are very attracted who has finally agreed to go with you. Unfortunately, the party is the night before your big test. Think aloud as you decide what to do.

Questions to Help You Analyze Your Think Aloud Protocols

1.   Did you generate enough good alternative choices?

2.   Can you identify any heuristics or decision-making strategies you used? Were they effective or could they lead to error?

3.   How did you select an alternative in your decision? Did you optimize? Did you satisfice?

4.   What are the risks and sources of uncertainty involved in making your decision?

5.   How will you evaluate the effectiveness of your decision?

Summary

In this chapter, we examined the sometimes severe consequences of faulty decisions. The consequences and uncertainty of decision making often produce stress and anxiety in decision makers. Decisions involve making choices between options. The process of decision making involves recognizing the need for a decision, identifying objectives and defining the problem, coming up with alternative courses of action, listing the relevant dimensions, evaluating the options, and selecting an option. Critical thinking resembles the decision-making process in that both are purposeful and deliberate. They both involve uncertainty and should be rational, in the sense that decisions and conclusions should be supported by good evidence and consistent with important goals.

People frequently use heuristics or rules of thumb to make judgments and decisions, but sometimes heuristics lead to errors. For example, people often use representativeness, which involves making a judgment about a sample based on the population or a known value or base rate; but sometimes people sample inadequately or fail to take base rate into account. Another heuristic, availability, helps us to estimate the frequency of certain events based on how easily we can bring an example to mind; sometimes, however, this ease of access is not a good indicator of the actual frequency of the event.

Other common judgment and decision errors discussed were confirmation bias, illusory correlation, and the halo effect. Confirmation bias is our tendency to pay attention to positive evidence and to not use evidence that could disconfirm a favored theory or hypothesis. Illusory correlation is an error in which people assert that two variables are correlated or related when in fact they are not. The halo effect is a tendency for positive evaluation on one dimension or item to spill over to the evaluation of another dimension or item.

Problems with judgment and decision making also occur because of a lack of awareness of the quality of decisions. For example, people are often overconfident of decisions that are based on very little information or evidence. The think aloud procedure is a useful technique for studying and making people aware of their decision processes.

Review Questions

Why do we need to make good decisions?

What is decision making?

What are decisions? What are judgments?

What are six steps or components of the decision-making process?

What is goals clarification? When is it important?

What is optimization?

What is satisficing?

What is a balance sheet? How do you set one up?

How are decision making and critical thinking related?

Compare heuristics to algorithms.

What is the representativeness heuristic? When might it fail?

What happens when a person fails to take into account base rate?

What is a conjunction fallacy?

What is availability? How can it contribute to faulty judgments?

How does confirmation bias influence how science is conducted?

What is illusory correlation? How can it affect clinical judgment?

What is the halo effect?

What is overconfidence? Why is it a problem?

How are the use of the think aloud procedure and metacognition related?

References

Beyth-Marom, R., Novik, R., & Sloan, M. (1987). Enhancing children's thinking skills: An instructional model for decision-making under certainty. *Instructional Science, 16,* 215–231.

Blackmore, S. (1992). Psychic experience: Psychic illusions. *Skeptical Inquirer, 16,* 367–376.

Bransford, J., & Stein, J. (1993). *The ideal problem solver* (2nd ed.). New York: W. H. Freeman.

Cooper, W. H. (1981). Ubiquitous halo. *Psychological Bulletin, 90,* 218–244.

Dawes, R. (1988). *Rational choice in an uncertain world.* New York: Harcourt Brace.

Dumont, F., & Lecomte, C. (1987). Inferential processes in clinical work: Inquiry into logical errors that affect diagnostic judgments. *Professional Psychology: Research and Practice, 18,* 433–438.

Ennis, R. H. (1987). A taxonomy of critical thinking dispositions and abilities. In J. Baron & R. Sternberg (Eds.), *Teaching thinking skills: Theory and practice.* New York: W. H. Freeman.

Ericcson, K. A., & Simon, H. A. (1984). *Protocol analysis: Verbal reports as data.* Cambridge, MA: MIT Press.

Franklin, B. (1887). *Complete works* (Vol. 4). J. Bigelow (Ed.). New York: Putnam.

Gambrill, E. (1990). *Critical thinking in clinical practice.* San Francisco: Jossey-Bass.

Halpern, D. F. (1996). *Thought and knowledge: An introduction to critical thinking* (3rd ed.). Hillsdale, NJ: Lawrence Erlbaum.

Harte, J. M., Westenberg, R. M., & van Someren, M. (1994). Process models of decision making. *Acta Psychologica, 87,* 95–120.

Hogarth, R. (1987). *Judgment and choice* (2nd ed.). Chichester, England: John Wiley & Sons.

Kahneman, D., & Tversky, A. (1973). On the psychology of prediction. *Psychological Review 80,* 237–251.

Laskey, K. B., & Campbell, V. N. (1991). Evaluation of an intermediate level decision analysis course. In J. Baron & R. V. Brown (Eds.), *Teaching decision making to adolescents.* Hillsdale, NJ: Erlbaum.

Mahoney, M. J. (1977). Publication prejudices: An experimental study of confirmatory bias in the peer review system. *Cognitive Therapy and Research, 1,* 161–175.

Matlin, M. (1994). *Cognition* (3rd ed.). Fort Worth: Harcourt Brace Jovanovich.

Medin, D. L., & Ross, B. H. (1992). *Cognitive psychology.* Fort Worth: Harcourt Brace Jovanovich.

Nisbett, R., & Ross, L. (1980). *Human inference: Strategies and shortcomings of social judgment.* Englewood Cliffs, NJ: Prentice-Hall.

Oskamp, S. (1965). Overconfidence in case study judgments. *Journal of Consulting Psychology, 29,* 261–265.

Ranyard, R., & Abdel-Nabi, D. (1993). Mental accounting and the process of multiattribute choice. *Acta Psychologica, 84,* 161–167.

Rosenthal, R., & Rosnow, R. (1991). *Essentials of behavioral research: Methods and practice* (2nd ed.). New York: McGraw-Hill.

Simon, H. A. (1957). *Models of man: Social and rational.* New York: Wiley.

Slovic, P., Fischoff, B., & Lichtenstein, S. (1976). Cognitive processes in societal risk taking. In J. Carroll & J. Payne (Eds.), *Cognition and societal behavior.* Hillsdale, NJ: Lawrence Erlbaum.

Smedslund, J. (1963). The concept of correlation in adults. *Scandinavian Journal of Psychology, 44,* 165–173.

Stapp, J., Tucker, A. M., & VandenBos, G. R. (1985). Census of psychological personnel: 1983. *American Psychologist, 40,* 1317–1351.

Wason, P. C. (1960). On the failure to eliminate hyptheses in a conceptual task. *Quarterly Journal of Experimental Psychology, 12,* 129–140.

Yates, J. F. (1990). *Judgment and decision making.* Englewood Cliffs, NJ: Prentice-Hall.

Zechmeister, E. B., & Johnson, J. E. (1992). *Critical thinking: A functional approach.* Belmont, CA: Wadsworth.

Do Emotions Hinder Critical Thinking?

Learning Objectives

• To better understand the relation between motivation, emotion, and cognition.

• To critically analyze a discussion of whether emotions interfere with rational and critical thinking.

• To apply knowledge of the influences of emotion on thinking so that you can identify and understand the effects of emotions on thinking in everyday situations.

What Do You Think?

Have you ever gotten so angry at someone that you could not think about anything else? Have you ever known someone who was so depressed that he or she could not bring himself or herself to do anything? Have you ever been so anxious before a test that you could not concentrate or remember anything that you had studied? Have you ever been so jealous of someone you cared about or loved that you continually looked for evidence that he or she was interested in someone else, perhaps even irritating the other person with your suspiciousness?

If you have had any of these experiences, then you are already well aware of how emotion can seem to interfere with the ability to think clearly. These examples also suggest that our emotions can affect our thinking in a variety of ways. But what does the scientific study of emotions tell us about the ways in which emotion can affect thinking, especially critical thinking? This chapter examines these effects and gives you practice identifying some ways emotions can affect thinking.

It is commonly thought that strong emotions interfere with clear thinking, causing people to think and behave irrationally (Parrott, 1995). Do our emotions interfere with the process of using and evaluating evidence so as to prevent our coming to a sound conclusion? If emotions do interfere with critical thinking, what specific effects do they have on our thinking and behavior? Before we examine these questions, it would be useful to define our terms—to understand what it means to have an emotion and to think rationally.

Defining Terms

First of all, what do we mean when we say that a person is having an emotion? One thing that we mean is that the person is in a particular **motivated state**— that is, that the person's behavior is aroused and directed toward some goal. To illustrate emotional and related states, let's take the case of a competitive athlete, such as a boxer. We would expect that his motivation would arouse and direct his behavior toward the goal of winning a boxing match, as indicated by his expenditure of effort in practicing and thinking about his upcoming fight.

Emotions often occur when we evaluate the meaning of a particular event in our lives with respect to our goals. Suppose the boxer was defeated by his opponent in the match. Which emotion he had would depend on how he evaluated the situation. If he attributed his loss to his having just recovered from the flu, then he would likely feel disappointment. If, however, the boxer attributed his loss to unfair scoring by the judges, then he would likely feel anger.

Anger is a good example of an **emotion,** which is a kind of motivated state marked by physiological arousal, expressive behaviors, subjective experience, and motivated dispositions to behave a certain way (Buck, 1988). Anger has all these characteristics. For example, the boxer experiencing the emotion of anger might show an increase in his heart rate (a physiological change); his lips might be compressed together in an angry facial expression (an expressive behavior); and he might have the subjective feeling that his body was tense. Also, he might have the behavioral disposition or tendency to strike out at someone, especially the perceived offender. Note that some psychologists use the more general term **affect** to refer to emotions, moods, and other emotional phenomena.

Suppose that the boxer just mentioned feels intense anger at having his goal of winning obstructed and so pounds his fist into a window. When I was in college, a similar event actually took place. A young and talented athlete I knew lost an event in which he was competing. In his anger and frustration, he smashed his fist into a glass window, severely injuring his hand.

From the perspective of critical thinking, the athlete's decision to slam his fist into the glass would seem irrational. The emotion of anger that led to this self-inflicted injury made the athlete behave in a way contrary to his goal of winning other matches or even practicing his sport for a while. In his anger that one goal was thwarted, he placed further obstructions in his way to reaching other goals. The assumption, of course, is that behaving in a way that furthers one's goals is **rational.** So to be rational means to behave in a way consistent with one's goals as well as to use reasons to draw a conclusion.

Goals, Outcomes, and Rational Behavior

The question becomes whether emotions help us to reach our goals or whether they interfere with or obstruct our efforts to reach our goals. This turns out to be a very complex question because we operate within the context of a multiplicity of goals. We may have more than one goal operating in the same situation, and sometimes our goals may be inconsistent and conflict (Baron, 1994).

≋ PRACTICE YOUR THINKING 10.1

Recognizing Goals and Outcomes of Emotions

To give you practice in identifying the relations between our emotions, goals, and thinking, you are presented with four cases depicting situations similar to the ones presented at the beginning of the chapter. Your task is threefold. First, determine what is the goal in each situation. Second, look for the outcome that seems to be occurring as a result of the emotional state. Third, use your knowledge of rationality and thinking errors we have covered to decide whether you think the emotion is making the person think or behave irrationally or is otherwise leading to some error in thinking. Explain. Write your responses in the spaces provided.

1. Rhonda got a letter from the registrar saying that a course she had taken would not count toward her graduation requirements and so she did not have enough courses to graduate. She got so angry that she went over and over in her mind how unfair they were being. She had given them the documentation of the course. Then she thought about how the financial aid office had notified her that her check was late at the beginning of the semester. Rhonda was so angry and upset that she did not study for a big test in psychology and failed it.

Goal: _____

Obstruction: _____

Outcome: _____

Irrational thinking/behavior: _____

2. Mark wanted to succeed at work, but he became so depressed that he could not bring himself to do anything. He would say to himself, "What's the use? No matter what I try, it doesn't work out." As a result, he would put off doing his work and sit around not getting anything done. His boss discussed Mark's low productivity with him.

Goal: _____

Obstruction: _____

Outcome: _____

Irrational thinking/behavior: _____

3. Lisa was very anxious about her statistics test. She studied for it, but she could not stop thinking about all the things she did not understand when she studied. When she got to the test she was so anxious that she could not concentrate or remember anything that she had studied. Lisa got a D on the exam, and she was disappointed because she needed a C in the course for her psychology major.

Goal: _____

Obstruction: _____

Outcome: _____

Irrational thinking/behavior: _____

4. Jim was very jealous of Tina, his girlfriend. He was very worried that she was interested in one of his good friends, Mario. The more Jim worried about this, the more evidence he found that Tina was interested in Mario, even though objectively there was little evidence that she was. Jim began to irritate Tina by being overly suspicious and inquisitive about her activities, and she talked to him about breaking up.

Goal: _____

Obstruction: _____

Outcome: _____

Irrational thinking/behavior: _____

Answers to Recognizing Goals and Outcomes of Emotions

1. Goal: *Rhonda's goal is to graduate from college.*
Obstruction: *The registrar's not counting Rhonda's credits is obstructing her graduation.*
Outcome: *Rhonda may not graduate on time, and she failed a test.*
Irrational thinking/behavior: *Rhonda's not studying for a big test further obstructs her goal of graduating from college.*

2. Goal: *Mark wanted to succeed at work.*
Obstruction: *Mark's depression and self-statements were getting in the way.*
Outcome: *Mark was very unproductive, and his boss talked to him.*
Irrational thinking/behavior: *Because he told himself he could not succeed, he began to believe it and engaged in a self-fulfilling prophesy.*

3. Goal: *Lisa wanted to do well on her exams and in her classes.*
Obstruction: *Her anxiety was making her unable to concentrate.*
Outcome: *Lisa got a D on her exam in a course she needed a C in.*
Irrational thinking/behavior: *Lisa became so anxious that all she was able to do was worry, which kept her from thinking about answering the questions on the test.*

4. Goal: *Jim wanted to continue to go with Tina.*
Obstruction: *His suspiciousness and jealousy got in the way.*
Outcome: *Jim irritated Tina, and she wanted to break up.*
Irrational thinking/behavior: *Jim's thinking and emotion led to actions that were bringing on what he wanted to avoid, similar to a confirmation bias or self-fulfilling prophesy.*

≋ PRACTICE YOUR THINKING 10.2

Critically Reading a Literature Review:
Do Emotions Make Thinking Irrational?

Does emotion make people think irrationally, as in these examples? Or are the effects of emotion on behavior and thinking more complex? To find out what kind of effects emotion actually has on thinking, it would be useful to examine the research literature. Before you examine the evidence, read over the following questions, which will prepare you to read the passage critically.

Questions to Prepare You for Critical Reading

1. What is the central question? What claim or claims are being made?

2. What evidence is relevant to evaluating the claim? Organize it under one category for evidence supporting the claim and another for evidence not supporting the claim. Then label each piece of evidence as to its kind.

3. Evaluate the quality and quantity of the evidence so that you can draw a sound conclusion based on the evidence presented.

4. Do any assumptions create problems for this conclusion?

5. What are some implications of this conclusion?

Appendix B contains a copy of these questions in a critical reading form. After answering them, you may consult the answers in Appendix C.

Do Emotions Make Thinking Irrational?

The idea that our emotions make us think and behave irrationally is an old one in Western thought that remains popular today. Since the time of Plato and Socrates, philosophers have viewed the emotions as in opposition to reason. The idea that emotion interferes with our judgment is reflected in the popular saying love is blind (Fischer & Jansz, 1995). In a recent informal survey, Parrott (1995) found that most people associate emotion with a disruption in thinking. Also, emotions are often viewed as involuntary while reason is thought to be voluntary. Our legal system reflects this view; for example, the penalties for premeditated murder (murder done in cold blood) are stiffer than for murder done in a fit of passion (Oatley, 1990). While popular and historical opinion both view emotion as interfering with reason, what does the research show?

Several lines of evidence suggest that emotional states, especially negative ones, impair the ability to think rationally. Ellis (1977a) argued that people become depressed because they hold irrational beliefs about themselves and the world. For example, depressed people who believe that they never can succeed look for evidence that success is not possible and in so doing create a situation that makes success very unlikely. Because they do not experience success, they continue to devalue themselves, confirming their belief in their own low value. This may lead to more failure and depression, and depression may, itself, lead to more negative thinking. A large body of literature supports the idea that negative, irrational thinking is related to depression (Ellis, 1977b). Other research by Tobacyk and Milford (1982) suggested that people who endorse irrational beliefs tend to show greater dogmatism and to make less critical inferences.

Other research on the effects of depression show mixed results, however. For example, Palfai and Salovey (1993) obtained results showing that the effects of emotion on performance on two reasoning tasks are complex. On the one hand, the researchers found that subjects who were experimentally induced to be in a depressed mood performed significantly more slowly on an inductive reasoning task than those induced to be in a neutral mood. On the other hand, those subjects experimentally induced to be in an elated mood performed significantly more slowly than depressed and neutral condition subjects on a deductive reasoning task. In another study by Camp and Pignatiello (1992), however, subjects induced to be in a depressed mood failed to show any impairment in their inferential reasoning using world knowledge as compared to subjects who were in either a happy mood group or a neutral mood group.

Fear has also been shown to interfere with rational thinking and behavior. Keinan (1987) found that when subjects were induced to be fearful by the threat of an electric shock they were less likely to examine alternatives to an anagram problem than subjects who were not made fearful.

Anxiety may also produce many negative effects on performance, including reasoning, especially when time pressure is involved, as in taking a test. Hembre (1988) reviewed a large number of studies in which test anxiety negatively impacted cognitive performance. Along these same lines, Wright (1974) found that subjects under extreme time pressure may have weighed negative evidence disproportionately and also may have paid attention to fewer dimensions in making their decisions.

Other research suggests that emotions and moods can have effects on a variety of kinds of judgments. For example, Johnson and Tversky (1983) found that subjects whose mood changed as a result of reading a tragic newspaper story increased their judgments of the frequency of other risks and undesirable events. On the other hand, subjects who read a positive story decreased their estimates of the frequency of risks. Another study found that happy subjects were willing to bet more on a long shot than subjects who were not made happy, suggesting that happiness can lead to greater risk taking under certain conditions (Isen & Patrick, 1983). Finally, Mayer, Gaschke, Braverman, and Evans (1992) showed that subjects tend to estimate the likelihood of events based on agreement between their mood and the affective quality of the event. So, for example, happy subjects tend to rate the chances of good weather as more likely than bad weather.

Not all experts agree that emotions always have negative effects on thinking. Scherer (1984) argued that low levels of positive emotion such as happiness may serve to maintain behavior, not interrupt it. According to Thorndike's law of effect, when a behavior leads to a pleasant outcome, organisms are more likely to engage in the behavior in the future, so affect may be linked to learning.

Although sometimes positive mood has helpful effects upon behavior and thinking, other research has shown that positive mood can bias thinking and judgment. For example, Isen and Daubman (1984) found that positive mood causes people to be more inclusive in grouping things into categories. In other words, if people have been put in a positive mood, they are more likely to say that a marginal example of a category was an instance of the category than subjects who were not put in a positive mood. For example, subjects were more likely to say that a ring was an example of the category clothing. Similarly, subjects in a positive mood gave higher ratings to poor instances of the category vehicle—such as elevator, camel, and feet—than did subjects who have not been put in a positive mood. Schwartz and Bless (1991) argued that when people are in positive moods, they are likely to use a processing strategy that lacks logical consistency and attention to detail.

Performance on tasks requiring logical, detail-oriented strategies may be impaired by a positive mood, but a positive mood may actually help a person on creative kinds of tasks (Isen, Johnson, Mertz, & Robinson, 1985). Creative thinking often requires that we see remote connections between stimuli, so a positive mood might be adaptive and helpful in solving some kinds of problems. In another study, Isen and Means (1983) found that subjects in a positive mood were more efficient in their decision making than were control subjects not put in a positive mood.

Mood has also been shown to have a variety of effects on persuasion, some of which are complex (Petty, Gleicher, & Baker, 1991). For example, Bless, Bohner, Schwartz, and Strack (1990) found that happy subjects were just as persuaded by weak arguments about a message that was opposite to their own attitudes on a topic as they were by strong arguments, unless they were told to pay attention to what the message said. Sad subjects, however, were more influenced by strong arguments than weak ones. Does being sad help you to think more critically?

If emotions really do disrupt rational processes and interfere with our thinking, what productive purpose could this serve? Some emotion theorists have argued that we can better understand the relation between emotion and rationality by understanding the function of emotion (Frijda, 1986; Oatley, 1990; Scherer, 1984). When behavioral scientists speak of the function of emotion, they may be talking about how a particular emotion evolved to serve an adaptive purpose or about how an emotion functions to regulate behavior (Bensley, 1993). Frijda's functional theory of emotion combines both of these senses in holding that emotions are tendencies toward specific modes of interaction with others, objects, and the environment.

Emotion might serve several functions. For example, emotion may facilitate learning, direct and redirect our attention to important environmental events, enhance expressive communication in our social interactions, or help maintain our goals and direct our actions toward them in general.

The function of rationality is quite different: to help us reason about evidence so that we can come to a logical conclusion (Oatley, 1990). Rationality would be better viewed as an ideal to be attained, not as something opposed to emotion, per se. Oatley (1990) correctly pointed out that thinking errors quite frequently occur outside of any particular emotional state. Also, Nathanson (1985) observed that the ideal of rationality, as it originated with Plato, proposes that effective reasoning requires an objective, cosmic perspective that is devoid of emotional attachment. Nathanson stated that while this view is prevalent in Western thinking, it is probably not possible to separate emotion and reason in this way.

Strong physiological arousal related to emotion may indeed interfere with thinking, and moods can affect our judgments; but our emotions should not be viewed as pitted against our rationality. Instead, we should view emotion as part of our ongoing processing, for which rationality is a goal.

A Classification of Emotional Effects on Thinking

To better understand ourselves as emotional beings with an ideal of rationality (not detached from our emotions), it would help us to become aware of some of emotion's effects on thinking and the uses of emotion in argumentation. The following describes several ways that emotions can affect thinking and can be misused in the critical thinking process.

1. **Interruption of thinking:** Strong emotions tend to shut down critical thinking, causing us to come to hasty and often irrational conclusions or to behave in ways that appear to be opposed to our goals.

2. **Distortion of judgment:** Judgments may be biased or altered by emotional states. For example, people who have a depressed outlook on life tend to expect failure even in situations in which failure is not likely. Also, people who are in a good mood tend to use categories in a more inclusive fashion than those not experiencing happiness.

3. **Appeals to emotion:** In persuasion and argumentation, a person may appeal to an emotion instead of providing a reason or evidence in support of some claim (see Neimark, 1987).

    a. **"Poisoning the well":** In this strategy, a person arguing for a position seeks to make it uncomfortable or embarrassing for another person to offer an opposing viewpoint or evidence. In this way disagreement and examination of all sides of an argument can be avoided.

    b. **Direct appeals to emotion:** Information is presented or situations are described for the purpose of arousing an emotion, such as pity or contempt, in order to influence or persuade.

    c. **Emotional language:** In making an argument, emotionally charged language is introduced in order to bias interpretation of the evidence or to color the argument.

≈ PRACTICE YOUR THINKING 10.3

Identifying Emotional Effects on Thinking

In each of the following examples, identify the specific kind of effect that emotion is having on thinking using the classifications just listed. Then, think of a strategy for overcoming the problem related to the emotion and the situation.

1. Tim has been dreading taking a math class for two years. When he finally takes his first exam for the class, his mouth is dry and he feels tense and jittery. He also has trouble concentrating on the questions being asked him, and he runs out of time. As a result, he fails the exam.

2. Bill and Paula were discussing the question of whether premenstrual syndrome should be considered a true mental disorder. Paula says, "Only an ignorant person who is insensitive to the changes that occur in women would think that PMS should not be considered a mental disorder."

3. Mary has just received news that she has been accepted into the sorority of her choice. She rushes off to tell the good news to her friend Yolanda. In telling Yolanda the news, Mary says she is already friends with all the other women in the sorority. In fact, however, just last week she got into a heated argument with one woman in the sorority, whom Mary previously has said she dislikes.

4. In an advertisement for a children's charity, a famous actress asks for support for the charity's good work in helping to eradicate a dreaded disease that is ravaging our children. Later in the ad, a child stricken by the disease says that he is sometimes in pain from the disease.

5.   In a speech, a political leader warns of the danger that a particular group of people pose to the country's way of life. The leader describes this group of people as "foreigners" who have "invaded" this "beloved" country in order to satisfy their own "greedy impulses."

Answers to Identifying Emotional Effects on Thinking

1.   The emotion of anxiety is *interrupting thinking.* The best way to prevent this problem is to not avoid the math class in the first place. If like Tim you had put off the math course, then you should study adequately for the test. Do not take caffeine or other stimulants and practice some form of relaxation training. It is very difficult to be anxious when you are relaxed.

2.   Paula is using the argumentative strategy of *poisoning the well.* Bill should point out that she is using this evasive strategy and that she is bringing in emotion to try to prevent a complete examination of the evidence.

3.   The happy experience of getting into the sorority is leading Mary to *distort her judgment.* She is thinking inclusively, ignoring her previous disagreement with one of the sorority sisters and including her among her friends. When one is happy, it is difficult to suppress it. In such cases, you should hesitate before you speak and listen to what you are saying, especially if there are negative consequences for misspeaking.

4.   The actress is using the argumentative strategy of *appealing to emotion,* in this case compassion or pity. This strategy is not altogether inappropriate, but if your finances are low and you cannot afford to give much, being aware of the use of this strategy may help you manage your budget.

5.   The leader is using *emotional language* in his argument to persuade and bias the judgments of his listeners. This should be pointed out to the speaker, and the listener should rephrase the argument with more emotionally neutral language.

These problems all illustrated how emotion might seem to derail rational thinking, but we have also examined situations in which emotion may improve thinking. Can you think of any examples?

Summary

Emotions have been shown to exert effects on thinking that may interfere with and interrupt rational thinking, as in the cases of jealousy, test anxiety, and depression. Emotions are motivated states and as such they direct and arouse behavior. They are marked by changes in subjective experience, such as feeling state, by expressive behaviors such as frowning, and by physiological changes such as changes in heart rate.

Emotions may interfere with rational thinking in at least two ways corresponding to the two meanings of *rational.* Emotions may interfere with a person's ability to reason or use evidence to draw sound conclusions. They may also direct or change a person's behavior in such a way that they obstruct a person from reaching his or her goals.

When we review the literature on the

effects of emotion on thinking, we observe complicated and mixed effects. There is evidence that strong negative emotion such as depression and anxiety may interrupt and interfere with organized behaviors and thinking. In fact, there is evidence that irrational thinking may help to maintain depression. Some research, however, has shown that depression may lead to better deductive reasoning than does happiness. Other research showed that happiness may also have both positive and negative effects on thinking. Positive mood may make a person more creative but also more inclusive in the use of categories. While emotions may interrupt and disrupt thinking, they also may serve useful functions such as regulating behavior and orienting the person to important events.

Affect also has other effects on thinking. It can be used in persuasion to derail an argument, as in the use of emotionally loaded language and in poisoning the well, an emotional personal attack against the person opposing an argument.

Review Questions

What are some examples of the effects of strong emotions on thinking?

What is a motivated state? An emotion? Affect?

What are the two meanings of "rational"?

Do emotions make us irrational?

> What are some examples of ways that emotions can interfere with thinking?

References

Baron, J. (1994). *Thinking and deciding* (2nd ed.). Cambridge, England: Cambridge University Press.

Bensley, D. A. (1993). Functions of emotion. In F. Magill (Ed.), *Survey of social science: Psychology*. Pasadena, CA: Salem Press.

Bless, H., Bohner, G., Schwartz, N., & Strack, F. (1990). Mood and persuasion: A cognitive response analysis. *Personality and Social Psychology Bulletin, 16,* 331–345.

Bodenhausen, G. V., Kramer, G., & Susser, K. (1994). Happiness and stereotypic thinking in social judgment. *Journal of Personality and Social Psychology, 66,* 621–632.

Buck, R. (1988). *Human motivation and emotion* (2nd ed.). New York: John Wiley.

Camp, C. J., & Pignatiello, M. F. (1992). Effects of induced dysphoric mood on fact retrieval and inferential reasoning from world knowledge. *Bulletin of the Psychonomic Society, 30,* 515–518.

Ellis, A. (1977a). The basic clinical theory of rational-emotion therapy. In A. Ellis & R. Grieger (Eds.), *Handbook of rational emotive therapy*. New York: Springer.

Ellis, A. (1977b). Research data supporting the clinical and hypotheses of ret and other cognitive-behavior therapies. In A. Ellis & R. Grieger (Eds.), *Handbook of rational emotive therapy*. New York: Springer.

Frijda, N. (1986). *The emotions*. Cambridge, England: Cambridge University Press.

Fischer, A., & Jansz, J. (1995). Reconciling emotion with Western personhood. *Journal for the Theory of Social Behavior, 25,* 59–80.

Hembre, R. (1988). Correlates, causes, effects, and treatment of test anxiety. *Review of Educational Research, 58,* 47–77.

Isen, A. M., & Daubman, K. A. (1984). The influence of affect on categorization. *Journal of Personality and Social Psychology, 47,* 1206–1217.

Isen, A. M., Johnson, M., Mertz, E., & Robinson, G. (1985). The influence of positive affect on the unusualness of word associations. *Journal of Personality and Social Psychology, 48,* 1413–1426.

Isen, A. M., & Means, B. (1983). The influence of positive affect on decision making strategy. *Social Cognition, 2,* 18–31.

Isen, A. M., & Patrick, R. (1983). The effect of positive feeling on risk taking: When the chips are down. *Organizational Behavior and Human Performance, 31,* 194–202.

Johnson, E. J., & Tversky, A. (1983). Affect, generalization, and the perception of risk. *Journal of Personality and Social Psychology, 45,* 20–31.

Johnson-Laird, P. N., & Oatley, K. (1992). Basic emotions, rationality, and folk theory. *Cognition and Emotion, 6,* 201–223.

Keinan, G. (1987). Decision making under stress: Scanning of alternatives under controllable and uncontrollable threats. *Journal of Personality and Social Psychology, 52,* 639–644.

Mayer, J. D., Gaschke, Y., Braverman, D., & Evans, T. (1992). Mood-congruent judgment is a general effect. *Journal of Personality and Social Psychology, 63,* 119–132.

Nathanson, S. (1985). *The ideal of rationality.* Atlantic Highlands, NJ: Humanities Press International.

Neimark, E. D. (1987). *Adventures in thinking.* San Diego: Harcourt Brace Jovanovich.

Oatley, K. (1990). Do emotional states produce irrational thinking? In K. Gilhooly, M. Keane, R. Logie, & G. Erdos (Eds.), *Lines of thinking.* West Sussex, England: John Wiley.

Palfai, T. P., & Salovey, P. (1993). The influence of depressed and elated mood on deductive and inductive reasoning. *Imagination, Cognition, and Personality, 13,* 57–71.

Parrott, W. G. (1995). But emotions are sometimes irrational. *Psychological Inquiry, 6,* 230–232.

Petty, R. E., Gleicher, F., & Baker, S. (1991). Multiple roles for affect in persuasion. In J. Forgas (Ed.), *Emotion and social judgments.* Oxford: Pergamon Press.

Scherer, K. R. (1984). On the nature and function of emotion: A component process approach. In K. Scherer & P. Ekman (Eds.), *Approaches to emotion.* Hillsdale, NJ: Lawrence Erlbaum.

Schwartz, N., & Bless, H. (1991). Happy and mindless, but sad and smart? The impact of affective states on analytic reasoning. In J. Forgas (Ed.), *Emotion and social judgments.* Oxford: Pergamon Press.

Tobacyk, J., & Milford, G. (1982). Criterion validity for Ellis' irrational beliefs: Dogmatism and uncritical inferences. *Journal of Clinical Psychology, 38,* 605–607.

Wright, P. (1974). The harassed decision maker: Time pressures, distractions, and the use of evidence. *Journal of Applied Psychology, 59,* 555–561.

Thinking Critically About Theories of Abnormal Behavior: Culture and Witches

Learning Objectives

• To understand how we use our personal theories, cultural assumptions, and stereotypes to make judgments about another person's behavior and character.

• To extract the important facts from a description of behaviors and interactions and then come up with hypotheses that might plausibly explain these.

• To analyze a discussion critically so that you can decide which hypothesis best accounts for the evidence when several possible explanations are offered.

What Do You Think?

Imagine that someone has been invited to give a guest lecture to your psychology class. Suppose that the speaker enters your classroom, turns toward the wall at the front of the classroom, and then begins to lecture facing the wall instead of facing you and the rest of the audience. What would you think about this behavior? Do you think it is unusual? Is it abnormal?

You might have thought to yourself, "This speaker is strange—a really weird person!" Social psychologists have emphasized that we tend to categorize people as whether they are like or unlike us, and like or unlike the group that we belong to (Festinger, 1954; Feldman, 1995). Although we tolerate some individual differences in behavior, the guest lecturer's behavior is so unusual that it practically begs for an explanation. In our culture, it is expected that a speaker will stand, most of the time, facing his or her audience; any deviation from that stance would probably set you to speculating about why the speaker was behaving this way. Perhaps you thought that the person might be from another culture and not know how to behave for an American audience. Or you might have thought, "How rude! This person does not even care enough to face the audience." Whatever you were thinking, your mental processes involved generating hypotheses to explain the speaker's unusual behavior.

Personal, Folk, and Implicit Theories of Personality

You were able to come up with hypotheses because, whether we are psychologists or not, we all seem to have our own personal theories about why people characteristically act, feel, and think the way they do. In other words, we each have our own theories of **personality.** These personal theories are sometimes called "implicit theories of personality," because we operate on their assumptions even though these assumptions are often not explicitly stated or taught to us (Schneider, 1973). For example, a person may use his or her implicit theory of personality to try to understand why someone who has been friendly to us in the past has now said something offensive to us. In such a case, we might speculate that something had gone wrong for the person and he or she was taking it out on other people. But we would probably not critically reflect on or examine the assumptions we were using to come to our conclusion. (Recall that assumptions are the premises of an argument that may be either stated explicitly or implied in the argument.)

Along the same lines, commonsense or folk "theories" of personality are based on common assumptions individuals share about why people act, feel, and think the way they do. Like personal theories of personality, when we use folk wisdom to explain behavior we often do not examine the assumptions made by the theory. Farina and Fischer (1982) reviewed research on people's beliefs about mental disorders and argued that these beliefs are very unstructured and vague, with many inconsistencies. In contrast, those who use scientific theories frequently do examine their assumptions explicitly. Scientists try to find consistency in their assumptions. For example, a great deal of clinical analysis and research has been done on defining what signs and symptoms are assumed to characterize particular psychological disorders and forms of abnormal behavior (American Psychiatric Association, 1994).

Just like scientific theories of personality, both personal and folk "theories" often include assumptions about which behaviors are normal and which are abnormal. These assumptions may be used to make predictions about how a person is expected to behave in a given situation and to explain why a person has acted differently from what was expected. In other words, the conclusion you draw about whether a particular behavior is normal or abnormal depends on your assumptions. To see that this is so, let's examine an example of behavior and try to determine whether it is abnormal or not.

≈ PRACTICE YOUR THINKING 11.1

Making Judgments About Behavior

This example comes from my experience as a young student attending Columbia University in New York City in 1971. When I wasn't studying, I often rode the subway to explore the city or to go to my part-time job. On one particular day, I sat down next to an elderly lady who was carrying on a conversation with someone—in and of itself a little unusual, since most travelers on New York's subways do not speak to other travelers. I looked over to see with whom she was talking—and there was no one there.

1. Was this person behaving abnormally? What do you think? Take a moment to think about how you made your decision.

2. What assumptions did you make about what is abnormal behavior in making your decision?

3. Did this person clearly demonstrate evidence that would lead you to conclude she was abnormal?

4. Can you think of examples of behavior like this woman's that would not be judged as abnormal in another context?

Answers to Making Judgments About Behavior

1.   Although this was before I had studied much psychology, I concluded this woman had a mental problem. You may have concluded the same thing.

2.   I made the assumption that speaking out loud in public to unseen persons is abnormal. You probably made a similar assumption. In fact, I expect that this assumption is probably part of the commonsense theories about abnormal behavior of most people now living in North America. My conclusion about this woman was probably also influenced by two other factors: first, assumptions in my culture about what behaviors are normal and abnormal and, second, the context of the behavior.

3.   While I concluded that the woman was abnormal, I drew my conclusion based simply upon my comparison of her behavior with my assumption that such a behavior is abnormal. I did not consider other possible explanations of her behavior, nor did I use any knowledge of psychology to make my judgment. From the perspective of making a good diagnosis, as discussed in Chapter 12, my conclusion was not based on sufficient evidence.

4.   When deciding whether a particular behavior is abnormal, one should also consider the context of the behavior. Under certain circumstances, people who speak to someone unseen are not believed to be crazy. Starting in the late 18th century, there was a revival of the idea in Europe and the United States that the spirits of dead persons could be contacted through a medium, a person with a special ability for communicating with the spirit world. In Africa, many people believe that spirits can cause mental and physical illness through witchcraft and that a victim can be rid of these effects by special exorcism rituals (Forssen, 1980). Also, Christian ministers and others around the world think of Jesus in personal terms and speak out loud to this unseen religious personage through public prayer. Moreover, in our modern technologically advanced world, we daily talk to people who are unseen by means of the telephone, and we take such communication for granted. This sort of communication would have appeared not just unusual but supernatural to people who lived prior to the 19th century. These few examples of people speaking to unseen others support the idea that whether or not a behavior is considered abnormal depends, not only on the assumptions of one's theory, but also on the social, cultural, and historical context of that theory.

Thinking Critically About Historical Questions

If it is true that people commonly use their own personal theories or folk theories to explain normal and abnormal behavior, then a historical question naturally arises: Have people always used such theories? Historical questions like this one pose special problems for the scientist and critical thinker. Recall that critical thinking involves evaluating evidence relevant to a claim or assertion so that a sound conclusion can be drawn. Because the theories we will examine are from people who died long ago, we must use evidence that they left behind, primarily their art, writings, and artifacts. Because we cannot ask these people questions about the meaning of the evidence and because they can produce no additional evidence, it is often difficult to come to a strong conclusion. Indeed, if these people from the past did not leave a record or other evidence behind, then it may be impossible to determine what actually did happen. We cannot survey them, conduct an experiment, or otherwise test them to find out about their theories as we can in psychological studies of living people.

To illustrate some of the problems in thinking critically about historical questions and to examine the influence of culture on theories of abnormal behavior, we will examine two cases, one from prehistoric times and the other from the late Middle Ages. The first example, concerning a possible primitive theory of abnormality, comes from the Paleolithic cave dwellers of Northern Europe. These people employed a method called **trephining** in which they used stone instruments to chip holes in the skulls of their group's members. This procedure may have been a therapy of some sort, because the skulls of the "patients" show that the bone tissue healed, indicating that they survived the procedure.

The specific purpose of Paleolithic trephining is not known. It may have been done to remove bone splinters resulting from fighting with primitive weapons; but the trephined skulls of many women and children, who were noncombatants, have also been found (Rogers, 1985). Perhaps, instead, trephining was done to let evil spirits out of the head, consistent with the common premodern belief that people behave the way they do because they are filled with a spirit or spirits. According to this view, called **animism**, a person could be possessed by a variety of spirits including the spirits of animals, ancestors, gods, and evil spirits. It was often thought that a person who behaved crazily was possessed by an evil spirit. Of course, although animism has been prevalent among many premodern peoples, we can only speculate what "theory" led to trephining, because no written records document Paleolithic beliefs. Our conclusion about the theory behind trephining is limited by the absence of any records of that theory.

We now turn to a second, later historical example for which there is more evidence, including written evidence—that is, the persecution of so-called witches starting in the late Middle Ages and the folk theory used to explain the "witches'" behavior. Before we do this, however, let's examine your own personal theory about witchcraft. When you think of a witch, what comes to mind? An old woman who comes out on Halloween? Someone who lures children into her gingerbread house and then bakes them? Or do you believe that witches are figments of overactive imaginations?

Most people living between the 14th and 17th centuries in Western Europe believed that witches actually existed (Connor, 1975). Perhaps, as many as several hundred thousand women were executed as witches. Many people believed that witches fornicated with the devil, flew through the air to secret meetings with other witches, and used magic and ritual to cause other people misfortunes, such as spoiled crops or even death.

"Impossible," you say? Let's use critical thinking to find out more about who these "witches" were. That will help us to decide which hypothesis explaining the witchcraft craze best accounts for the evidence.

Witchcraft: An Explanation for Various Troubles

In Western Europe and America during the 14th through 17th centuries, a common explanation for all kinds of misfortunes, afflictions, and other disastrous outcomes was the involvement of unseen evil forces. A prevailing notion at the time was that people could be possessed by evil spirits, like Satan, that would cause them to behave in very peculiar ways, often doing evil things to others. It was not uncommon to accuse a neighbor of witchcraft in order to account for some otherwise inexplicable event, such as the sudden death of a horse or child. During this time, a great number of people were tried and executed for witchcraft. Most of the accused were women. While people from all walks of life were accused, many were unmarried and widowed women (Williams, 1978).

The idea of the witches' crimes and powers came to be increasingly elaborated, culminating in the publication of the *Malleus Maleficarum* (*The Hammer of Witches*), a guidebook for finding, testing, prosecuting, and punishing witches (Kramer & Sprenger, 1971). Written by two Dominican priests involved in the Inquisition, this book also included superstitions and folktales not strictly of Christian origin. (The Inquisition was an institution within the Catholic Church that provided the legal mechanism for accusing, trying, sentencing, and executing people accused of witchcraft.)

Witches were thought to sign a compact with the devil and to engage in various evil activities. The devil would then have sexual intercourse with them and mark them in their private areas with his special mark. This intercourse was thought to be painful because the devil's organ was large and icy. Witches were thought to prepare flying ointments and then to fly at night to Sabbats, or gatherings of witches. At these secret, orgiastic meetings, witches were purported to drink blood, to engage in wild dancing and sexual intercourse, and to sacrifice and eat children. By the 15th century, the Sabbats were viewed as a profane, anti-Christian celebration (Spanos, 1978). Witches were also thought to be able to fly through the air by magic and to cause physical harm simply by looking another person in the eye. They were thought to be able to cause other people harm just with their glance or by means of a curse. They often were seen with animal companions called familiars that were really devils in animal form.

Mair (1976) pointed out that witches are usually a challenge to the social order and in many cultures are viewed as rebels against important social rules. This relationship to society took a very legalistic turn in witchcraft prosecution in Renaissance Europe. In the 13th century, the Catholic Church viewed belief in witchcraft as an illusion, but by the 15th century such a belief was viewed as a serious crime punishable by death. As Currie (1968) noted, by the 15th century the witch was thought to sign a contract with the devil and to renounce the Christian faith (in almost a legal fashion, by signing a book or making a pact with the devil): heresy of the highest order.

As in other cultures, if witches are perceived as a threat to the social order and to particular individuals, then there must be a means for identifying them and prosecuting them. The *Malleus Maleficarum* gave explicit instructions for how to identify and prosecute witches. At the same time Pope Innocent VIII decreed the establishment of the Inquisition to investigate heretics and those deviating from Catholic doctrine. This group was empowered to torture those accused of witchcraft and heresy. An elaborate set of tests was developed to determine whether individuals were witches. The Inquisition encouraged people to turn in anyone they knew who was suspect. Not to do so was to act as a witch's accomplice.

Once a person was accused, she could be interrogated using torture, such as thumbscrews and the rack, and given other dubious tests to detect the devil's influence. Often the accused was stripped naked with her hair shaved off, and her private areas were searched for a devil's mark. When such a mark was found, the investigator would often stick pins in it, because a witch was not supposed to show pain when the mark was probed. Inquisitors also immersed the accused in a river as a test of innocence. If she floated, this was a sign that the substance of her body was different from ordinary water because of the devil's influence, and she was guilty; if she sank, she was innocent (of course, she could also drown). Another test involved poking needles into the flesh to find areas of the body that were insensitive to pain, supposedly a sign that a woman was a witch. Sometimes, a needle was thrust into the same place repeatedly, and if the accused no longer showed pain, this was taken as a sign that she was guilty even though an area may become less sensitive as nerves are damaged by the repeated jabbing. In addition, professional witch-finders, paid to identify potential witches, sometimes used trick needles that would collapse in the hand. These needles would only appear to go into the flesh, but would lead observers to believe that the accused was not experiencing pain from a painful jab.

The *Malleus Malleficarum* was used for more than 200 years by both Catholics and Protestants to try witches. The results of this systematic inquisition resulted in probably hundreds of thousands of deaths. In continental Europe the usual mode of execution was burning—preferred because it was thought to destroy the evil force inside the accused. In Britain the preferred method was hanging.

Sometimes, those accused of witchcraft confessed to a number of these crimes. In many cases in Europe, the accused witches confessed to these misdeeds after torture. These misdeeds were considered crimes and sometimes tried by the civil authorities. By the 15th century, there was no sharp distinction between the concerns of the church and the civil laws for these kinds of moral questions and affronts. Often both civil and church authorities were involved in prosecuting witch cases.

Examining Witchcraft Accusations in Colonial New England

It is instructive to examine the behavior and accusations of a group of young girls who were the main accusers of witches during an outbreak of witchcraft in Salem village in the Massachusetts colony in 1692. This incident is better documented than many of the earlier European outbreaks, so we can use it to examine various hypotheses about witchcraft (Woodward, 1969).

The episode in Salem appears to have started with 9-year-old Betty Paris, the daughter of Samuel Paris, the minister of Salem village (Weinstein and Gatell, 1981). Young Betty began to show unusual behaviors, such as bouts of uncontrollable weeping. At other times, she would wander about or even sit for hours oblivious to everyone around her. When she came out of the trancelike state, she would scream frantically. Then, her cousin Abigail Williams began to show similar but even more dramatic symptoms. Soon, several of the girls' friends also showed symptoms and behaviors that alarmed the whole Salem community. The girls showed sudden convulsive fits in which their arms, necks, and backs were turned abruptly as if out of their own control.

Apparently, the first of the afflicted girls had listened to tales about spirits told them by Tituba, the servant woman of Samuel Paris. Reverend Paris had acquired Tituba and her husband in the West Indies, where African beliefs about spirits had coalesced with Christianity and other influences to form the voodoo religion. To entertain Betty and Abigail, Tituba had told them strange spirit stories; later other young girls from Salem also visited to hear the stories. After this, the girls began to show the symptoms.

Ministers from nearby communities were summoned to offer their opinions and prayers concerning the afflicted girls' conditions. At the time, accusations of witchcraft were not uncommon, and witch trials and even hangings had taken place in Boston and other New England towns. In fact, ministers often gave sermons that warned their audiences of demons and witches, and the famous minister Cotton Mather gave just such a sermon in Salem two years prior to the outbreak (Silverman, 1983). The suspicion arose that the Salem girls were afflicted by the influence of witches. The afflicted girls were questioned relentlessly until they named three women of questionable reputation: the slave Tituba, a sharp-tongued younger woman, and an older woman known for her lying and poor church attendance.

At the trials of the accused witches, the girls claimed that the accused had appeared to them in the form of apparitions seeking to get them to write their names in the book of the devil. Each time one of the accused moved, the girls would thrash their bodies about as if reacting to the accused's movement. The girls claimed they were bitten, pinched, bruised, and otherwise physically tormented by the specters of the witches (Weinstein & Gatell, 1981).

Generating Other Explanations for "Witches'" Behaviors

How would you explain these unusual behaviors and symptoms of the "witches'" accusers? Critical thinkers are willing to consider any plausible explanation and to examine the evidence for each explanation. Recall from Chapter 2 that a plausible explanation is one that not only is a possible cause, but reasonably could have produced the effect and is consistent with the evidence. Plausible explanations are like hypotheses, in that both are educated guesses based on certain assumptions and knowledge. Here, a plausible explanation for the accuser's symptoms and behaviors is one that is consistent with the important facts in the case. Before you can come up with a plausible explanation, you must be clear about what the facts are. In the next section, we will first try to identify the facts to be explained.

≋ PRACTICE YOUR THINKING 11.2

Identifying the Facts to Be Explained

To help you find the facts to be explained, let's examine the following questions. Simply write down facts that seem important to understanding the witchcraft phenomenon.

1. What characteristics, special abilities, and experiences did those accused of witchcraft have?

_____

_____

_____

_____

_____

_____

_____

2. How did members of the community and others interact with the accused witches?

_____

_____

_____

_____

_____

_____

_____

Answers to Identifying the Facts to Be Explained

1. What characteristics, special abilities, and experiences were witches thought to have? *Witches had special powers: flying through the air, causing bad things to happen to people through magic, such as rituals and potions. They got their power from the devil. They went to ritual meetings and engaged in wild dancing, sex, ritual killing, and sacrifice. They were heretics believing ideas opposite to Christianity.*

2. How did members of the community and others interact with the accused witches? *Witches were viewed as evil by the community. Institutions for identifying them were established. They were charged and had to go to court to defend themselves. They were identified by people who were paid to stick them with pins in order to identify them. They were tortured severely, often until they confessed. The accusers in Salem listened to stories about magic and then showed strange behaviors such as throwing their bodies at the trial in response to movements of the accused. When witches were convicted, they often were executed, and large numbers of women, especially, were killed.*

 PRACTICE YOUR THINKING 11.3

Generating Plausible Hypotheses

First, think of two plausible explanations for the unusual behaviors of the afflicted girls who accused the women of being witches; then, write your hypothesis about what caused the unusual behaviors in the space provided below.

1. _____

_____

2. _____

_____

Second, how could you account for the bizarre behaviors that the women on trial were accused of? Sometimes accused witches confessed to the accusations—what would explain these confessions? Using your knowledge of psychology, think of three plausible explanations for these unusual behaviors of the accused witches, and write your hypothesis about what caused the unusual behaviors in the space provided below.

1. _____

_____

2. _____

_____

3. _____

_____

In the next sections we will examine how one might come up with hypotheses to explain the witchcraft phenomenon.

Note that the kinds of hypothesis you generate depend on the prior assumptions you make. For example, if you assumed that witches did not actually exist, then you would look for different explanations than if you assumed that they did. Of course, one possibility is that the accused actually were witches. Margaret Murray (1921), relying heavily on evidence from the confessions of English witches, argued that witchcraft was the remnants of the pre-Christian religion of Britain and Western Europe. She said this pre-Christian religion was the basis for the rituals of the witch's Sabbat or Sabbath, as well as the origin of the devil in animal form.

It may help you to ask yourself what could make a person hallucinate that she was communicating with the devil, that she could fly through the air, or that she could cause a misfortune through indirect, magical means. Think about it before reading on.

After pondering this first question, it might have occurred to you that hallucinations may occur when a person's brain chemistry is disturbed. This could occur if the person had ingested a drug. Hallucinogenic substances may have been put into brews and herbal concoctions the accused prepared as part of folk medicine they used. Caporael (1976) proposed that the bizarre behaviors of the accusers in Salem village may have been caused by ergot poisoning from the ergot fungus infesting the grains of the village. The hallucinogenic drug LSD derives from one form of the ergot fungus. This may have led to the symptoms of the accusers, including stomach cramps, convulsions, and hallucinations. A biochemical imbalance could also occur if the accusers or accused had developed a serious mental disorder, such as schizophrenia, in which auditory hallucinations are common. In fact, this hypothesis that witches actually had mental disorders has been very popular with psychiatrists and psychologists over the last several decades. It is found in many psychology textbooks (e.g., Rosenhan & Seligman, 1989) and has been reviewed by Spanos (1978).

Another way to generate alternative hypotheses to explain the witch persecutions is to change your assumptions. Ask yourself, if the accused was not actually a witch, what might have made her say she was a witch. Think about it before reading on.

By making the assumption that some people may have confessed to crimes and experiences they did not have, another possibility may have occurred to you. The accused may have been forced to make a confession through torture or social pressures.

In this chapter, we will explore four theories that have been proposed to explain the witch craze of this period. These are as follows:

1.   There really were witches.

2.   Chemical substances account for the "witches'" strange behaviors.

3. "Witches" actually suffered from mental disorders.
4. "Witches" were the victims of sociopolitical forces, including religious and economic factors, and the witch craze was the product of the culture.

Let's critically examine each of these theories to see which best explains the witchcraft phenomenon.

Analyzing a Complex Psychological Question: The Witchcraft Phenomenon

We have accomplished the first step in answering the question by generating potential explanations of it. The next step involves examining how each hypothesis explains the witchcraft craze and then evaluating the evidence for it. Finally, we will decide which explanation best accounts for the evidence.

Now that we have examined some background information on witchcraft, let's examine how each of the four theories seeks to explain various facts of the witchcraft phenomenon.

Theory 1: Witches Really Did Exist

Let's first consider the possibility that witches did exist. Our modern scientific and materialistic theories provide little room for the idea that witches really did have intercourse with the devil or could fly through the air on a broom. Perhaps, as the anthropologist Murray (1921) proposed, witches really existed as the remnant of an earlier, pre-Christian cult. She based this conclusion largely upon the confessions of several witches and the remarkable similarity of their accounts of witches' rites.

It is true that witches are found in many cultures around the world and are apparently archaic in origin. Recall that Odysseus was lured by the sirens, witches who drove men crazy and changed his men to pigs. The Bible mentions witches, and Exodus 22:17, a very early book of the Bible, admonishes, "Thou shalt not suffer a witch to live." Jesus and his disciples exorcised demons that possessed people.

Murray argued that many women who were called witches were actually members of an agrarian cult that worshipped the Greek goddess of the hunt, Diana (Murray, 1921). Many of the rituals, rites, and cures that cult members believed Diana had passed along to them were concerned with fertility, which the Christian judges of the witch trials took to be examples of licentiousness and an overemphasis on sex. According to Murray, the idea of a ritual parody of the sacraments, such as the Black Mass in which Christian rites were turned upside down or reversed, was really a creation of the Christians of the late Middle Ages.

Later, a Roman Catholic priest and scholar, Montague Summers, agreed with Murray's idea that witches actually existed, but he argued they were indeed vile devotees of an obscene creed who did cause all kinds of crimes. He agreed that the confessions were true and that the Sabbat did take place (Summers, 1956).

Similarly, Russell (1972) argued that the idea of witchcraft developed out of the Christian church's response to heretics, those who would disagree with church doctrine. Russell disagreed with Murray that witches were part of an agrarian fertility cult, because the early origins of the witchcraft craze were in the most industrialized and advanced, most well-educated areas of Europe in the late Middle Ages: France, northern Italy, the Rhineland. In general, this idea that witches of the late Middle Ages were the remnants of a cult who worshipped Diana has received little support from scholars in the area. Murray's evidence cannot be trusted, because much of it was confessions from tortured persons (Mair, 1976; Spanos, 1978). Ginzburg (1992), however, provided evidence of groups like the Bennetati who believed that they were called to protect their villages from the witches who flew to Sabbats, engaged in abominable behaviors, and caused problems in their region. This further suggests the common people, not just religious and legal authorities, believed that there were witches who attended Sabbats and posed a real threat.

Nevertheless, it should be noted that there is a long folk tradition of women practicing lay medicine using herbal cures. Before the advent of modern medicine, women often played informal roles as healers and midwives (Ehrenreich & English, 1973). Some of these herbal cures may have had psychoactive properties.

Theory 2: Chemical Substances Caused Witches' Strange Behaviors

Perhaps, then, the mental disturbance and bizarre behaviors of so-called witches were actually caused by psychoactive properties of chemicals they ingested. Some of those accused of witchcraft did create their own mixtures, usually from herbs and other vegetable sources, to treat ailments and perhaps to have some magical effect. There are records of aphrodisiacs and love potions, of flying ointments that witches supposedly used to help them fly through the air to Sabbats, even of potions for killing other individuals. We do not know the precise recipes for these concoctions, partly because this information was not readily disseminated by witches and was actively suppressed as heretical by those in authority during this time. Johannes Weyer in the 1560s was one of the first people to argue that witches were simply confused old women suffering from mad imaginations and that witches' brews and unguents had no magical properties. In his books he included invocations, recipes, and symbols used by witches; for this he was called a blasphemer by Zilboorg (1969).

Hansen (1983) and others have examined the ingredients of these potions. Many of the substances are psychoactive at low doses and poisonous at higher doses, such as henbane, hemlock, mandrake, moonshade, tobacco, and opium. Some may have mild hallucinatory effects, like opium and thorn apple. Others may have soporific effects that lead to an increase in dreamlike reveries. Clark, a pharmacologist (cited in Hansen, 1983), argued that some ingredients, like aconite, make heart rate irregular and may produce a sensation of falling through space as one falls asleep, perhaps fostering the imagined sensation of flying. Interestingly, some researchers have tried the flying ointments, and one reported an erotic dreamlike reverie. Another researcher died in testing one of the witch potions (Hansen, 1983).

Another biochemical hypothesis ascribes the strange hallucinations and symptoms of those involved in the accusations of witches as due to the effects of the ergot fungus growing in the rye flour of this time. Caporeal (1976) argued that in Salem village, the scene of the 17th century Massachusetts witch craze, conditions were right for ergot to have grown in rye grain. Ergot (the fungus from which LSD is synthesized) produces a number of symptoms including vomiting, diarrhea, convulsions, and sensory disturbances. The young accusers claimed they felt nauseous and as if their intestines were being torn out of them. They convulsed when they saw the accused and apparently hallucinated apparitions of the accused witches. At the trial, every time the accused witch would move, the girls would convulsively throw their bodies as if in sympathetic pain.

Spanos and Gottlieb (1976), however, argued persuasively against this interpretation. They argued that if the girls had been poisoned with ergot then their families should have also shown symptoms, too; but the record makes no mention of this. They also argued that the girls' convulsions were not actual convulsions, but rather were more like symptoms of conversion disorder. A person suffering from conversion disorder shows physical symptoms such as numbness when there is no physical cause. The first symptoms the girls showed were bizarre behaviors such as hiding in holes. However, as the girls learned more and more about what the symptoms of witchcraft were, their symptoms became more and more consistent with those communicated to them from social expectations.

Theory 3: Witches Had Mental Disorders

Now let us turn to the theory that witches actually suffered from mental disorders. Since the rise of psychology and psychiatry in the latter part of the 19th century, many have speculated that witches actually suffered from mental disorders (e.g., Zilboorg, 1969). According to this view, the premodern people of the late Middle Ages did not understand or recognize the signs of severe mental disturbance in witches, but instead mistook these for indications of supernatural forces at work. At the same time, they argue that there was a great upsurge in mental illness in the late Middle Ages (Alexander & Selesnick, 1966). These were difficult times during which to live. The plague had killed more than one-third of the population. The feudal system was breaking down to be replaced by a still forming new economic system. The Catholic Church was being challenged by Protestants and a number of so-called heretical sects and splinter groups. Modern science was having its beginnings. All of these changes led to social unrest and confusion that precipitated widespread mental illness.

A variety of mental disorders have been summoned up to explain the strange behaviors and symptoms of witches, as summarized by Spanos (1978). For example, the delusions or hallucinations about flying through the air were the result of severe psychotic disorders like schizophrenia. The fact that some of the accused witches did not experience pain when a needle was inserted into a devil's mark suggested that they had conversion disorder, often characterized by local insensitivities to pain. People with conversion disorder are usually susceptible to hypnosis as well. This might account for the influence of the male sorcerer at Sabbats or even the influence of the leading questions of interrogators on the confessions of hysterics (usually women). Also, the painful intercourse at Sabbats reported by some of the accused is also a symptom of conversion disorder. The reported sexual orgies occurring at Sabbats could be due to the accused having sexual disorders. The idea that a witch could change forms or that the devil could possess individuals could be a sign of severe dissociative disorder, like multiple personality.

The theory that witches really suffered from mental disorders can be subjected to several criticisms, however. First of all, accurate diagnosis of a disorder requires information from a variety of sources, such as behavioral observation, the person's self-report, even physiological tests. None of these is available from the witchcraft cases. The reports of the accused, who were often illiterate, come to us through the literate inquisitors. The behavioral observations of the accused witches come to us second- or thirdhand. Moreover, as Spanos (1978) noted, psychiatric diagnosis is often not reliable even under better conditions than these. Third, as Spanos (1978) and others noted, many of the "witches'" accounts of bizarre behaviors were obtained under conditions of deprivation and severe torture.

Finally, suppose we assume that the explanation for the witches' bizarre behaviors was mental illness that went unrecognized at the time. Based on the incidence of psychoses, hysteria, and sexual disorders among women today, we would not expect so many more women than men to have been accused of witchcraft. Although hysteria (conversion disorder) is more common in women, psychoses in general are not.

Foucault (1987) argued that the idea that people with mental disorders were possessed is a fairly recent one. Prior to the 19th century, when possession became associated with the idea of mental illness, madness had many forms. To be sure, from Greek medicine came an association between madness and pathology. But madness was sometimes also viewed as folly and as a part of the human condition, and such people often went unrestricted in society. Only later did the mad come to be separated from the rest of society, interned in institutions that also held the infirm, the poor, the idle, and those who could not fit into or cope with society. These early institutions were more forced labor facilities for isolating outcasts than treatment facilities.

Witchcraft came to be associated with madness only later and only by some in society. In the 16th century, Johan Weyer, as was noted, argued that witchcraft was more a product of a mad imagination than an evil collusion with the devil (Zilboorg, 1969). Also, church authorities, in response to challenges from Protestant and Jansenist mysticism, called upon doctors to show that heretics' ecstasies and supposed possession by the holy spirit were due to violent movements of the humors, an old medical explanation for illness (Foucault, 1987).

Theory 4: Sociocultural Factors Explain the Witch Craze

A number of researchers in this area have argued that social and political factors led to the persecutions of witches in continental Europe, in England, and in colonial America (e.g., Karlsen, 1987; Mair, 1976; Spanos, 1978; and Trevor-Roper, 1969). This sociocultural explanation views the influence and power that groups exercise upon individuals as broad. It assumes that individuals can be regulated through economic means and through belief systems such as organized religion. Spanos (1978), summarizing many of these ideas, argued that the institutionalized persecution of witches arose in part from political and economic changes as feudalism declined. Religious groups were spawned in response to the political and economic inequalities of feudalism in which lords or large landowners controlled the lives and economic welfare of the serfs and vassals below them.

During the Middle Ages, as the Christian religion moved into pagan countries, it relegated the spirits of the pagan religions, such as gnomes, fairies, and leprechauns, to the status of lesser demons. Individuals who were witches were considered to be simply deviant nuisances. The idea of demonic possession was not strongly associated with witchcraft; the church simply wanted to deemphasize such superstitious beliefs. As feudalism declined, however, religious interpretations associated with it as a social system came to be challenged. Increasingly, groups who deviated from Christian practices and belief and who were perceived to be challenging the Christian social system came to be ostracized, even attacked by those in authority (Russell, 1972; Trevor-Roper, 1969).

As Russell and others have pointed out, the term *witch craze* is somewhat of a misnomer. Undoubtedly, many church representatives and citizens were afraid that the evil conspiracy of witchcraft was about to overtake Christendom, and so we may say that they acted irrationally. The prosecution of witches, however, was a deliberate policy and program endorsed by the pope himself and various monarchs. The Inquisition was an institution supported by people in power with the express purpose of identifying witches and eliminating them. The killing of witches was not considered murder but rather a legally justified action to stop the use of the witches' evil power.

Misogynist Trends in Western Culture

An important question is raised by the fact that in witch persecutions in Europe and America from the 14th to the 17th century, the great preponderance of those tried and executed—at least 85%—were women. One important source of misogynist influence in the development of the concept of witchcraft comes from Judeo-Christian religion, beginning with the story of Eve as seductress, temptress of Adam, the first man. While the Bible contains some stories that portray women in positive ways, many other stories, such as that of Jezebel and of Samson and Delilah, portray women in the role of wicked seductresses and betrayers who lead men to their downfall.

Emphasizing these themes are numerous misogynist statements in the *Malleus Mallificarum* (Williams, 1978); for example: "What else is a woman but a foe to friendship, an unescapable punishment, a necessary evil, a natural temptation, a desirable calamity, a domestic danger, a delectable detriment, an evil of nature, painted with fair colors." Before publishing the *Malleus Mallificarum*, the two Dominican priests Springer and Kramer had tried 50 witches, 48 of whom were women. Frequently, men tried as witches were accused because of their association with female witches. The *Malleus* also singled out midwives as connected to witchcraft. This may have been part of the opposition to female lay healers by the growing male medical profession (Ehrenreich & English, 1973).

Others have emphasized the apparent sexual repression in this pervasive hatred and persecution of women. In fact, in the demonology of the West, other out-groups besides witches, such as Jews, were accused of engaging in sexual orgies, as well as other outrageous behaviors such as human sacrifice and eating children.

The study of in-groups and out-groups in social psychology has shown that groups of similar people often maintain stereotypes about the attributes of their own group that tend to distinguish them from outsiders. Race and gender have often been used as the basis for the perception of group identity, and people can readily make judgments using information from these two dimensions (McCann, Ostrom, Tyner, & Mitchell, 1985). The labeling of Jews and women as heretics can be seen as an example of the male Christian hierarchy's maintaining their in-group identity by differentiating themselves from other groups who were viewed as increasingly different and more deviant. Dressler (1985) documented that levels of belief in witchcraft increase with increases in cultural change. Staub (1990) argued that the increasing polarization of in-groups and out-groups can lead to treating out-group members, such as witches, as morally inferior or even as not part of the moral order.

The Economics of Witch Persecution

Economic persecution of women or those supporting them also occurred during this period. Frequently, convicted witches lost their property. Let's briefly examine several examples. First is the story of Lady Alice Kyteler, a noblewoman of the Anglo-Norman aristocracy in Ireland, who had inherited much property from her deceased husband. At this time, however, the marriage cere-mony made women legally dead. Knights, noblemen, and even her own chil-dren went after her inheritance. Her servant woman was beaten until she proclaimed that Lady Kyteler practiced ritual magic. Her conviction of witch-heresy would allow redistribution of her holdings (Williams, 1978). Similarly, a religious sect called the Waldensians had taken a stand in favor of women in the priesthood. The French King Louis XIV and others accused the entire order of witchcraft, and their holdings were confiscated.

Incentives were also given for identifying witches. Itinerant witch finders were given a reward for finding a witch. The Inquisitors received compensation from the property of convicted witches that was confiscated from them. Also, some religious groups were attacked because of their power and wealth, not just because of their heretical religious views. For example, members of the Knights Templar, a wealthy religious order, were falsely accused of Satanism and tor-tured until many made false confessions. Their wealth was confiscated in an action instigated by King Phillip IV of France (Spanos, 1978).

Other evidence suggests that economic and political motives may have led to accusations of less wealthy individuals, and often the accused were women. In England, the accused were often older, poor women without good means of supporting themselves (Laslett, 1971); these women may have been viewed as a burden to those around them. In addition, more women had survived the plagues and were competing for the same resources. In the Salem village out-break, accusations may have been related to competition and divisiveness of fac-tions within the village as well as social instability created by changing views of women's property rights in colonial Massachusetts (Karlsen, 1987).

What Is the Best Explanation?

It appears that women accused of witchcraft lacked power because of low social status, the difficulty of acquiring wealth, and a political and religious system that portrayed them as innately evil and threatening—a patriarchal system that was willing to enforce its prejudices through the institutions of the Inquisition. At the psychological level, women may often have been forced through torture to confess to deeds they did not commit. In some cases, individuals who were sug-gestible or hypnotically susceptible may have come to believe that they actually were witches.

The psychology of accusers is much more varied and complex. Although some, because of conversion disorder or suggestion, may have believed that they were tormented by witches, others may have played their roles for wealth and position. Other accusers, such as some in Salem, may have made these false accusations as a game. Most people probably believed that witches were a real threat, although this threat was often more in the form of heresy to established beliefs than the actual practice of evil magical rituals. At the same time, the labeling of Jews and witches as heretics, the confiscation of property from women and religious fringe groups, and the elimination of these people from positions of any influence—all within the changing social structure of the late Middle Ages—suggest that the witch craze phenomenon functioned to maintain social control of individuals in out-groups (Currie, 1968).

The three other hypotheses we explored may be able to explain in some cases the reported experiences of witches, such as flying through the air, as due to a drug-induced or psychotic state. Healers and users of herbal cures may have been in this group, but it does not appear that ancient pagan practices were followed on a scale large enough to account for the vast numbers of witches brought to trial. While these other explanations may account for some accusations of witchcraft, they do not seem to be able to account for women's being singled out to be labeled and persecuted as witches. Rather, a sociocultural explanation that encompasses socioeconomic, political, and religious factors better accounts for more of the facts.

If a culturally based explanation of witchcraft is best, then how are witches viewed in other cultures? In many other cultures witches are male; examples are some African witches and Indian witches of the highlands of Chiapas, Mexico. In some places, witches are viewed as sometimes using their magic for evil purposes, but not as necessarily being evil, in contrast to the thinking behind the European and American witch craze of the 14th to 17th centuries.

Many take a broader view of witchcraft. In modern culture in the United States and Europe, Luhrmann (1989) documented a group of witches (magicians) in the United Kingdom who are professional people—lawyers, computer programmers, even a psychologist—who practice magical rituals. Many present-day witches belong to Wicca, an organization of witches who follow neo-pagan practices in the tradition of the worship of Diana, Isis, and Demeter. These neo-pagans value freedom and harmlessness, and they practice magic for healing and self-improvement.

In contrast, during the 1980s there was much concern among various groups and individuals concerning outbreaks of Satanism and Satanic practices in the United States and Great Britain. Stories of the activities of these Satanists show striking resemblance to the practices of accused witches of the 14th to 17th centuries: human sacrifice, worship of the devil, blood rituals and cannibalism, and abduction and sacrifice of children. These contain some of the same elements of the old Western demonological tradition.

These days, however, many people would apply a psychiatric model to explain this phenomenon in one of two ways. Those who espouse the medical model of psychological problems would explain the beliefs of some in Satanic ritual phenomena as due to disturbance in the normal biochemical processes in their brains (Turner & Edgley, 1983). Others would explain belief in such things as delusional and due to psychological disturbance. Some of these clinicians, perhaps the modern-day exorcists, help clients to recover repressed and dissociated memories of Satanic ritual abuse that are supposed to have occurred as a result of belief and practice of Satanism.

Although some researchers in the area, like Hill and Goodwin (1989), have suggested that the striking similarities between recent accounts of participation in Satanic rituals and pre-Inquisition historical accounts may indicate the reality of Satanic ritual events, there are other explanations for such similarities. Victor (1993) did a lengthy study of the spread of the rumor of Satanic cult activity in a small New York town and found that the spread of very similar accounts of alleged ritual activity was due to informal communication among groups of individuals who passed along similar elements of the ancient blood legend in the form of modern urban legend. None of these people who passed along these stories bothered to check them out or to substantiate them with other evidence, but rather passed them along uncritically.

Summary

People have their own implicit theories about personality or why people characteristically think, feel, and act the way they do. They also have their own beliefs about what is abnormal behavior. They use these beliefs and "theories" to explain other people's behavior, but these beliefs often do not have the consistency of scientific theories, and their assumptions are not examined the way scientific theories are.

Witches were accused of many things. They were blamed for all kinds of misfortunes. They were thought to have supernatural powers through their compact with the devil so that they could fly through the air and exert magical control over natural phenomena. They were also thought to engage in many evil practices, such as ritual killing, and other acts that were opposed to Christian practices, including licentious dancing and sexual activity. The religious and legal establishment increasingly viewed witches as a heretical threat to the Christian social order. Witches were systematically sought out and prosecuted, especially by the Catholic Inquisition but also by Protestant groups.

Four theories were discussed that might account for the witches' behavior. The first,

that witches actually existed, is mostly supported by confessions of the accused, many of which were extracted through torture. The theory that psychoactive chemicals and drugs accounted for the witches' strange experiences is not supported by much evidence, partly because there is a severe lack of evidence; and the possibility of ergot poisoning was shown to be inconsistent with the facts. The third theory, that witches actually had mental disorders, cannot easily be verified because most of the records come to us through prosecutors and do not directly inform us about the lives of the accused. Also, the great number of people, and the disproportionate number of women tried for witchcraft, make the possibility of mental disorders a somewhat less plausible explanation. The fourth theory, that accused witches were the victims of sociocultural forces, receives considerably more support. In particular, the special persecution of women and some wealthy groups with divergent beliefs and the emphasis on the accused's heresy suggest social factors were involved. Women and other groups were stereotyped and labeled as posing a particular kind of threat to the eroding social order, making the gap between in-group and out-group members wider. Recent Satanic cult outbreaks suggest that these kinds of social forces, and persistent ancient ideas about evil forces recast as modern urban legends, continue to exert their effects.

Review Questions

Compare commonsense, folk, and implicit "theories" to scientific theories.

How do context and cultural assumptions affect our judgments about people?

What special problems are involved in trying to answer questions about witchcraft and other historical questions?

How does a person generate a hypothesis to explain some behavior?

> What are some of the important facts that need to be explained?

How well does the evidence support the theories that there really were witches? That chemical substances accounted for their strange behaviors? That witches actually suffered from mental disorders? That witches were the victims of sociocultural forces?

What is the best explanation and why?

How are witches viewed in other cultures and in our own time?

References

Alexander, F. G., & Selesnick, S. T. (1966). *The history of psychiatry*. New York: HarperCollins.

American Psychiatric Association (1994). *Diagnostic and statistical manual* (4th ed.). Washington, DC: Author.

Burket, R. C., Myers, W. C., Lyles, B., & Carrera, F. (1994). Emotional and behavioral disturbances in adolescents involved in witchcraft and satanism. *Journal of Adolescence, 17*, 41–52.

Caporeal, L. R. (1976). Ergotism: The Satan loosed in Salem? *Science, 192*, 21–26.

Connor, J. W. (1975). The social and psychological reality of European witchcraft beliefs. *Psychiatry, 38*, 366–380.

Currie, E. P. (1968). Crimes without criminals: Witchcraft and its control in Renaissance Europe. *Law and Society Review, 3*, 7–32.

Dressler, W. W. (1985). Stress and sorcery in three social groups. *International Journal of Social Psychiatry, 31*, 275–281.

Ehrenreich, B., & English, D. (1973). *Witches, midwives, and nurses: A history of women healers*. Oyster Bay, NY: Glass Mountain Pamphlets.

Farina, A., & Fischer, J. D. (1982). Beliefs about mental disorders: Findings and implications. In G. Weary & H. Mirels (Eds.), *Integrations of clinical and social psychology*. New York: Oxford University Press.

Feldman, R. S. (1995). *Social psychology*. Englewood Cliffs, NJ: Prentice-Hall.

Festinger, L. (1954). A theory of social comparison processes. *Social Relations, 7*, 117–140.

Forssen, A. (1980). Illness and helping in a traditional East African tribe. *Psychiatrica Fennica*, 57–66.

Foucault, M. (1987). *Mental illness and psychology*. Berkeley: University of California Press.

Gambrill, E. (1990). *Critical thinking in clinical practice*. San Francisco: Jossey-Bass.

Ginzburg, C. (1992). *Ecstasies: Deciphering the witches' sabbath*. Harmondsworth, England: Penguin Books.

Hansen, H. A. (1983). *The witch's garden* (Muriel Crofts, Trans.). York Beach, ME: Samuel Weiser.

Henningsen, G. (1980). *The witches' advocate*. Reno: University of Nevada Press.

Hill, S., & Goodwin, J. (1989). Satanism: Similarities between patient accounts and pre-Inquisition historical sources. *Dissociation, 2*, 39–44.

Karlsen, C. F. (1987). *The devil in the shape of a woman: Witchcraft in colonial New England*. New York: W. W. Norton.

Kemp, S. (1989). Ravished of a fiend: Demonology and medieval madness. In C. Ward (Ed.), *Altered states of consciousness and mental health*. Newbury Park, CA: Sage.

Kramer, H., & Spenger, J. (1971). *The Malleus Maleficarum* (M. Summers, Ed. and Trans.). New York: Dover.

Laslett, P. (1971). *The world we have lost.* New York: Scribner's.

Luhrman, T. M. (1989). *Persuasions of the witch's craft.* Cambridge, MA: Harvard University Press.

MacDonald, M. (1981). *Mystical Bedlam: Madness, anxiety, and healing in seventeenth century England.* Cambridge, England: Cambridge University Press.

Mair, L. (1976). *Witchcraft.* New York: McGraw-Hill.

McCann, C. D., Ostrom, T. M., Tyner, L. K., & Mitchell, M. L. (1985). Person perception in heterogeneous groups. *Journal of Personality and Social Psychology, 49,* 1449–1459.

Monter, E. W. (1969). *European witchcraft.* New York: John Wiley.

Murray, M. (1921). *The witch-cult in Western Europe.* London: Oxford University Press.

Nash, M. (1967). Witchcraft as social process in a tzeltal community. In J. Middleton (Ed.), *Magic, witchcraft, and curing* (pp. 127–133). Garden City, NY: The Natural History Press.

Pearl, J. L. (1982). Humanism and satanism: Jean Bodin's contribution to the witchcraft craze. *Canadian Review of Sociology and Anthropology, 19,* 541–546.

Rogers, S. L. (1985). *Primitive surgery: Skills before science.* Springfield, IL: Charles C Thomas.

Rosenhan, D. L., & Seligman, M. E. (1989). *Abnormal psychology* (2nd ed.). New York: W. W. Norton.

Russell, J. B. (1972). *Witchcraft in the Middle Ages.* Ithaca, NY: Cornell University Press.

Schneider, D. J. (1973). Implicit personality theory: A review. *Psychological Bulletin, 79,* 294–309.

Silverman, K. (1983). Letters of thanks from hell. *Social Science Information, 22,* 947–968. Beverly Hills: Sage.

Spanos, N. P. (1978). Witchcraft in histories of psychiatry: A critical analysis and alternative conceptualization. *Psychological Bulletin, 85,* 417–439.

Spanos, N. (1989). Hypnosis, demonic possession, and multiple personality: Strategic enactments and disavowals of responsibility for actions. In C. Ward (Ed.), *Altered states of consciousness and mental health.* Newbury Park, CA: Sage.

Spanos, N. P., & Gottlieb, J. (1976). Ergotism and the Salem witch trials. *Science, 194,* 1390–1394.

Spanos, N. P., & Gottlieb, J. (1979). Demonic possession, mesmerism, and hysteria: A social psychological perspective on their historical interrelations. *Journal of Abnormal Psychology, 88,* 263–282.

Staub, E. (1990). Moral exclusion, personal goal theory, and extreme destructiveness. *Journal of Social Issues, 46,* 47–64.

Summers, M. (1956). *The history of witchcraft and demonology.* New Hyde Park, NY: University Books.

Trevor-Roper, H. R. (1969). *The European witch-craze of the sixteenth and seventeenth centuries and other essays.* New York: HarperCollins.

Turner, R. E. & Edgley, C. (1983). From witchcraft to drugcraft: Biochemistry as mythology. *The Social Science Journal, 20,* 1–12.

Victor, J. S. (1993). *Satanic panic: The creation of a contemporary legend.* Chicago: Open Court.

Weinstein, A., & Gatell, F. O. (1981). *Freedom and crisis: An American history* (3rd ed.). New York: Random House.

Williams, S. R. (1978). *Riding the nightmare: Women and witches from the Old World to colonial Salem.* Williams, NY: HarperCollins.

Woodward, W. E. (1969). *Records of Salem witchcraft.* Roxbury, MA: Da Capo Press.

Zilboorg, G. (1969). *The medical man and the witch during the Renaissance.* New York: Cooper Square Publishers.

CHAPTER TWELVE

Critical Thinking and Diagnosing Mental Disorders

Learning Objectives

• To learn about how psychologists use critical thinking and hypothesis testing to diagnose mental disorders, evaluating the severity of psychological problems and whether an individual has a mental disorder.

• To learn about the diagnostic signs of various mental disorders.

What Do You Think?

Imagine that you are a clinical psychologist meeting with a new client for the first time, and you are trying to determine the nature of his problem. At your first meeting, your client, a young man in his early 20s, looks nervous and tense. You ask him how he is doing and he replies, in a quiet and hesitant voice, "OK." He averts his glance from you and seems to be preoccupied with his own thoughts. What do you think is the person's problem?

With only this three-sentence description you were probably already beginning to think of questions, to speculate, to form hypotheses about the nature of the young man's problem. You may appreciate that this task is very difficult. The client presents you with different kinds of information about his past, his emotional state, his own perception of his problem, his attitudes and beliefs. What's more, you learn only fragments of information, and even these pieces of data may be untrue or biased. To elaborate on Dumont's (1993) analogy, this is very much like putting together the pieces of a puzzle with many thousands of pieces. What fits with what? How do you find out what you need to know in order to decide what your client's problem is? A great deal of uncertainty is involved in this process, and there is much room for error in coming to a decision.

The clinician who is making a diagnosis of a psychological disorder engages in critical thinking very much like that of the scientist who is testing a hypothesis. Recall that critical thinking involves evaluating the evidence relevant to a claim so that a sound conclusion can be drawn about the claim. Scientists, too, evaluate research evidence to decide whether some hypothesis (claim) is true. Along the same lines, a clinical psychologist, psychiatrist, or other clinician gathers evidence to evaluate the hypothesis that a person has a psychological disorder (Synder & Thomsen, 1988). Like the critical thinker and researcher who searches for a causal explanation for some phenomenon, the clinician also gathers and evaluates evidence to eliminate possible alternative explanations for a behavior or pattern of behavior.

Many clinicians assume that the diagnosis of a mental disorder is an important first step in identifying the causes or etiology of a client's mental disorder. According to this view, once a diagnosis has been made and the causes of the mental disorder are identified, the therapist is in a position to treat the problem. Note, however, that although a diagnosis may be useful to finding the causes of a disorder, a diagnostic label does not necessarily pinpoint the cause of a behavior (Gambrill, 1990). For example, it should not be concluded that the depression of a person diagnosed as having a major depression caused his or her difficulties in getting along with loved ones.

Beyond the role diagnosis can play in identifying causes of behavior problems, there are other good reasons to study the diagnosis of mental disorders within the context of critical thinking. First of all, because diagnosis is frequently necessary for insurance and legal purposes, it has economic and social implications. Although you and some clinicians may not agree that people can be put into categories, this does not remove the social and economic reality requiring clinicians to do just that. Second, the consequences of applying incorrect diagnostic labels can have many negative effects. Saying that a person has a disorder that he or she does not have may lead to the wrong treatment intervention or, in some cases, to a client's being needlessly stigmatized for a nonexistent problem. A third reason to study diagnosis within the context of critical thinking is that frequently clinicians have been shown to fail to think critically in making diagnoses (Gambrill, 1990). Consequently, it is prudent to remember critical thinking as you are introduced to diagnosis of mental disorders.

The Task of Diagnosis

The task of diagnosing a client is really a classification task in which the clinician puts a client into one diagnostic category or another: "well" or "having a mental disorder," perhaps "schizophrenia" or "anxiety disorder." To aid in this process of classifying clients into diagnostic categories, clinicians frequently use the *Diagnostic and Statistical Manual of Mental Disorders*, 4th edition (DSM-IV) (American Psychiatric Association, 1994). The DSM-IV is a classification system that associates common and important symptoms with particular disorders. For example, extreme, prolonged sadness is a primary symptom of major depression. Other symptoms, such as a disturbance in sleeping patterns, change in weight, and lack of energy, also indicate major depression. The DSM-IV has five axes or dimensions for classifying mental disorders: Axis I for most types of disorders; Axis II for personality disorders and mental retardation; Axis III for the person's general medical condition; Axis IV for the person's level of psychosocial stress; and Axis V for the person's global functioning. By using all these axes, the clinician may develop a good **multi-axial** classification of the client that can help develop an understanding of the person's problem from many perspectives or dimensions. As noted by Dumont (1993), this approach can help clinicians consider various potential causes of the client's problem, making it less likely that a clinician will conduct a narrow, ineffective search for causes.

Since diagnosis is a very complex process, the present discussion will focus on critical thinking and diagnosis using Axis I. This will help you become more familiar with the major categories of disorders. A complete diagnosis requires making decisions that would identify and categorize an individual on each of the five axes. Clinicians should do a **differential diagnosis**—a diagnosis that shows that the person's signs, symptoms, and behaviors meet the criteria for a particular diagnostic label, eliminating other possible labels for the same set of signs, symptoms, and behaviors.

TABLE 12.1

Preliminary questions to determine the existence of a severe psychological problem

1. Is the person's behavior abnormal—for example, of excessive or high magnitude, or of long duration? Can the behavior be explained by the context in which it appears?
2. Is the behavior maladaptive? Does it bother other people or get in the way of the person's effectiveness in his or her environment?
3. Does the behavior cause personal distress? Does it bother the person with the problem, making his or her life unpleasant or troubled?

Clinical Assessment

To classify a client on Axis I and the other axes, a clinician gathers a variety of kinds of evidence to assess the client using various evaluation devices and methods. Clinicians use clients' self-reports of symptoms; behavioral observations; paper-and-pencil psychological inventories; and psychological interviews, along with other methods. Taken together, the methods and techniques used in evaluating clients' problems are called **clinical assessment procedures.** The clinician uses the evidence from assessment to decide whether the client has a psychological disorder and then to decide which disorder the client has, using the evidence to eliminate possibilities.

What particular assessment procedure or procedures a clinician uses depends on a number of factors, including his or her training and theoretical perspective. For example, a behavior therapist is much more likely to use observation of the problem behaviors of a client than a psychoanalyst. A behavior therapist would assume that the best way to treat a psychological problem is to change the maladaptive behaviors involved. On the other hand, a psychoanalyst would much more likely use a projective technique such as the Rorschach inkblot test, which assumes that the client's interpretation of ambiguous figures reveals unconscious conflicts to resolve in psychoanalysis. Other clinicians take an eclectic perspective and may use a variety of assessment methods depending on the problem. Recall, though, that psychotherapy has been called the talking cure: Most clinicians use talk and interview techniques in some phase of their assessment and treatment.

Whatever the assessment procedure, evaluating psychological problems and making accurate diagnoses require asking appropriate questions to obtain relevant evidence. If clinicians, who get much of their information about psychological problems from clients or patients, do not ask appropriate questions in a clinical interview, then they will not find out about symptoms and signs that would help identify disorders. Appropriate questions are an efficient guide in the process of acquiring and evaluating signs and symptoms.

Table 12.1 contains some sample basic questions that could be used to determine the severity of a client's problem and to identify the possible presence of a psychological disorder. If the answer to all three questions is yes, then the person likely has a psychological problem that may require diagnosis.

TABLE 12.2

Some general questions to help in a preliminary diagnosis of some common psychological disorders (from Axis I of DSM-IV)

1. **Does the person show unusual and/or dramatic changes in emotion?**
   a. Is it primarily related to anxiety? If so, then an anxiety disorder. If anxiety not specific, then generalized anxiety disorder. If repetitive thoughts or behaviors, then obsessive-compulsive disorder.
   b. Is it primarily related to a fear? If fear is specific, then a phobia.
   c. Is there depression?
      If only depression, then may indicate major depression.
      If depression, mania, and mood swings, then bipolar disorder.
2. **Does the person show severe cognitive, perceptual, or thought disturbance, such as hallucinations and delusions, suggesting lack of contact with conventional reality?**
   If this is in combination with little or flat affect and social withdrawal, then may indicate schizophrenia. If in combination with depression or mania, then may indicate a mood disorder with psychosis.
3. **Does the person dissociate part of his or her experience or personality from another part?**
   If the person appears to become one other person for a relatively longer period of time, then psychogenic fugue state. If the person appears to take on multiple personalities, then dissociative identity disorder.
4. **Does the person have physical symptoms without a physical basis?**
   If so, then may be a somaticization disorder, such as malingering or conversion disorder.
5. **Is the problem drug or substance-induced?**
   If so, then could lead to hallucinations and other symptoms induced by the substance or to maladaptive behaviors due to addiction to the substance.
6. **Does the person engage in maladaptive sexual practices or have a sexual disorder?**
   Depending on the specific signs, could be a sexual arousal disorder, a sexual desire disorder, or sexual dysfunction.
7. **Is the problem due to difficulties in adjustment?**
   If adjustment problem lasts longer than 6 months, then adjustment disorder.

Other questions useful in diagnosing specific disorders on Axis I are found in Table 12.2. These questions provide a heuristic, or rule of thumb, for searching through the DSM-IV's classifications of disorders and associated symptoms. When a certain number of symptoms that go with a particular disorder are present, then the classification of the client as having that mental disorder is indicated.

Note that a clinician would seek information with other useful questions to make a differential diagnosis, including questions such as whether the disorder might have an organic or physical basis, perhaps due to nervous system damage or deterioration. Answering this question could help eliminate or identify physical problems that can cause symptoms like those of a mental disorder, such as the deterioration in mental functioning due to Huntington's disease. Another useful question is whether the person's problem comes from the development of personality characteristics that are maladaptive or dysfunctional. Answering this question could eliminate or identify a personality disorder, such as antisocial personality disorder. While many other useful questions could be asked to make a complete multiaxial diagnosis, we will focus on some of the main disorders associated with Axis I.

The list of questions in Tables 12.1 and 12.2 should of course not be taken as a complete list that would lead to an accurate diagnosis in any individual with a psychological problem, but it does help organize important distinctions in many psychological disorders. Also, you should note that a clinician may not directly ask the client all of the questions in Tables 12.1 or 12.2 or in this particular order but rather seeks information in assessment to answer the questions. As noted before, the questions in Tables 12.1 and 12.2 refer to Axis I; often, however, a clinician in actual diagnosis might want to eliminate right away the possibility of a general medical condition or physical origin to the problem, which is Axis III.

Take a moment to read over the questions in Table 12.1 and 12.2. Think about how these questions relate to the different psychological disorders and problems you know about from studying abnormal psychology and from other sources.

≈ PRACTICE YOUR THINKING 12.1

Identifying and Diagnosing Cases

Let's practice using the questions in Tables 12.1 and 12.2 on some hypothetical cases. The first one is based in part on an actual case reviewed in Spitzer, Gibbon, Skodol, Williams, and First (1989). Imagine that this person comes into your clinic and you must ascertain his or her problem. What would you do? Use the questions from Tables 12.1 and 12.2 as starting points to analyze Bill's problem in Case 1. First, decide whether he has a psychological problem based on your answers to the questions in Table 12.1. Then, if he has a problem serious enough to warrant a diagnosis, what is his preliminary and partial diagnosis based on Table 12.2? After you have diagnosed each case, you can check your solution against the one in Appendix C.

Case 1: "It's Not Good Enough Yet"
Bill came to the clinic complaining that stress at work was getting him down. He graduated from college two years ago with an English/business major and is now employed at an advertising agency as a copywriter. From interviewing Bill, it is discovered that his boss has threatened to fire him if he does not begin to get his work done on time. Bill does many preparations for writing but does not begin to write his advertisements until shortly before they are due. For this reason, they frequently are turned in late and sometimes not at all. In preparing to write, Bill keeps rearranging the things on his desk, neatening up his papers and reorganizing his folders of assignments. Often he will agonize over the choice of a word for several minutes. He corrects the punctuation and then changes it back again. He reads

and rereads what he has written until he puts aside what he is working on when he becomes too uncomfortable and nervous. Then he moves on to rearranging the work on his desk or to another unfinished project as the thoughts about the quality of his work on this other project make him more and more agitated. He saves all drafts of his previous writing—even from completed projects, saying that they could be improved, too. When he does write, he is afraid to show his work to anyone, saying that "it's not good enough yet." The work he does complete is generally of high quality.

His perfectionistic tendencies dogged him in college, as well. He had to graduate a semester late because of incomplete work in several courses. In general, Bill works very slowly. At home, his wife says that he puts off paying the bills until they are past due and will not let anyone else help him with these because they could not do as good a job. Although he does not pay the bills or even sometimes open the mail, he saves all the papers stacked neatly in a corner of his home. Sometimes, he rearranges the papers to organize them, but he does not pay the bills or take care of this business.

Sometimes, Bill feels very discouraged by his job and thinks of getting a new one. He clips out many want ads from the newspaper but cannot decide which job he could do better and so he seldom writes or calls about another job.

Now try Case 2 using the questions from Tables 12.1 and 12.2 to analyze Jim's problem. First, decide whether Jim has a psychological problem based on your answers to the questions in Table 12.1. Then, if he has a problem serious enough to warrant a diagnosis, make a preliminary and partial diagnosis based on Table 12.2.

Case 2: "The Walls Have Earrings"

Jim Nelson, a 20-year-old college student majoring in English, reported difficulty concentrating. He was referred to the college counseling center by Ed, a friend of his, who noticed some disturbing changes in Jim's behavior. Jim refused to go, however, until one of his professors, after an "unusual" conversation with Jim, also suggested that he visit the counseling service.

In his first clinical interview, Jim mentioned no headaches or unusual physical symptoms, but he did mention that sometimes he had swarms of ideas flying through his mind at once. Jim, whose favorite pastime was creative writing, said that this flight of ideas reminded him of the inspired state he sometimes went into before beginning to write a poem or short story. Lately, he has begun to spend more and more time by himself, writing. He had stopped attending his classes and frequently failed to turn in his assigned work. He said he was doing this to concentrate on his writing. In fact, he did spend much time sitting by himself, apparently absorbed in the creative process.

In addition, the language he used in his poetry had begun to change. Jim said that he was seeking new ways to express himself. Jim's unusual use of language had begun to creep into his conversations with others, like Ed, as well. For example, he had once said, "The walls have earrings." When the psychologist asked what Jim meant, he said, "I have this ringing in my ears, and it is as if the sound is bouncing off the walls back to my ears." Later, he asserted that his ex-girlfriend was listening to him from behind the walls and sometimes hitting the walls, making them ring. She did this to keep him from concentrating on his work. He said that she had been plotting to get him to fail ever since she broke up with him. He also said that he knew this was true because one time he heard her thoughts come to him through the walls of his dormitory room.

As time went on, Jim became very unresponsive. It was as if there was an emotionless mask over his face. For example, at one session he told the psychologist that he was going to have to move to another room because the thoughts coming through the wall were becoming too disturbing. As he described this disturbance, however, he showed no negative emotion.

Now try Case 3 using the questions from Tables 12.1 and 12.2 to analyze Karen's problem. First, decide whether Karen has a psychological problem based on your answers to the questions in Table 12.1. Then, if she has a problem serious enough to warrant a diagnosis, make a preliminary and partial diagnosis based on Table 12.2.

Case 3: "I'm Not Ready"

Jason and Karen liked each other, but in only a month they would be going to their respective colleges, 400 miles apart. They had been going out together only for about two months, since right after their graduation from high school. By this time, they had both already enrolled in their respective colleges. As summer moved along, they had begun to see each other more and more and were becoming increasingly intimate. Jason wanted to have sex with Karen, and it seemed that they were headed in that direction. However, they had not had a good talk about it, and both were reluctant to bring up the subject of birth control. Karen realized this was a problem and resolved to talk to Jason about it, which she did.

Lately, Karen had begun to worry about all the talk about the danger of AIDS when having sex without a condom. But most of all, she was worried about getting pregnant. She was not on the pill, and having sex with Jason seemed to be a big step in many ways. But Jason was being pretty insistent. Karen also worried about doing the right thing. Karen came from a traditional religious background that discouraged premarital sex, and she respected these views while not always agreeing with them.

Karen felt torn. What should she do? She tried to talk to her closest friends about it. One said, "Go ahead, everybody does it." Another said that she should wait until it seemed right to her. But the more she thought about it, the more confused she felt. Her stomach felt as if it were tied in knots. She worried that if she didn't have sex with Jason he would get impatient and leave her or find someone else at college. At the same time, she was afraid she would get pregnant. These nagging fears bothered her all the time. Her muscles seemed to be constantly tense, and she began to have severe headaches.

She finally decided to see her physician, a woman general practitioner, whom she had known for several years. Her physician found no organic basis for her headaches apart from muscle tension. After listening to Karen describe the conflicts she was experiencing, her physician recommended that she talk to a psychotherapist about her problems. She also told Karen that if after thinking through the matter she wanted a prescription for birth control pills she would write it for her.

Now try Case 4 using the questions from Tables 12.1 and 12.2 to analyze Marilyn's problem. First, decide whether Marilyn has a psychological problem based on your answers to the questions in Table 12.1. Then, if she has a problem serious enough to warrant a diagnosis, make a preliminary and partial diagnosis based on Table 12.2.

Case 4: "What's the Use?"

Marilyn was upset by academic pressures at college. She found the work more demanding than in high school. Although she had been an above average student in high school, she found that she had to work harder in college to get almost the same grades; and twice she had gotten low grades, a C- and a D+. Lately, she had become increasingly doubtful about her ability to succeed. She often said to herself: "I can't do it," or "It's too hard," or "What's the use? Even when I work harder, I only do as well as I did in high school, never better." Other times, she would say to herself, "It's hopeless"—even, "I'm no good."

During the next few months, Marilyn began to spend less time studying and more time lying around and sleeping. She seemed not to care much about her personal appearance, and she put on some weight. Everything she did, she seemed to do in slow motion, and everything she did looked as if it took extreme effort. Her facial expression often looked sad, and sometimes she would cry for an hour at a time. Other times, she appeared anxious and even angry.

Then after a period of reduced activity and energy, she seemed to revive herself. During these times, she would say things like the following to herself, "I'm a very intelligent and creative individual. I can do this stuff. They don't know how good I am. Lots of times people with brilliant ideas are not recognized." During these phases, she would stay up all night and work on her homework, She would also talk nonstop until her roommates either chased her out of the room or themselves went somewhere else to sleep.

Then, after a day or so of being in this highly active, energized condition, she would return to her more inactive, negative state. During these times, she often blamed her roommates for preventing her from studying and succeeding. Her roommates were getting to the point that they wanted to switch rooms. They confronted Marilyn about this and they all discussed the matter with their dormitory hall adviser. She suggested that Marilyn visit the counseling service since she was having difficulty both with her schoolwork and with her personal relationships.

Summary

Diagnosis of mental disorders is difficult because the clinician must evaluate a complex variety of symptoms and behaviors. The clinician sees only fragments of a person and sometimes sees only what the client reveals.

In some ways, trying to understand a client's problem is like hypothesis testing in science. Diagnosis involves putting people into categories consistent with their symptoms. Making a diagnosis does not mean one has found the cause of the person's problem. Diagnosis is necessary for insurance and legal reasons. It is important not to misdiagnose clients because labels can stigmatize people.

Before making a diagnosis, the clinician must do assessment, or gather information on the person. Methods of assessment include behavioral observations, psychological inventories, and psychological interviews. Clinicians should do a differential diagnosis—that is, a diagnosis that shows that the person's signs, symptoms, and behaviors fit a particular diagnosis, eliminating other possible diagnoses for the same set of signs, symptoms, and behaviors.

To help determine the severity of a person's problem and the kind of disorder a person has, several preliminary questions may be asked. To assess the severity of the problem, one can ask whether the problem or behavior appears to be abnormal, whether the behavior is maladaptive, and whether the problem causes the person personal distress. To help determine the kind of disorder from DSM-IV's Axis I, one can ask whether the problem involves changes in emotion, severe thought disturbances, dissociation, physical symptoms without physical causes, the use of substances, maladaptive sexual practices, or difficulties in adjustment.

Review Questions

Why is the task of diagnosis so difficult?

How does the clinician engage in hypothesis testing like a scientist?

What is assessment?

How does one do a differential diagnosis?

What is DSM-IV?

What are axes, and what is Axis I?

What questions might you ask to help you determine the severity of a person's problem?

What questions would help you to determine what Axis I disorder a person had?

References

American Psychiatric Association (1994). *Diagnostic and statistical manual of mental disorders (DSM-IV)* (4th ed.) Washington, DC: Author.

Dumont, F. (1993). Inferential heuristics in clinical problem formulation: Selective review of their strengths and weaknesses. *Professional Psychology: Research and Practice, 24,* 196–205.

Gambrill, E. (1990). *Critical thinking in clinical practice.* San Francisco: Jossey-Bass.

Snyder, M., & Thomsen, C. J. (1988). Interactions between therapists and clients: Hypothesis testing and behavioral confirmation. In D. Turk & P. Salovey (Eds.), *Reasoning, inference, and judgment in clinical psychology* (pp. 124–151). New York: Free Press.

Spitzer, R. L., Gibbon, M., Skodol, A. E., Williams, J. B., & First, M. B. (1989). *DSM-IIIR Case book* (revised). Washington, DC: American Psychiatric Press.

Thinking Critically About Repression and Recovered Memories of Abuse

Learning Objectives

• To learn how a complex question, such as whether people can accurately remember repressed memories of sexual abuse, can be broken down into the smaller questions for analysis.

• To critically read the discussion of a complex question by analyzing the parts of the larger question.

• To apply what we have learned from critically reading the literature to solving a practical problem, such as determining the best way to recover previously unrecalled memories of sexual abuse.

What Do You Think?

Can a person who has been sexually abused or otherwise traumatized at first not be able to recall the experience, but then years later be able to recall it accurately? What do you think?

A century ago, Sigmund Freud introduced the term **repression,** the idea that the memories of unpleasant or threatening experiences, such as the experience of childhood sexual abuse, could be pushed into the unconscious part of the mind. In this chapter, we will see that this question is actually a complex one related to other fascinating questions.

For example, here's a related question: Is there a vast international conspiracy of satanists who abduct children, sexually abuse them, and then sacrifice them, as some people claim? Here's another one: Can a person, in reaction to a severe trauma such as sexual abuse, develop separate personalities with one or more of these personalities unaware of the trauma? What do you think? These related questions make it clear that the larger issue—whether a person can years later accurately recall a previously unrecalled traumatic experience—is a very complex question indeed.

To help you appreciate the difficult problems repressed memory presents for clinicians, let's suppose you are a psychotherapist. Someone comes to you with severe mental problems, and you suspect that this person may have been sexually abused as a child, but so far the person has not reported this to you. Can a therapist come to a sound conclusion about whether or not the person has been sexually abused? What do you think? How would you decide whether the person had been abused but repressed the memory of this traumatic incident?

These days, clinicians and law enforcement officers confront this question frequently. To find out whether abuse has occurred, one must not only think critically about the relevant information and evidence, but also about how information on a person was acquired. If a police officer used leading questions to extract information from a person, for example, the memory report obtained would be less trustworthy than a memory report obtained freely. To answer any of the complicated questions raised here, we need to think critically and to draw sound conclusions based on the evidence.

The Need for Critical Thinking About Repressed Memories

To illustrate one consequence of misuse of one memory recovery method, take the example of Joseph Cardinal Bernadin, the late archbishop of Chicago, who needlessly suffered false accusations of sexual abuse by Steve Cook, a former parishioner. As part of his psychotherapy, Cook had been hypnotized and recalled "memories" of abuse that formed the basis of the charges against

Bernadin—memories Cook later came to doubt were authentic. On the other hand, of course, if we conclude that a person cannot accurately recall a repressed memory of abuse when in fact she can, then a serious crime could go unpunished. This high-stakes question is perhaps the most controversial issue in psychology today. Because the consequences are so serious, critical thinking about the issue is especially important.

What is needed are effective methods that clinicians and people in the legal system can use to recover accurate memories of abuse. But before we can develop effective recovery methods, we must understand repressed memories of abuse, which requires that we be familiar with the relevant research literature on this question. We will see that the complexity of this question demands that we examine several parts of the literature. Development of effective methods requires that we apply knowledge from research and other sources; appropriate application of knowledge requires both critical thinking and knowledge of the area of application. We may find that some methods for recovering repressed memories cause people to recall false memories or to fail at effectively recalling true ones.

How This Chapter Is Different

You may have noticed that the learning objectives for this chapter are somewhat more ambitious than for other chapters. This chapter is more complex because, first, the question we are addressing has more parts to it and, second, we will be seeking to apply what we learn about recovery of repressed memories of abuse to the practical problem of deciding whether a particular person has suffered abuse. Accordingly, in this chapter we will review the relevant research and other information about the question of recovering repressed memories of sexual abuse by separately discussing different aspects of this complex question. You will practice drawing conclusions from each of these discussions. Next, we will discuss how to apply the conclusions we have drawn to develop methods for recovering accurate memories of sexual abuse. Finally, you will have an opportunity to practice applying your knowledge to analyze client-therapist interactions concerning the recovery of memories of sexual abuse.

Issues in the Recovery of Repressed Memories

The question whether people can accurately recall repressed memories of sexual abuse is actually very complex. Often, in psychology and other areas of inquiry, an important question actually encompasses a number of questions. To successfully address the big question, we must unpack, or break down, the complex question into the smaller questions it contains. We can break our question down into the following three questions:

1. What is childhood sexual abuse, and how often does it occur?
2. Does repression of unpleasant experiences actually occur?
3. Can people accurately remember repressed memories?

The literature review that follows does not review all the studies relevant to these questions. Instead, it is a selective review—it includes studies that represent different positions on these questions, but not all the studies that could be reviewed. For more exhaustive reviews of the literature on repressed memory of abuse, see Lindslay and Read (1994) or Loftus (1993). After the selective review concerning each of these three questions, conclusions and implications for that section will be presented. We will apply these findings toward developing the most accurate possible methods for recovery of experiences from memory.

≈ PRACTICE YOUR THINKING 13.1

Drawing Conclusions from the Research: Defining and Estimating Childhood Sexual Abuse

This first section reviews the literature on the occurrence of sexual abuse. Read over the following questions before you critically read the passage, and keep them in mind as you read. Then after you have read the passage, check your conclusions against those set out in the conclusions and implications section at the end of the passage.

1. From the evidence presented here, what can you generalize about the occurrence of sexual abuse?
2. Can you draw the same conclusion for the various kinds of sexual abuse? Why or why not?
3. What do you think are the implications of your conclusions for the larger question of determining whether someone who cannot at first recall having been sexually abused actually has been?

What Is Childhood Sexual Abuse and How Often Does It Occur?

Before we can determine the frequency of childhood sexual abuse, we must first define what it is. Wyatt (1985) offered a general and inclusive definition of childhood sexual abuse that will allow it to be measured. Her definition specifies sexual abuse as any sexual advance by an individual 5 or more years older than the child or victim. A child is legally defined as a person under 18 years of age. Her definition also includes any unwanted sexual advance by a perpetrator involving some degree of coercion even when the difference between the perpetrator and victim was less than 5 years. This definition would include actual sexual contact such as fondling, intercourse, and oral sex, as well as exhibitionist behaviors and solicitations to engage in sexual behavior. Childhood sexual abuse most often occurs within the family (incest). It may also occur with an acquaintance; less often, a stranger is the offender. More recently, it has been claimed that it may occur with multiple offenders as part of a child sex ring, often to exploit the child for some purpose such as for pornography, child prostitution, or for cult purposes as in satanic ritual abuse (SRA).

Estimating Childhood Sexual Abuse

There is little doubt among those in the helping professions and in law enforcement that sexual abuse, in general, is fairly common in the United States. Estimates vary widely, however. An early study by Weinberg (1955) estimated the incidence of childhood sexual abuse at one in one million. Recent studies have shown its prevalence to be much higher. (Estimates of **prevalence** look at any occurrence of sexual abuse during a time period, such as any unwanted sexual advance before the age of 18; estimates of **incidence,** in contrast, take into account recurrence and severity of abuse.) Stinson and Hendrick (1992) estimated the prevalence of sexual abuse among college students in counseling centers to be 31% of men and 37% of women, or 35% overall, based on responses to a childhood sexual experience questionnaire. They found that significantly fewer persons—only 8%—reported childhood sexual abuse on their own without any direct questioning. Another study by Wyatt (1985) of 248 randomly selected women in Los Angeles showed that 62% of them had at least one instance of sexual abuse before age 18, using a broad definition of sexual abuse.

Estimates sometimes differ based on respondents' race and educational background and on how broadly sexual abuse is defined. The general conclusion is that sexual abuse is alarmingly frequent, much more frequent than previously estimated. Russell (1983), in a study of both the prevalence and incidence of childhood sexual abuse in 930 San Francisco women, obtained lower estimates than Wyatt (1985). She found the prevalence of childhood sexual abuse to be 38%.

While many of the people reporting sexual abuse in these and other studies have always been able to recall their abuse, increasing numbers of people could not recall their abuse until they were in psychotherapy. According to Freud's repression theory, childhood traumas, like early sexual abuse, could be pushed out of awareness, resulting in various symptoms including depression, anxiety, and sexual problems, even though the victim is not aware of the traumatic experience. Later, Janet (1898) argued that victims of trauma might use a different defense mechanism called **dissociation.** In dissociation, the person splits off the memory of the traumatic experience from the rest of awareness. According to early theory, dissociation occurs involuntarily and outside of awareness. In extreme cases, dissociation can result in the victim's developing a severe mental disorder. For example, in psychogenic fugue states, a person forgets who he or she is. The person may take on a new identity, move to another city—even commit bigamy—while in a fugue state. In dissociative identity disorder, the memory of the traumatic material is split off into a separate personality that does not remember the abuse. What may result is multiple personalities in the same person, each functioning separately within the main, host personality. Often these separate personalities are unaware of one another.

Frequently it is assumed that each personality has a distinct pattern of feeling, thinking, and acting. Multiple personality may be frequently found in clients with histories of sexual abuse, although this view is somewhat controversial.

Treatment of victims with dissociative disorders involves at least two steps: (1) the recovery of the memory of the traumatic experience, and (2) abreaction or reexperiencing the traumatic experience in the safe environment provided by the psychotherapist (Mulhern, 1991). This therapeutic process will be impeded if a client either fails to remember repressed experiences of abuse or remembers experiences inaccurately.

Estimating the Incidence of Satanic Ritual Abuse

Most researchers agree that childhood sexual abuse is very prevalent. There is less agreement about the prevalence of satanic ritual abuse, hereafter referred to as SRA. In the 1980s the idea emerged that an international network of blood cult groups worshipped Satan. These groups were thought to commit heinous crimes such as the ritual sacrifice of animals and children, desecration of Christian rituals, cannibalism, and sexual abuse. Stories appeared of people who survived and escaped SRA that included vivid descriptions of sexual abuse. They suggested that children were abducted and sacrificed and that some of the victims of the cults served as "breeders"—women impregnated for the purpose of creating infants for human sacrifice in satanic rituals. As these stories accumulated, some people concluded that the threat was of great proportions, with groups like the Cult Crime Network estimating 50,000 human sacrifices a year (Lotto, 1994). Estimates of the numbers of SRA cult members varied depending on the source. Briggs, cited in Hicks (1990), estimated there were 300,000 adherents in the United States. Of the 7000 cases in which people have claimed to have been falsely accused of being sexual abuse offenders, 17% of them were accused of SRA (Lotto, 1994).

Only very limited efforts have been made to verify specific cases of SRA (Lotto, 1994). Many cases, once investigated, have not supported claims of SRA. For example, in the United Kingdom, child protective workers removed children who were claimed to be SRA victims from their parents' home, but a thorough investigation revealed no SRA. Similarly, of 29 cases of SRA studied by Coons (1994), not one was corroborated by examination of old records or statements of relatives interviewed. One study by Femina, Yeager, and Lewis (1990) did provide limited physical evidence of SRA; satanic ritual scars were found on two individuals' heads and backs. No efforts were made, however, to contact relatives or the police to verify the claims of SRA.

In spite of elaborate efforts by law enforcement personnel to obtain material evidence to substantiate the claims that ritual abuse murders had occurred, very little material evidence has been produced (Hicks, 1990). Kenneth Lanning, an FBI officer with the Behavioral Science Unit, involved in investigating crimes of sexual abuse in children, reported that the FBI had found no evidence of human sacrifices or cannibalism in their investigations of child sex ring cases (Lanning, 1992).

What could account for this lack of material evidence in support of SRA? The dramatic increase in the number of ritual abuse cases reported and the estimates of as many as 50,000 annual ritual abuse murders suggest that the SRA is very prevalent. One explanation is that the children who are sacrificed are often runaways and so are not missed when cult members abduct them. Another explanation is that SRA members are kept in the group and prevented from divulging information about it by the use of drugs, hypnotic control, brainwashing, and threats of retaliation against the victims. Another common explanation is that members of cults are very good at hiding the bodies and other evidence of their ritual ceremonies from authorities.

All three of these explanations are weak. First, there are many times fewer runaway children in the United States than the 50,000 annual ritual abuse murders that some estimate. During a 4-year period in the late 1980s, there were only a few more than 4000 runaways and missing children documented during the entire period; the total average number of homicides was about 25,000 each year (Lanning, 1992). And while threats of retaliation, hypnosis, and brainwashing techniques can be effective in controlling individuals, this does not explain why the claims of SRA victims have not been substantiated once the victims have moved out of the control of the abusing group. Lastly, if as many people are involved in SRA as has been claimed, it would be very difficult for at least some of the illegal activities of certain individuals to go undetected. Even members of organized crime sometimes become informants, and illegal activities are subsequently detected. Not so with claims of SRA.

If the absence of material evidence really does indicate that SRA does not exist, then what could explain the great number of reported cases of SRA? A common explanation of SRA stories is that they are part of the social construction of reality. Belief in the reality of SRA may be constructed from a variety of sources (Victor, 1990). We will examine two important kinds of evidence that have been used to support claims of SRA: the rumor-story and the self-reported cases of SRA, especially within the context of psychotherapy.

A second important kind of evidence for the reality of SRA has been the stories of individuals purporting to have been victims of SRA groups. These stories have appeared extensively in the popular press and also are reported to mental health care providers. For example, one early book by Stratford (1988) described her escape and experiences in a SRA group that forced her to breed babies for ritual sacrifice. But an extensive investigation of her claims by *Cornerstone,* a Christian magazine, revealed basic contradictions between her story and facts from her family history. Also, the physical scars that she claimed were part of her abuse were self-inflicted, and she was apparently never pregnant despite her claims of having been a "breeder" for the group (Mulhern, 1991). The stories of self-professed cult survivors have also appeared on television programs on satanism and SRA, such as *20/20* and Oprah Winfrey's and Geraldo Rivera's talk shows. These stories may have influenced others in claiming victimization by SRA groups.

Therapists and clients may also form informal communication networks for transmitting ideas about SRA. Psychologists and others report on the symptoms of mental problems like those related to SRA at conferences and workshops, in journals and books. Mulhern (1992) argued that SRA training workshops present information on SRA to workshop attendees in a very uncritical fashion. Bucky and Dalenberg (1992) found that symptoms of a number of problems such as ritual abuse and multiple personality may become more related in the minds of those clinicians who have attended SRA workshops. It may, therefore, be premature to classify satanic ritual abuse as a clinical disorder, as some have claimed it is (Young, Sachs, Braun, & Watkins, 1991).

Yapko told a story about the therapeutic interaction between a troubled man and one of Yapko's colleagues, a psychotherapist (Yapko, 1994). The troubled man seems to have become very agitated by the sneakers his wife wore. When he calmed down, he told her that his captors, at his prisoner of war camp in Vietnam, had worn sneakers like hers. His captors humiliated and abused him, locking him in a bamboo cage, regularly beating him, and urinating on him. In fact, the guard he strangled when he escaped from the POW camp had worn those kind of shoes. Finally, he went to a therapist for help. His therapist diagnosed him as having post-traumatic stress disorder, a common diagnosis for people who have suffered severe traumatic experiences, such as those soldiers suffer during wartime. Despite treatment, three years later the man committed suicide. His wife petitioned for his name to be placed on the state's Vietnam memorial because she felt that the war had caused his death even though he had not died overseas, and his therapist wrote a letter of support. Her petition was denied after a search of the records revealed that her husband had never been to Vietnam.

This story reveals an important problem in the dual roles of the psychotherapist or counselor. One important role is investigative—to find out what has happened to a client and to document the facts related to a client's problem. These facts have been called the "historical truth" of a client's life. At the same time, the other important role of the counselor is to provide a safe, supportive environment for the client, reassuring and taking the side of the client when necessary. This is reflected in the common saying among child abuse counselors in reference to children's claims of abuse: "Believe the child." This statement is intended to place the therapist squarely on the side of children's claims of abuse. It is like the assumption commonly made about survivor stories in general—that is, that no one would make up such a traumatic story filled with such ghastly detail.

Nevertheless, people do make up stories and tell them to therapists. People who are very confused about who they are, such as those with multiple personalities, may tell stories that seem true to them. Also, people with factitious disorder may present false symptoms of abuse or other mental problems in order to play the role of a mental patient (Coons & Grier, 1990). Coons also found that 14% of SRA clients he observed had factitious disorder (Coons, 1994). These stories that clients tell, which are true to them, are said to have "narrative truth." They may or may not be historically true, but clients may think that they are.

Conclusions and Implications

Childhood sexual abuse is clearly very prevalent. Estimates have ranged as high as 62%, although a more conservative estimate of 38% is justified. Estimates depend on other factors, such as the gender and economic status of the individuals, as well. Estimates vary in part because of the definitions they use: The 62% estimate is based on an inclusive definition of sexual abuse. Also, prevalence estimates may overestimate clinically important incidents of sexual abuse, such as recurring and severe incidents, because prevalence estimates include any incident—even a single incident. Since the prevalence of abuse is estimated as much lower when clients are not requested to report on sexual abuse, they should be asked objective but not leading questions in a standardized way, perhaps using a questionnaire such Wyatt's (1985). The clinician should take into account the base rate or the expected rate of occurrence for the particular kind of abuse in helping to decide whether it did occur. While estimates vary, a number of research studies and authorities suggest that the base rate for prevalence of sexual abuse (defined as one incident or more, regardless of severity) in female Americans is between 30% and 40%.

If we use the base rate of sexual abuse in the population to help us decide how likely it is that a particular individual has been sexually abused as a child, then we must examine other factors as well. While it is very difficult in general to verify that sexual abuse has occurred in a particular case, some types of abuse like SRA may be less credible than others. For the most part, when efforts have been made to verify the reports of victims of SRA, little good evidence has been found to corroborate these reports. Consequently, the incidence of some kinds of abuse like SRA is probably much rarer than the believers in this phenomenon would suggest. The clinician should take this into account when deciding whether the person was abused. Also, clinicians should keep in mind the distinction between the historical and narrative truth of clients' stories, so as to draw reasonable conclusions about the meaning of the evidence presented.

≈ PRACTICE YOUR THINKING 13.2

Drawing Conclusions from the Research: Is Repression Real?

In this second critical reading passage concerning whether repression actually occurs, read over the following questions before you read the passage, and keep them in mind as you read. After you have read the passage and written your answers on a separate piece of paper, check your conclusions against those in the conclusions and implications section at the end of the passage.

  1. From the evidence presented here, what can you generalize about whether memory can actually be repressed?

  2. What are the implications of your conclusions for the larger question of determining whether someone who cannot at first recall having been sexually abused actually has been?

Does Repression Actually Occur?

We have seen that much evidence from cases of sexual abuse shows that victims who do not at first remember abuse may later come to remember such incidents. But we also know from Chapter 2 that the use of cases as evidence has a number of problems and limitations. For example, the victim may be lying about the abuse in order to get attention or constructing a story as part of a self-presentation in a dissociative disorder. From case evidence alone we could not infer that sexual abuse could lead to repressed memories of the experiences. Cases leave many other variables uncontrolled that could be accounting for the repression, such as the motivation to try to remember.

A stronger argument for repression could be made if we could conduct an experimental demonstration of the recovery of repressed memories of childhood sexual abuse. If we could manipulate sexual abuse as an independent variable and eliminate other extraneous variables in the situation, then we would be in a better position to decide if sexual abuse could cause repression of memory for the experiences.

Of course, for ethical reasons we could not conduct such an experiment. Nevertheless, it is possible to conduct experiments that test memory for negative or unpleasant information without actually creating conditions of sexual abuse. Holmes (1990) reviewed a number of these kinds of repression studies in which researchers examined the forgetting of information that caused the subjects pain. For example, he found that in studies that asked subjects to list positive and negative experiences, subjects tended to recall fewer negative than positive experiences, consistent with repression theory. The results of other experiments, however, suggested that the intensity of the experience determined whether or not the experience was recalled, not the positive or negative nature of the experience. Moreover, other research showed that negative experiences declined in intensity faster than positive experiences. Consequently, as time passed, negative experiences would be harder to remember than positive experiences because of this loss of intensity, not because of selective forgetting of unpleasant experiences as repression theory proposes. His review of other experimental research on repression also failed to support repression theory.

Holmes (1990) concluded that the 60 years of research that he reviewed contained no evidence for repression other than case study evidence. He amusingly suggested that the concept of repression carry a product warning with it: "Warning: The concept of repression has not been validated with experimental research and its use may be hazardous to the accurate interpretation of clinical behavior." (Holmes, 1990, p. 97). Because repression has not been clearly demonstrated but most would agree that a person, for some reason, may not recall an event at some point after it occurs, it would seem wise to change what we call such memories. Recently, Emms, McNeilly, Corkery, and Gilbert (1995), and others working in this area, have begun to call them *delayed memories*; this term need not directly evoke the concept of repression, but it does describe the kind of memories under discussion.

Because repression of childhood sexual abuse is thought to differ from repression of the everyday unpleasant experiences studied in the laboratory, many have thought that repression of memories of abuse does not lend itself to generalizations from those experiments. Other studies have used nonexperimental methods to examine repression of sexual abuse. Loftus (1993) reviewed studies in which subjects were asked to report on whether they have ever been unable to remember their experiences of sexual abuse for at least some period of time. Estimates ranged from 18% to 59% who reported that they had been unable to remember the experience for at least part of the time. These kinds of studies are problematic because it is unclear why subjects were unable to remember the experience; perhaps they were just trying not to think about it. Also, in some studies those reporting were clients in psychotherapy; they may have been influenced by information suggesting that memories frequently are repressed.

Another method that avoids these problems and may test repressed memory of sexual abuse more directly was used in a study by Williams (1994a). Although not a true experiment, this study was a prospective study, which allows the researcher to establish the causal criterion of time order—that is, that sexual abuse did indeed occur prior to attempts at remembering. In this study, several girls were identified from hospital records as having been sexually abused. Years later, these same individuals were contacted and interviewed to determine whether they could remember having been sexually abused. Williams (1994a) found that 38% of the women did not remember the abuse experiences they had reported as children, as indicated by their failure to report the abuse when interviewed later about the reason for their being at the hospital. For example, one woman who had been abused by her uncle recalled that he had abused a little boy but no longer remembered that he had abused her, as well. Williams also found that victims were more likely to forget the abuse when the perpetrator was a family member than when the perpetrator was a stranger.

Loftus, Garry, and Feldman (1994) argued that Williams (1994a) did not demonstrate repression of memories of sexual abuse because it was not clearly shown that the participants in the Williams study had actually stored the experience of the abuse in memory in the first place. The authors supported this assertion with the idea that sometimes children and other clients in psychotherapy do not really understand what problem they are in treatment for; the authors speculated that parents who took their children to the hospital for sexual abuse may have protected their children from this truth by not telling them why they were there. Loftus, Garry, and Feldman (1994) also argued that the estimate of the number of women who failed to remember their childhood sexual abuse should also take into account how many of the girls had originally fabricated their story of sexual abuse. In response, Williams (1994b) argued that only 2% of her subjects reported to have fabricated their memories; this is less than the fabrication rate of 4% to 8% reported in a review by Emerson and Boat (1989).

Conclusions and Implications

Much anecdotal evidence from case histories and survivors' stories supports the claim that people can repress memories of sexual abuse. In addition, between 18% and 59% of subjects reported that they were unable to remember their experiences of sexual abuse for at least some period of time. No experimental evidence, however, supports the idea of repression. A prospective study did indicate that perhaps 38% of women who were sexually abused as children did not remember their abuse several years later. This failure to remember does not necessarily indicate repression, but it does suggest at least a problem in remembering or memory testing in a more general sense. The research also suggests that estimates of the occurrence of abuse must take into account that between 2% and 8% of those supposed to have been abused may have fabricated their stories.

These findings have a number of implications for clinicians and others who must evaluate claims of repressed memories of abuse. One implication is that the term *repressed memory* should perhaps be replaced with the term *delayed memory*. When therapists and others use such concepts, it gives them a certain reality. People may come to expect that they have memories of which they are unconscious, which in turn may lead them to reconstruct memories based on inaccurate sources of information. Another implication is that therapists should be cautious in suggesting to clients that some level of delayed memory occurs in the population. Finally, the person evaluating delayed memories of abuse should keep in mind that some of these memories may be fabricated.

≈ PRACTICE YOUR THINKING 13.3

Drawing Conclusions from the Research:
Accuracy and Repressed Memories

In this third critical reading passage about whether people can accurately remember repressed memories, read over the following questions before you read the passage, and keep them in mind as you read. After reading the section, write your responses on a separate piece of paper, then check them against the conclusions and implications section at the end of the passage.

1. From the evidence presented here, what can you generalize about the reliability of human memory and various methods used to recover memories?

2. Can you draw the same conclusion for all methods of recovering memories?

3. What are the implications of your conclusions for the larger question of determining whether someone who cannot at first recall having been sexually abused actually has been?

Can People Accurately Remember Repressed Memories?

Although there is room for doubt that memories of abuse are repressed, victims nevertheless may fail to remember abuse. If subjects do recover memories that they previously did not remember, are these recovered memories accurate? This passage examines issues related to the accuracy of memory and methods used to recover memories.

Reconstruction in Memory

As discussed in Chapter 8, memory is not a reproductive process that makes a virtual copy of whatever is happening in the environment, like a videotape. Rather, memory is a reconstructive process more like an editor of that videotape— selecting portions of what is happening, putting together pieces, rearranging the parts, reinterpreting the story, and showing only the parts consistent with the story. What ends up in the story recorded by our memory system can be influenced by the learner's expectations, suggestions made to the learner at the time an event occurs, and other knowledge the person has. Since memory is assumed to be reconstructive, in general, we would expect survivors' memories of abuse to be no different.

Recovering Memories with Hypnosis

The use of hypnosis has a long and problematic history as a method for recovering memories of traumatic events, as discussed in Chapter 6. Freud used hypnosis to help patients recall traumatic memories, but later abandoned it after observing that patients sometimes did not accurately recall information about their experiences when hypnotized (Mulhern, 1991). As we also saw in Chapter 6, contrary to popular opinion hypnosis may not be an effective method for bringing back accurate memories. Although after being hypnotized, people sometimes recall things they did not previously recall, the recall of new information may be due simply to repeating the attempt to recall. What's more, the new information people recall may be inaccurate, but people recalling under hypnosis are nevertheless more confident in their recall (even when they are mistaken) than they are under ordinary conditions. In addition, pseudomemories are very easily formed during hypnosis; events that did not actually happen, when suggested during hypnosis, afterward may be recalled as memories of actual events.

Research evidence suggests that individuals interviewed with the aid of hypnosis may produce false confessions. For example, Coons (1988) reported the case of a woman who confessed to shooting her two children after being hypnotized by a police hypnotist who used particularly suggestive interview techniques. The woman produced a secondary personality under hypnosis, and this personality confessed to the crime; little other evidence was found against her, however.

Hypnosis can pose other problems for the therapist. Some people who are very susceptible to hypnosis may be especially likely to show dissociation and memory distortions. Speigel (1972) identified what he called "grade fives," highly hypnotizable individuals, who are especially likely to fill in missing gaps in their memories and to confabulate (Mulhern, 1991). Another problem with hypnosis as a method for recovering memories is that the person who has been hypnotized during a session may not be able to tell whether an event occurred during hypnosis or outside of hypnosis (Whitehouse, Orne, Orne, & Dinges, 1991).

There is also evidence that persons with dissociative disorders like multiple personality often have sexual abuse in their backgrounds and often are very susceptible to hypnosis. Researchers have been able to use hypnosis to create multiple personalities in hypnotized subjects (Kampman, 1976).

In a similar study (also described in Chapter 6), Spanos, Menary, Gabora, DuBreuil, and Dewhirst (1991) gave each of their subjects the suggestion during hypnosis to regress past his or her birth to a former life. Many subjects showed alternative or secondary personalities from previous lives when suggested to regress to a former life. These researchers found that subjects tended to pick personalities with whom they were somewhat familiar. For example, one subject who claimed to have been Julius Caesar was studying him in school. The personalities constructed by the hypnotized subjects were not historically accurate, however, as one would expect if the subjects really had regressed to a former life. For example, the person who claimed to be Julius Caesar said he was the emperor of Rome and that the year was A.D. 50. In fact, Julius Caesar never was crowned emperor, and he died in 44 B.C.—many years before the convention for naming the date as B.C. or A.D. was even established.

Spanos, Menary, et al. also found that subjects incorporated characteristics into their created personalities that they were led to believe were characteristic of past-life personalities. In particular, in one experiment, subjects, who were told that children in the past were frequently abused by their parents and others, were subsequently much more likely to report that they had been abused as children in a former life than were subjects who were not given this information beforehand. In another experiment, the credibility of reincarnation was manipulated. The researchers found that subjects who were told beforehand that scientific evidence supported the validity of reincarnation rated their past life experiences as significantly more credible than subjects who were told beforehand that they would be engaging in fantasy, not actually going back to a former life.

Spanos, Burgess, and Burgess (1994) argued that these experimental results suggest that the pseudomemories of a hypnotized person may be of an entire story, not just a single detail as previous research had found. Spanos (1989) also argued that hypnosis, multiple personality, and demonic possession are similar in important ways. In all three, the actor temporarily loses voluntary control over his or her actions; control over those actions is transferred to another part or agency. In each case the actor also is unaware of or cannot remember information from this hidden self. These agencies or hidden selves can be revealed, however, as in the case of the hypnotized person who regresses to a previous lifetime, the client with multiple personality who reveals a secondary personality in psychotherapy, or the possessed person whose demon is exorcised by a priest. Spanos viewed the actor's behavior in all three of these cases as the result of the actor's social role enactment. Role enactments—patterns of action identified with a particular social status, social position, or social value—may be voluntary, involuntary, disinterested, personally involving, or characterized by faking (Spanos, 1989).

Returning to the example of satanic ritual abuse, the role of a survivor might include patterns of action specified by satanic legend as interpreted by the media, notions of how to behave as a mental patient, as well as internal feeling states associated with being an abuse victim. This complex role could be consciously enacted to simulate a person with a mental disorder, or it could be firmly believed.

Ofshe (1992) documented the case of Paul Ingram, whose adult daughters accused him of raping them. Though Ingram did not actually go through a hypnotic procedure, a relaxation technique that may have induced a state resembling hypnosis was used on him. He was interrogated by police and a psychologist over a period of several days. Ingram, the police officer, and his family all believed in a satanic conspiracy and SRA. He was diagnosed as having multiple personalities, and the investigators began looking for a repressed memory of the sexual abuse. Due to the combination of Ingram's extreme suggestibility to hypnosis, his dissociative state during the relaxation procedure, and the pressures exerted upon him during interrogation, Ingram came to believe that he had sexually abused his daughters as part of his membership in a satanic cult. He persisted in this belief for six months although no other evidence was found to incriminate him.

An important implication of this study is that a highly hypnotizable subject like Ingram may inadvertently be hypnotized during interrogation procedures and then construct pseudo-memories based on suggestions made within the interview session. In fact, Loftus and Coan (in press) showed that a pseudo-memory can be planted in a young person who is unhypnotized. In their study they had a graduate student, Jim, in a conversation, casually ask his 14-year-old brother, Chris, the leading question, "Remember when you were lost in the mall?" The young man not only believed the event suggested to him by a trusted adult, his brother, but also viewed the pseudo-event as arousing mild fear and trauma. Also, the event seemed as if it actually happened even a year after Chris was told that it did not actually occur.

Other Memory Recovery Methods

Sometimes, instead of hypnosis, a therapist will use a guided imagery technique to help a client recover memories. **Guided imagery** is much like hypnosis in that the subject is instructed to close his or her eyes and relax, and given imagined scenarios to develop. Perry and Nogrady (1985) found that, like hypnosis, guided imagery may lead to dissociation and hence to reduced accuracy of memory.

Since the time of Freud, clinicians have been using dream analysis to uncover repressed material. As Lindslay and Read (1994) noted, no evidence suggests that the presence of sexual abuse imagery in a client's dreams necessarily means that the client was sexually abused. Dreams are frequently filled with concerns, issues, and talk from people's daily lives. If a client is receiving therapy for sex abuse, it would not be surprising for such images to appear in the client's dreams. Also, there is always the danger that a therapist's own theoretical beliefs may bias the interpretation of dream content, which is often somewhat ambiguous.

Some therapists try to get subjects to examine their body memories of sexual abuse. Body memories may begin as vague discomfort, pains, and the memories of other unpleasant sensations localized in some part of the body. Often, the client looks for the source of these feelings and how they relate to abuse. It is unclear how these fragments can become associated with a person or experience without being prone to the same problems of reconstruction seen in other recovery methods.

Informal Therapy: Mixed Methods

Sometimes, therapists suggest that their clients use one of the self-help books for survivors of sexual abuse such as *The Courage to Heal* (Bass & Davis, 1988). *The Courage to Heal* employs a number of potentially problematic memory recovery techniques, including guided imagery, dream work, journal writing, and recovery of body memories. Books like this one take a very uncritical approach to the recovery of memories of abuse. For example, in response to a potential survivor's comment that she didn't have any such memories, Bass and Davis advise: "If you don't remember your abuse, you are not alone. Many women don't have memories and some never get memories. This doesn't mean they aren't abused." (Bass & Davis, 1988, p. 81). This statement presumes that memories are repressed. Also, logically it is not necessarily the case that such a person must have been abused. If we pursue this line of reasoning further, an important question arises concerning verification of sexual abuse.

Suppose a person has no memory of sexual abuse after considerable effort in trying to remember. Suppose further that no other person or material evidence can corroborate sexual abuse in this case. Finally, suppose that the person has anxiety, depression, problems with sex, vague feelings that something is wrong. No specific set of symptoms invariably indicates sexual abuse. In fact, there is no diagnostic category to classify the symptoms of sexual abuse as a mental disorder in any diagnostic system conventionally accepted by professional clinicians. Given only a set of symptoms without awareness of sexual abuse, what other evidence indicates that this person was actually sexually abused? While *The Courage to Heal* contains much advice that might help people feel better about themselves, it also contains many statements exhorting readers to reconstruct memories because their healing depends on recovery of memories of abuse. In the presence of these kinds of social cues and incentives to believe, an unsure person looking for the certainty of answers to unanswered questions may reconstruct memories of sexual abuse even when no abuse had occurred. Books like these, widely available to the public, could lead to recovery of false memories.

Childhood Amnesia

A phenomenon called childhood amnesia is also relevant to the issue of accuracy in the recovery of memories of childhood sexual abuse. Pause for a moment, and try to recall your earliest memory. Try to remember an incident that you remember experiencing—some event that you were not told about or shown pictures of later. How old were you when this event took place? On average, people report that they were 4 years old. Some remember an event from when they were 3 years old, but hardly anyone can be shown to remember accurately before the age of 2. Freud coined the term **infantile** or **childhood amnesia** to refer to this early part of our lives that we are unable to remember. Recently, Usher and Neisser (1993) showed that almost 60% of the children in their study were able to recall the important events of hospitalization and the birth of a sibling that occurred when they were between 2 and 3 years of age—a younger age than was previously thought to be the lower age limit for childhood amnesia. Only a little more than 20% of the subjects could recall the birth of a younger sibling that occurred when they were between the ages of 1 and 2.

Conclusions and Implications

Even under ordinary conditions, human memory is reconstructive and so may not remember accurately. Some memory recovery methods, like hypnosis, may lead to even more inaccurate memory. Highly hypnotizable individuals may be especially susceptible to the effects of suggestions during an interview and may even inadvertently become hypnotized and appear to have secondary personalities. They may develop and recall pseudo-memories and even confess to crimes they did not commit. Consequently, leading questions and other cues during an interview may lead to inaccuracies in memory even when the subject has not been hypnotized, as in the use of methods like guided imagery. The misuse of these recovery methods in self-help books and by untrained individuals in recovery groups may lead especially to the reconstruction of false memories of sexual abuse.

≋ PRACTICE YOUR THINKING 13.4

Drawing Conclusions from the Research: Summary

Now that you have read these three passages and tried to draw sound conclusions from the reviewed evidence, try to integrate all of your conclusions by answering the following questions. Then check your answers against the summary of conclusions and implications that follows the questions.

1. Based on the reviews of evidence in all three passages, what can you generalize about the complex question of whether people can accurately recall repressed memories of abuse that they could not previously recall?

2. What are the implications of your conclusions for the larger question of determining whether someone who cannot at first recall having been sexually abused actually has been?

Conclusions and Implications of the Reviewed Research

The following summary reviews some of the important conclusions found in each of the three literature reviews and examines their implications for clinical practice. First of all, estimates vary concerning both the prevalence of sexual abuse and of people being unable to recall the number of incidents of abuse during some point in their lives. The prevalence of sexual abuse among women and girls is thought by many to be 30% to 40%. The therapist should be aware of the base rate for various kinds of childhood sexual abuse, realizing that claims of certain forms, such as SRA, are less likely to be credible.

Support for the idea of memory repression has come from research in the form of case studies, but not from the experimental literature. Although it is impossible to experimentally test whether occurrences of sexual abuse become repressed, other research has shown little support for a broader form of repression theory involving memory of unpleasant material. One implication is that clinicians should not use the term *repressed memories* and perhaps instead use the term *delayed memories.*

Research on the accuracy of memory and recovery methods such as hypnosis and guided imagery suggests that memories of abuse may be especially inaccurate under some conditions. In general, people often reconstruct memories of events in their lives that are inaccurate. Leading questions and suggestions, both inside and outside hypnosis, have been found to produce false memories. Other techniques like guided imagery have also proved unreliable.

The large amount of research on reconstruction in memory and suggestion effects with hypnosis, and the lack of evidence for repression in memory, has led some scientists to conclude that false memories of sexual abuse may be created. Terming this **false memory syndrome,** these researchers cite instances of people who have discovered that they developed false memories in therapy. They argue that clinicians offer very little good research evidence to support the idea of repressed memories of abuse, mostly supporting these claims with anecdotes and case studies. At the same time, Pope (1996) argued that supporters of the false memory syndrome hypothesis must also be careful about interpreting evidence of cases where false memories may have been developed through therapy.

A general implication of all the literature reviewed is that the clinician and others should proceed with caution in deciding whether a particular memory of sexual abuse is true in the historical sense. There is no valid test for deciding whether a particular memory report is true. Since self-reported memories are frequently false, the clinician should be cautious about these and look for other evidence that could corroborate these stories. Only therapists who are well trained in avoiding leading suggestions and other sources of bias should use recovery methods like hypnosis and guided imagery—and then only with extreme caution. Biased interpretation of dreams and other ambiguous information about clients' experiences should be avoided, as well as the confirmatory bias of the therapist's own beliefs. A client should only be sent to a survivors' support group when it is clear that the client has been sexually abused. The therapist should use direct questioning or a sexual abuse inventory to assess the potential for abuse. In addition, the therapist should provide a supportive therapeutic environment within which a client may feel safe to divulge information about a history of abuse. Lastly, the therapist, who is only concerned about the reports of his or her client and not in corroborating these reports, should interpret recovered memories of abuse as true in a narrative and not historical sense.

≋ PRACTICE YOUR THINKING 13.5

Evaluating Client-Therapist Interactions

Following are two case descriptions of interactions between clients and their therapists, in which previous sexual abuse of the client may be suspected. As you read each case, apply your knowledge from the previous discussions and exercises to analyze and evaluate the interaction. Use your knowledge about recovery of memories of abuse to identify possible problems in the therapists' interactions with their clients that would make it difficult to conclude validly from the case that sexual abuse had occurred. Then answer the following two questions. (As a final step, check your answers against those in Appendix C.)

1. Evaluate the quality of the therapist's decision; note how any problems in interviewing and the use of memory recovery methods might be avoided.

2. Do you agree with the psychotherapist's conclusion? Why or why not?

Interaction 1: Jennifer and Her Therapist
Jennifer is a 20-year-old junior in college who sought counseling because she fears intimacy with her boyfriend of six months. She comes from a protective family that has allowed her few opportunities to make important life decisions. She has been reluctant to talk about her past despite repeated attempts by her therapist to uncover details about her life. She is showing signs of anxiety and depression, low self-esteem, and sexual problems.

Her therapist suspects that she is repressing memories of sexual abuse from her childhood. He suggests to her that clients with her pattern of symptoms often have a history of sexual abuse during childhood. Then he asks her to try to recall any memories of abuse that she has perhaps forgotten. For two weeks, Jennifer probes her memory but cannot remember any such incident. She tells him that she cannot recall any memories of abuse. Then her therapist tells her that 60% of all women experienced sexual abuse in their childhood, that very many survivors of sexual abuse have trouble recalling having been abused, and that this did not mean that they were not abused.

He suggests that she further explore her memories of her family and early life with an imagery technique. From a previous interview, he learned that her father was frequently angry with her; so they begin the session with her in a room with her father, who is angry. She thinks about this for a while and seems to be very absorbed in her imaginings. She is quiet and describes mundane things in the room vividly. She says she can see the angry expression on her father's face. Then, after a while, she imagines that her father is yelling at her.

At the next session, her therapist goes over the memories that she recalled during the previous week. With encouragement from her therapist, her memories begin to fill in with other details such as her father yelling at her, holding on tightly to her hand, and standing over her. She recalls that for as long as she can remember, her father has had a bad temper and a drinking problem that seem to accentuate his fits of rage. When asked if any of her memories were of a sexual nature, she says no, but that she can remember seeing her father naked one time.

Her therapist tells her that this sounded like part of a memory of sexual abuse from her father that she is recalling but is afraid, or at least reluctant, to discuss. He recommends that she seek to further explore her memories of abuse in a support group of people recovering from sexual abuse. After two months in the group she becomes more and more convinced that she has been sexually abused by her father. She begins to have memories of a pressure on her body. She thinks she is remembering the weight of her father's body. Her memories of abuse extend further and further back in time, with her earliest memory of abuse beginning when she was in her crib at the age of six months. Her therapist encourages her to confront her father about the abuse.

She confronts her father with accusations of sexual abuse. He acts shocked by the allegation and denies that he had ever done it. Her two sisters are also shocked, professing no knowledge of any abuse.

Interaction 2: Laura and Her Therapist

Laura is a 31-year-old woman who is married with two children. She has sought the help of a counselor because she has been depressed lately and is having trouble with the sexual part of her relationship with her husband. This has been a recurring problem during her 10-year marriage with her husband. She becomes very tense and her heart pounds whenever her husband gets physically close to her.

She has been depressed on two other occasions, and once she had to be hospitalized because of an attempted suicide. She complains of frightening nightmares in which she is being chased by an evil person whose face she cannot see. She occasionally has a flashback, an intrusive vivid memory in which her father is yelling at her in a threatening manner. She appears to have ambivalent feelings toward her father, although she professes to love both her parents.

As part of her assessment, she is given the MMPI. It shows that her depression subscale is elevated, $T = 85$ (scores greater than 70 suggest depression). She is also given a brief questionnaire on her sexual experiences, and her responses suggest that she may have been sexually abused as a child. When asked directly if she has been abused, Laura denied having any recollection of such an experience.

Her therapist decides to focus on her thoughts and feelings when Laura is anxious with her husband. The therapist asks Laura to record her thoughts and feelings during these times, to read over her notes, and to think about these before their next session. She reassures Laura that whatever she noticed and wrote would be all right. She also tells Laura that if she has any trouble she should get in touch. The next week they discuss her notes and comments. The therapist reassures Laura that her observations are good and that she is a good person with some problems that they would explore together. Then the therapist teaches Laura a relaxation technique that she can employ if she begins to get anxious.

At the next session, the therapist helped Laura to relax as she held a pillow, closed her eyes, and imagined her husband hugging her. As they continued with this practice, Laura became very agitated at one point and began to cry. She sobbed uncontrollably and cried no several times. She then pushed the pillow away. Her therapist asked Laura what was wrong. She said that she had just had an image of her older brother fondling her after hugging her. Her therapist asked Laura if she was remembering something that had actually occurred. She replied, "Maybe."

Her therapist proceeded with her relaxation therapy as before, and more images returned to Laura. After some weeks Laura began to recall two different episodes of sexual abuse by her 14-year-old brother when she was 6 years old. Laura decided that she wanted to find out more about what had occurred. She confronted her brother and asked her mother. Her brother confessed, and her mother acknowledged that her brother had severe problems during this period of time.

At this point, her therapist initiated other treatments besides the relaxation training that were more specifically designed to help her recover from her abuse.

Review Questions

How should sexual abuse be defined?

What is the base rate for sexual abuse of female persons?

Is the prevalence of sexual abuse the same for all groups?

What is repression? How does it relate to memory?

What is dissociation? How does it relate to memory and psychological problems with identity?

Does research evidence support the idea of repression?

Instead of *repressed memories*, should we use the term *delayed memories*?

How does reconstructive memory relate to the memory of sexual abuse?

Can we trust memories recovered through the use of hypnosis?

What other methods create problems for recovery of memories of abuse, and why?

What are the implications of the research reviewed in this chapter for clinicians and law enforcement investigators?

References

Bass, E., & Davis, L. (1988). *The courage to heal.* New York: HarperCollins.

Briere, J., & Conte, J. (1993). Self-reported amnesia for abuse in adults molested as children. *Journal of Traumatic Stress, 6,* 21–31.

Bucky, S. F., & Dalenberg, C. (1992). The relationship between training of mental health professionals and the reporting of ritual abuse and multiple personality disorder symptomatology, *Journal of Psychology and Theology, 20,* 233–238.

Claridge, K. (1992). Reconstructing memories of abuse. A theory-based approach. *Psychotherapy, 29,* 243–252.

Coleman, L. (1990). False accusations of sexual abuse: Psychiatry's latest reign of terror. *Journal of Mind and Behavior, 11,* 545–556.

Coons, P. M. (1988). Misuse of forensic hypnosis: A hypnotically elicited false confession with the apparent creation of a multiple personality. *International Journal of Clinical and Experimental Hypnosis, 36,* 1–11.

Coons, P. M. (1994). Reports of satanic ritual abuse: Further implications about pseudomemories. *Perceptual and Motor Skills, 78,* 1376–1378.

Coons, P. M., & Grier, F. (1990). Factitious disorder (Munchausen type) involving allegations of ritual satanic abuse: A case report. *Dissociation, 3,* 177–178.

Emerson, M. D., & Boat, B. W. (1989). False allegations of sexual abuse by children and adolescents. *Journal of American Academy of Child and Adolescent Psychiatry, 28,* 230–235.

Emms, C. Z., McNeilly, C. L., Corkery, J. M., & Gilbert, M. S. (1995). The debate about delayed memories of child sexual abuse: A feminist perspective. *The Counseling Psychologist, 23,* 23–101.

Femina, D. D., Yeager, C. A., & Lewis, D. O. (1990). Child abuse: Adolescent records vs. adult recall. *Child Abuse and Neglect, 14,* 227–231.

Herman, J. L., & Shatzow, E. (1987). Recovery and verification of memories of childhood sexual trauma. *Psychoanalytic Psychology, 4,* 1–14.

Hicks, R. D. (1990). Police pursuit of satanic crime. *Skeptical Inquirer, 14,* 378–389.

Holmes, D. S. (1990). The evidence for repression: An examination of sixty years of research. In J. Singer (Ed.), *Repression and dissociation.* Chicago: University of Chicago Press.

Janet, P. (1898). *Neuroses et idees fixes* (vols. 1–2). Paris: Alcan.

Josephson, G. S., & Fong-Beyette, M. L. (1987). Factors assisting female clients' disclosure of incest during counseling. *Journal of Counseling and Development, 65,* 475–478.

Kampman, R. (1976). Hypnotically induced multiple personality: An experimental study. *International Journal of Clinical and Experimental Hypnosis, 24,* 215–227.

Lanning, K. V. (1992). A law enforcement perspective on allegations of ritual abuse. In D. Sackheim & S. Devine (Eds.), *Out of darkness: Exploring satanism and ritual abuse.* New York: Lexington Books.

Lindslay, D. S., & Read, J. D. (1994). Psychotherapy and memories of childhood sexual abuse: A cognitive perspective. *Applied Cognitive Psychology, 8,* 281–338.

Loftus, E. F. (1993). The reality of repressed memories. *American Psychologist, 48,* 518–537.

Loftus, E. F., & Coan, D. (in press). The construction of childhood memories. In D. Peters (Ed.), *The child witness in context: Cognitive, Social, and legal perspectives.* New York: Kluwer.

Loftus, E. F., Garry, M., & Feldman, J. (1994). Forgetting sexual trauma: What does it mean when 38% forget? *Journal of Consulting and Clinical Psychology, 62,* 1177–1181.

Loftus, E. F., Polonsky, S., & Fullilove, M. T. (1994). Memories of childhood sexual abuse: Remembering and repressing. *Psychology of Women Quarterly, 18,* 67–84.

Lotto, D. (1994). On witches and witch hunts: Ritual and satanic cult abuse. *Journal of Psychohistory, 21,* 373–396.

Mulhern, S. A. (1991). Satanism and psychotherapy: A rumor in search of an inquisition. In J. Richardson, J. Best, & D. Bromley (Eds.), *The satanism scare.* New York: Walter de Gruyter, 145–172.

Mulhern, S. A. (1992). Ritual abuse: Defining a syndrome versus defending a belief. *Journal of Psychology and Theology, 20,* 230–232.

Nurcombe, B., & Unutzer, J. (1991). The ritual abuse of children: Clinical features and diagnostic reasoning. *Journal of American Academy of Child and Adolescent Psychiatry, 30,* 272–276.

Ofshe, R. J. (1992). Inadvertent hypnosis during interrogation: False confession due to dissociative state; misidentified multiple personality and the satanic cult hypothesis. *International Journal of Clinical and Experimental Hypnosis, 40,* 123–156.

Olio, K. (1989). Memory retrieval in the treatment of adult survivors of sexual abuse. *Transactional Analysis Journal, 19,* 93–100.

Pendergast, M. (1995). *Victims of memory: Incest accusations and shattered lives.* Hinesburg, VT: Upper Access Books.

Perry, C., & Nogrady, H. (1985). Use of hypnosis by the police in the investigation of crime: Is guided imagery a safe substitute. *British Journal of Experimental and Clinical Hypnosis, 3,* 25–31.

Pope, K. S. (1996). Memory, abuse, and science: Questioning claims about false memory syndrome. *American Psychologist, 51,* 957–974.

Russell, D. E. (1983). The incidence and prevalence of intra familial and extra familial sexual abuse of female children. *Child Abuse and Neglect, 7,* 133–146.

Spanos, N. (1989). Hypnosis, demonic possession, and multiple personality: Strategic enactments and disavowals of responsibility for actions. In C. A. Ward (Ed.), *Altered states of consciousness and psychopathology.* Newbury Park, CA: Sage.

Spanos, N. P., Burgess, C. A., & Burgess, M. F. (1994). Past-life identities, UFO abductions, and satanic ritual abuse: The social construction of memories. *International Journal of Clinical and Experimental Hypnosis, 42,* 433–446.

Spanos, N. P., Cross, P., Dickson, K., & DuBreuil, S. C. (1993). Close encounters: An examination of UFO experiences. *Journal of Abnormal Psychology, 102,* 624–632.

Spanos, N. P., Menary, E., Gabora, N. J., DuBreuil, S. C., & Dewhirst, B. (1991). Secondary identity enactments during hypnotic past-life regression: A sociocognitive perspective. *Journal of Personality and Social Psychology, 61,* 308–320.

Spiegel, H. (1972). The grade five syndrome: The highly hypnotizable person. *International Journal of Clinical and Experimental Hypnosis, 22,* 303–319.

Stevens, P. (1991). The demonology of Satan: An anthropological view. In J. Richardson, J. Best, & D. Bromley (Eds.), *The satanism scare* (pp. 21–39). New York: Walter de Gruyter.

Stinson, M. & Hendrick, S. (1992). Reported childhood sexual abuse in university counseling center clients. *Journal of Counseling Psychology, 39,* 370–374.

Stratford, L. (1988). *Satan's underground.* Eugene, OR: Harvest House.

Usher, J. A., & Neisser, U. (1993). Childhood amnesia and the beginnings of memory for four early life events. *Journal of Experimental Psychology: General, 122,* 155–165.

Victor, J. (1989). A rumor-panic about a dangerous satanic cult in western New York. *New York Folklore, 15,* 23–49.

Victor, J. (1990). Satanic cult rumors as contemporary legend. *Western Folklore, 49,* 51–81.

Victor, J. (1991). Satanic cult "survivor" stories. *Skeptical Inquirer, 13,* 274–280.

Weinberg, S. K. (1955). *Incest behavior.* New York: Citadel.

Whitehouse, W. G., Orne, E. C., Orne, M. T., & Dinges, D. F. (1991). Distinguishing the source of memories reported during prior waking and hypnotic recall attempts. *Applied Cognitive Psychology, 5,* 51–59.

Williams, L. M. (1994a). Recall of childhood trauma: A prospective study of women's memories of child sexual abuse. *Journal of Consulting and Clinical Psychology, 62,* 1162–1186.

Williams, L. M. (1994b). What does it mean to forget child sexual abuse? A reply to Loftus, Garry, and Feldman (1994). *Journal of Consulting and Clinical Psychology, 62,* 1182–1176.

Wyatt, G. E. (1985). The sexual abuse of Afro-American and white-American women in childhood. *Childhood Abuse and Neglect, 9,* 507–519.

Yapko, M. (1994). *Suggestions of abuse.* New York: Simon & Schuster.

Young, W. C., Sachs, R. G., Braun, B. G., & Watkins, R. T. (1991). Patients reporting ritual abuse in childhood—A clinical syndrome: Report of 37 cases. *Child Abuse and Neglect, 15,* 181–189.

Critical Thinking and Writing

Learning Objectives

• To learn about how writing and critical thinking are related.

• To learn about effective approaches to writing.

• To learn how to think critically through writing answers to critical thinking essay questions, short term papers that critically review the research on a question, and introductions and literature reviews for a research report.

What Do You Think?

Do you think writing about an idea helps you to think more clearly about that idea? I have often had the impression that I thought more clearly about a question or idea after I had written about it, and I have heard other people say that they thought so, too. In fact, I posed this question informally to my colleagues in the psychology department and to my students. Read the following question I asked them and then indicate your opinion by circling the appropriate number.

In your experience, when you have written about an idea, did your writing about it help you to think more clearly about that idea?

Never   *Sometimes*   *Always*
1   –   –   2   –   –   3   –   –   4   –   –   5   –   –   6   –   –   7

How did you answer? I found wide agreement among the faculty, graduate students, and undergraduates that writing had helped them to think more clearly about some idea. The mean (arithmetic average) of all the groups was 5.84 with a standard deviation of 0.77. This result suggests that although they did not always find writing helpful, they did find it to help considerably more often than just sometimes.

Critical Thinking and Writing

Although it is informative to know that people believe writing helps them think more clearly, this does not mean that writing necessarily does improve people's thinking. Nisbett and Wilson (1977) found that people are often unaware of their own thinking processes as they answer a question like this one. We should look for evidence besides people's self-reports that writing improves thinking. In fact, there are many other good reasons to conclude that writing helps improve thinking, and it is to these reasons that we now turn.

How Writing Enhances Critical Thinking

One reason we might expect that writing would improve critical thinking is that for some kinds of writing tasks, such as persuasive or argumentative writing, the act of writing is very much like critical thinking itself. In **persuasive writing**, for example, the writer offers reasons to convince the reader of the merit of some idea or claim and often encourages the reader to draw some conclusion or to make some decision. In a persuasive essay, a writer should offer the best reasons available to support a position on a question so the reader will draw some favored conclusion. This effort is like what the critical thinker does—that is, gather and evaluate the evidence relevant to a claim. Too often, however, persuasive essay writers focus almost solely on the evidence favoring their position and do not seriously examine counterarguments and negative evidence. Critical thinking involves evaluating all the relevant evidence on *all* sides of a question in order to draw a sound conclusion. So, to write a **critical essay,** the writer gathers and organizes the evidence relevant to all sides of the question, evaluates that evidence, including counterarguments, and then is led to and writes a conclusion consistent with the evidence. This is critical thinking, in the form of writing.

Another reason critical thinking and writing are often closely related has been stated by researchers and others working in the area. Several have argued that the processes involved in critical thinking are similar to those involved in scientific and rational writing (e.g., Langer & Applebee, 1987; Nickerson, Perkins, & Smith, 1985). Both involve manipulating language, focusing on a specific question, planning and organizing evidence, evaluating evidence critically, and communicating arguments effectively. Even revising your written work involves a critical evaluation of what you have written (Glathorn, 1985).

Many people, such as teachers, who evaluate other people by means of their writing, take good writing to indicate good thinking. For example, the forms that college teachers complete for recommending their undergraduate students to graduate programs frequently ask them to evaluate their students' communication and writing skills. I suspect that, like myself, most instructors take a student's clearly written paper as an indication of the student's clear thinking. Similarly, getting hired for a job sometimes requires that job applicants offer good reasons in writing why an employer should hire them. What is judged to be a clearly written and reasonable application may suggest that the applicant is capable of clear and reasonable thinking.

Unfortunately, the results of large-scale assessments of students' ability to think critically through writing suggest that the U.S. educational system may not be adequately preparing its students (e.g., Langer & Applebee, 1987; National Assessment of Educational Progress, 1986). Fortunately, other research evidence suggests that critical thinking can be improved through special writing assignments (e.g., Bensley & Haynes, 1995; Roussey & Gombert, 1996; Scardamalia, Bereiter, & Steinbach, 1984).

You too may have observed the connection between your writing and thinking when you experienced difficulties in thinking while trying to do a writing assignment. For example, perhaps after writing a response to an essay question you have said something like this: "I wish I knew if I were answering this question right. I know the material, but I'm not sure how to answer. What kind of an answer is my instructor looking for, anyway?" On several occasions, I have heard students make comments such as these. In fact, your uncertainty about whether you are writing and thinking effectively is, in a way, a good sign. It means you have been thinking about your own thinking and monitoring its effectiveness. In other words, you have been metacognitive, or aware of your own thought processes, and are trying to evaluate them relative to a standard. In this case, you may need to become more aware of what the standards for good writing are. Becoming aware of your thinking in your writing is an important way in which writing can help make your thinking become more effective (McGuinness, 1990; Swartz, 1989).

Writing can be an excellent tool for you to improve your thinking because it allows you to externalize and make visible the usually invisible process of thinking. By reflecting on the arguments you have made in your own writing, you may be able to revise them, strengthen them, and make them clearer. In other words, you can actually see your thinking improve as you improve your writing. We will return to this idea shortly when we discuss revision, but now it would be useful to review what you probably already know about writing so that your critical writing skills can be developed in new ways.

Using What You Know to Write Critically

This section reviews what you know about writing to help you learn some special features of critical writing. First, you should keep in mind your **purpose** for writing. As you probably realize, writing can have several purposes: to describe, inform, entertain, explain, persuade. Common purposes in critical writing are to analyze, evaluate, interpret, and persuade. The important idea here is that your purpose in writing should determine, in part, both what information you include and how you structure your writing. In a later section, you will see that in critical writing tasks, such as responding to an essay question, your specific purpose and approach will be determined by whether the question asks you to explain, to analyze, or to respond to some other kind of question.

Another issue related to good critical writing of which you may already be aware is the need to keep your audience in mind as you write. The **audience** is the intended reader of your critical writing. It is often difficult to know what to include and what not to include in writing. In general, you should be able to assume your reader has some basic knowledge of psychological terminology and concepts. For example, in writing an essay on the question of whether people are basically selfish you would not typically need to define the term *psychology;* however, you might need to define some basic terms in social psychology, such as *prosocial behavior* and *altruism*. In general, you should define the most important terms relevant to the specific question you are trying to answer. When you are writing, you should keep in mind that you are asking the reader to think with you. You should ask yourself, "What do I need to tell the reader so that the reader can follow my thinking and line of reasoning?" If you are writing a response to a critical thinking writing assignment, then your audience is your instructor. Even though you can assume your instructor has more familiarity with the subject area than you do, you need to make it clear to the instructor that you are familiar with the ideas related to your question.

You should also attempt to use the relevant psychological terminology and concepts appropriately, avoiding everyday terminology for psychological terms, so that your instructor can understand your discussion as one based on the science of psychology. Often, you will need to define your terms carefully at the outset of your paper, beginning with the way these terms are typically defined in your textbook or in the literature, in order to make effective arguments. Of course, if you are writing a literature review for an article or for a scientific research report to be submitted for publication, then you can assume that your audience will have greater expertise in the subject area, since your readers will likely be people knowledgeable in the specific area of psychology related to your research report. Similarly, as you move to higher-level psychology courses, your questions will become more specifically focused and you will define fewer basic terms and more higher-level terms related to your question.

Another consideration in effective writing of which you may already be aware is tone. **Tone** is the style and approach an author takes in presenting ideas. In critical writing on psychology questions, your tone should be objective and generally serious—that is, more formal than informal (Cavender & Weiss, 1987). Although occasionally I have been amused by a student joke in a writing assignment, it is a tricky thing to tell a joke that is relevant and really adds to the discussion. Most of the time, the joke simply detracts from the rest of the discussion, taking valuable space away from more important ideas and evidence. In a similar vein, personal anecdotes may contribute to illustrating a point, but they should not be taken necessarily as good evidence upon which to draw a conclusion, as noted in Chapter 2.

You should also use what you know about **organization** to make a more coherent and readable text. You can communicate your arguments more effectively if you present them using conventional formal organization, such as good sentence and paragraph organization. Because you are probably already familiar with this, we will discuss it only briefly before moving on to constructing the plans for critical writing. Beyond the simplest level of individual words, the most basic structural unit of your paper is the sentence. Make sure that you have both a subject and a verb in all your sentences. At the next level, your sentences should be organized into paragraph form. Write a topic sentence to begin each paragraph that presents one basic idea or main point (Cavender & Weiss, 1987). Every sentence in the paragraph should be related to the topic sentence. At the next level of organization, use transition words to connect ideas from paragraph to paragraph. For example, one paragraph might begin, "Early research showed that . . ."; a later paragraph might start out, "More recent research found that . . ."

Most important, you should develop a conceptual plan for developing arguments in your critical writing. Plans have been shown to be an important part of successful writing (Flower & Hayes, 1981; Hayes, 1989). Making plans for your writing requires your thinking about your question and your reasoning to be focused. As you begin the discussion, you tell the reader what question you are focusing on and how you are going to discuss it. In other words, you tell the reader the plan for your discussion, which helps you to organize it. In the next part of your discussion, you present your analysis or the evidence related to the various sides of the question.

Just as the sentence and paragraph are basic units of organization at the formal level, the argument and extended argument are the basic units for organizing your critical writing discussion at the more conceptual level. Of course, any argument you make must be composed of an assertion and the relevant evidence that is presented with it. You must decide what your main argument is and whether you will make any less important but related arguments. For example, in the critical reading passage in Chapter 3 about whether people are basically selfish, the main argument was that people are basically selfish and that they will only help if they stand to gain in some way. A subordinate argument was that people behave the way they do, not just because of a trait that they have, but also because of something that happens in the situation. In this case people will help not just because of the tendency to be selfish or unselfish but because of the possibility of getting a reward for helping. This subordinate argument, that people help not just because of their trait but also because of the details of the situation, supports the main argument that people help when they stand to gain something and so is also a counterargument.

Clearly, arguments like these can become quite complex. Sometimes, subordinate arguments are part of long strings of arguments that are related to or support a general conclusion. To keep all these parts organized, it may help you to outline your arguments before you write a draft. You may wish to organize the relevant evidence into two categories, one for evidence supporting a position and one for evidence not supporting a position, as you plan how to write your discussion of the question.

Paying Attention to Both Process and Product

Much research on composition suggests that emphasizing process in writing is important to improving people's writing (e.g., Applebee, 1986; Hayes & Flower, 1986; Hillocks, 1986). Process is the change or changes involved in moving from one state to another. Rather than treating a writing assignment as a single task, a **process approach** breaks the entire task of composing a final draft into a number of subprocesses or stages. This breakdown is useful because it makes the process leading to the final product more manageable. Research suggests that writing is a complex, effortful task that is a bit like juggling (Hayes, 1989) and that critical and persuasive writing may be even more effortful than other kinds of writing (Kellog, 1992). Consequently, to help people learn how to do this complex task, it should be useful to divide the task up into smaller, more manageable components.

Frequently, composition teachers divide the writing task into three stages: prewriting, drafting, and revising. While this ordering of the three stages is convenient for discussing the process of writing, you should not assume that these three stages are necessarily sequential. To help you learn how to manage your own critical writing, when possible this chapter breaks writing assignments down into manageable parts, encouraging you to take a process approach to your writing. Now, let's examine more closely what's involved in each of these stages in the writing process.

Prewriting involves finding out about your topic, focusing on a question, planning, and organizing the information before you write. Students generally have trouble focusing on a question (Marzano et al., 1988). One of the best things you can do to narrow down your approach to a question, refining it and making it more specific, is to read and think about the question. Students also have trouble with planning in their writing. Even though planning has been shown to be correlated with quality of writing (Hayes, 1989), unskilled college student writers engage in little high-level planning before they write (Perl, 1979). If you do not form adequate, well-elaborated plans before you write, it may be that your previous educational experiences failed to provide you with both the opportunity and the means for developing such plans. In this chapter, you will be given sample plans and strategies for doing critical writing assignments in the form of an outline, writing objectives, and samples of well-written assignments.

What is traditionally thought to be the next step in the writing process, drafting, involves making an actual attempt at writing the essay, term paper, or other written product. You should concentrate on getting the ideas from your prewriting, such as notes from research you have done, onto paper. The important thing is to get your ideas down in an organized fashion, not to worry at this point about the best possible wording of your ideas.

Revision, the next important component of the critical writing process, means different things to different people. In the traditional view, the act of **revision** involves making corrections, sometimes substantial ones, to a draft. More modern, process views of revision assume that revision can go on at any stage of writing. Research on revision in writing also suggests that when given the opportunity to revise, students frequently make small cosmetic changes, such as changing a word or sentence, rather than making more substantial changes in the organization of their writing (Fitzgerald, 1987). In contrast, expert writers are much more likely than novice writers like students are to reorganize presentation of ideas when revising a draft (Scardamalia & Bereiter, 1991). Revision presents you with the opportunity not only to fine-tune the communication of your ideas, but also to reorganize your writing and even to restructure your thinking. Consequently, I would strongly urge you to revise drafts of your writing, trying to better understand and reorganize the ideas you are trying to communicate. You can do this even if your instructor requires you only to submit one draft for an assignment.

While taking a process approach is important to improving your writing, keeping writing objectives and goals in mind as you write is also important. Hillocks (1984), who reviewed the literature investigating what makes writing instruction effective, found that when combined with product guidelines, a process approach improved writing more than the process approach did by itself. **Product guidelines** are goals and objectives that the writer keeps in mind and tries to take into account in his or her writing. In other words, they are targets for the final form and content of your written products. So, in addition to taking a process approach, the writing assignments described in this chapter also emphasize your seeking to attain specific writing objectives that should help make what you write even better. You will find these objectives in the following three forms in this chapter: (1) suggestions for things to keep in mind when writing an answer to an essay question; (2) a suggested general outline format to organize the final draft of the short term paper; and (3) objectives found in the checklist for writing the introduction to a research report. You should be aware of these goals even as you begin to write, but most important, make sure you reach these goals in your final draft.

Critical Thinking and Essay Questions

Frequently, we are called upon to compose a written response to a question posed to us, such as a response to an essay question. Instructors ask essay questions because they value written communication, and they realize that a written essay response provides a special window into student thinking. From your perspective as a student, you can use your writing to examine and reflect upon your own thinking and to show your instructor that you know how to think using the psychological concepts you have been studying.

When writing an effective essay response, the writer uses relevant knowledge to discuss a specific question. Writing critical essays involves discussing evidence relevant to the various sides of a question and often persuading the audience that one position is better than another.

As mentioned previously, critical writing is actually a very complex process. Similarly, writing a response to an essay question really involves a number of steps. These steps include identifying the kind of essay question being asked; prewriting tasks such as gathering and organizing the evidence relevant to the question; planning how to present your evidence and ideas; and actually writing or drafting a written response. We will discuss each of these steps in turn.

Kinds of Essay Questions

First, the writer must **focus** on the question, which helps the reader follow the writer's reasoning. Focusing on the question involves identifying any claims made or implied by the question. It also involves deciding on the kind of approach to take in answering the question. In order to focus correctly on the question to be answered, one must read the question carefully through and look for clues as to the form of response and the kind of thinking the instructor is seeking. As noted by Stiggins, Rubel, and Quellmalz (1988), instructors asking essay questions commonly assess six important thinking abilities of students: (1) knowledge, (2) comprehension, (3) application, (4) analysis, (5) synthesis, and (6) evaluation. Each of these types of essay questions will be discussed in turn along with the words that often signal such a question and the approach to take in answering each.

If an essay question is intended to assess your **knowledge,** then your instructor is asking mostly what you remember pertaining to the question. Words like *list, describe, name, define, identify, who, what,* and *when* suggest that the instructor is trying to see what you can recall of the content you studied.

Similarly, a **comprehension** essay question asks you to remember content pertinent to the question, but also to show that you understand what it is that you remember. Words like *paraphrase, summarize, explain, review, discuss, interpret, how,* and *why* are clues that the essay question is a comprehension question. In general, knowledge and comprehension essay questions require mostly memory of the material and little in the way of critical thinking. But beware. Suppose you are asked the following question: "Explain why the 'dopamine hypothesis' is the best explanation of schizophrenia." To answer the question adequately, you may have to do much more than simply recall and understand the dopamine hypothesis. Besides knowing that dopamine is a chemical messenger found in excess in the brains of schizophrenics and that this excess may lead to schizophrenic hallucinations and delusions, you must also be able to compare and evaluate the effectiveness of the dopamine hypothesis as against other hypotheses used to explain schizophrenia.

Other questions require **application;** these questions also require that we go beyond simple recall and understanding to use the knowledge we have. Words like *apply, construct, simulate, employ, predict,* and *show how* are clues that a concept should be applied. For example: "Predict what would happen if a schizophrenic did not take his antipsychotic medication based on what you know about the dopamine hypothesis."

Another type of essay question requires **analysis.** These analysis questions require that something be broken down into component parts so that it can be better understood. Words like *classify, distinguish, differentiate, compare, contrast, categorize,* and *break down* are clues that analysis is called for. For example: "Differentiate cognitive development into as many different stages as you think are appropriate to explain it." In this case, the instructor is probably trying to find out whether you understand the changes in cognitive development overall and can break the process down into separate stages. Analysis is often used in critical thinking. For example, we analyze a phenomenon into cause and effect, distinguish between two concepts to clarify an argument, or compare two positions on a question.

Answers to **synthesis** questions require you to bring together different knowledge or concepts in a unified response. Words that provide clues that this kind of a response is needed include *combine, relate, put together,* and *integrate.* For example: "Combine what you know about stress and health and then briefly describe the kinds of behaviors that increase stress and threaten health." Synthesis is used in critical thinking when we must integrate information in order to draw a single conclusion.

The last type of essay question requires **evaluation.** In evaluation questions, you must make a judgment about whether something is good or bad. Frequently, some kind of evidence must be evaluated as the basis for a judgment. So evaluation is closely related to critical thinking. We can see this in the overlap of some of the language of argumentation and words that signal evaluation, such as *judge, argue, assess, appraise, decide, defend, debate, evaluate,* and *choose.* For example: "Decide whether you think people who watch violence on television are more likely to behave aggressively than those who do not."

≋ PRACTICE YOUR THINKING 14.1

Identifying Kinds of Questions

Students frequently go wrong in answering essay questions when they fail to identify or do not pay attention to the kind of question being asked. They may not read the question carefully, or they may not know what kind of answer is indicated by the clues in the question. As a result, they fail to organize their response around the appropriate purpose for writing and then do not include the appropriate reasons, evidence, and other information that would appropriately respond to the request for writing. To help you avoid these kinds of problems, practice identifying what kind of response is being sought in each of the following essay questions: knowledge, comprehension, application, analysis, synthesis, or evaluation.

1. Differentiate between the way in which the eye and ear transduce energy—that is, convert physical energy from the environment into neural signals.
2. Describe the basic characteristics of short-term memory.
3. Summarize the process of how a nerve impulse is transmitted from one nerve cell to another.
4. Compare and contrast some basic differences between classical and instrumental conditioning.
5. Show how you could use what you have learned about memory to advise a student on how to study for an essay test. What would you tell the student to do?
6. Decide whether the following statement is true: "Positive reinforcement is the best way to motivate people." Explain your conclusion.
7. Relate the assumptions of psychoanalysis to the use of projective tests in assessment of personality and psychological problems.

Answers to Identifying Kinds of Questions

1. analysis
2. knowledge
3. comprehension
4. analysis and synthesis
5. application
6. evaluation
7. synthesis and application

≋ PRACTICE YOUR THINKING 14.2

Analyzing an Essay Response

Now, let's examine an essay question response to see whether the writer succeeded in correctly identifying the kind of question and in providing the appropriate information in response. Let's assume that Lenny, a college student, has written the following brief essay to answer the following question: "Decide whether you think people who watch violence on television are more likely to behave aggressively than those who do not." What do you think of how Lenny answered the question? Critically analyze his response based on what you know about argumentation and the different kinds of essay questions.

> Aggression is a behavior or pattern of behavior in which someone deliberately tries to inflict injury on another person, either verbal or physical injury. It is a growing problem in our nation. Gangs roam the streets and commit murders over drugs. People engage in countless violent crimes in the movies and on television. Also, children play with guns and pretend they are shooting each other. Children see these acts of violence on television, in the movies, and in the media.
>
> Some of the murders are just crazy, such as the senseless "drive-by" shootings that don't seem to have a purpose. Other acts of aggression are for a purpose, such as when a person shoots a clerk at a convenience store to rob the store, and these acts are called instrumental aggression. Other acts of aggression are motivated out of strong emotions, such as anger; this is called affective aggression. In conclusion, someone should do something about all the violence on television and in the media to reduce the rate of violent crime.

Answer to Analyzing an Essay Response

Lenny included some correct information in his essay, but you probably found many problems with the essay. For example, Lenny's use of the word *crazy* is not appropriate for a scientifically trained audience. But his main problem may be that he has failed to realize that this essay question was calling for an evaluative response; the question called for a response setting out evidence that could provide the basis for a decision. Lenny failed to provide this kind of evaluative answer. For example, he began by defining aggression, and he mentioned many observations related to aggression, but then he did not use the definition to build an evaluative answer. Later, with even less relevance to the question, he defined instrumental and affective aggression. In so doing he failed to focus on the question. His response comes closer to answering a different kind of question—namely, a knowledge question that asks you to define something. Even if the question were of that type, Lenny recalled few specific facts and details related to the question. The clue word in the question is *decide,* but Lenny did not even assert a connection between TV violence and aggressiveness in order to make a decision about the truth of the claim. He merely mentioned that there is a lot of violence in the media. In a separate sentence, he wrote that children watch this violence. At the end he wrote, "In conclusion, someone should do something about all the violence on television and in the media to reduce the rate of violent crime." This conclusion does not follow from the evidence Lenny presented, since he provided almost no evidence for the claim that viewing violence in the media leads to aggressive behavior.

In order to decide this question, Lenny should have presented evidence relevant to the question. Let's see how this is done in the following, more successful, essay response that appropriately responds to the request for an evaluative response.

> An important social question facing our country today is whether or not viewing violence on TV or in the movies makes a person likely to engage in aggression. There is much evidence to support the claim that violence viewed on television

or in the movies leads to aggressive behavior. There are many real-life examples of this connection. For example, Geen reported that three people, who repeatedly watched *Magnum Force,* a movie in which criminals forced other people to swallow a caustic solution like Drano, subsequently committed their own murders forcing their own victims to drink the substance. Also, I have noticed that after watching Saturday morning cartoons with aggressive scenes that my little brother will get up during commercials, run crazily around the house, and even hit his sister.

Stronger evidence for the effect of observed violence on later aggressive behavior comes from many experiments. In an early experiment, Bandura and his colleagues found that children who were shown an adult model beating up on a "Bobo" doll were more likely to later engage in aggressive behaviors than were a group who did not see the adults playing aggressively with the doll. Many other experiments have found the same type of effect, even when a person does not directly observe another person modeling the aggressive behavior but only sees it on television. While occasionally a study does not obtain these results, most of the studies have.

Other research has shown that children and people who prefer to watch violent television are the most vulnerable to the effects of violence on TV. Also, because other studies have shown that children watch many hours of TV per week and many programs have several acts of violence on each episode, this puts the nation's youngsters at risk. With all the violence in the media, it is not surprising that our country has such a severe problem with violent crime. In conclusion, there is much evidence to show that watching violence on TV or in the movies leads to later aggression in those viewing it, while little evidence contradicts this.

Notice how the writer of this second essay followed good argumentative form and succeeded in answering the evaluative question posed. The writer first introduces the question. Then, she presented different kinds of relevant evidence in support of the claim. The writer stated that little evidence supports the position that viewing violence does not lead to aggression. She made it clear that this is a real problem because people view so much violent television. She concluded that watching aggressive acts can lead to increases in aggression, and she stated the implication of this conclusion for the present social situation.

Notice too, that the essay used words from the language of argumentation found in Appendix A. Words such as *question, claim, evidence, support,* and *conclusion* signaled important parts of the argument. Also, words such as *example, studies, research, experiment, found,* and *effect* described the evidence used to evaluate the claim. When an important study or expert's idea was mentioned, the name of the principal investigator or expert was also given, making these ideas more credible as evidence. You are encouraged to use this language in your own essays because it helps to communicate your arguments more effectively. This kind of language, used correctly, tends to make your arguments more persuasive.

Preparing to Answer an Essay Question

Of course, the ideal situation for preparing to answer an essay question is to know the question in advance. If your instructor gives you your question in advance, even when you have to write your answer in class, then you will have time to find the relevant information you need and to organize the points you want to make.

First, you must focus on the kind of question that you are asked to answer so that you will gather the appropriate information to answer it. For example, if it is a knowledge question, then you must collect factual and other relevant information to demonstrate your knowledge. If it is an evaluative question, however, then you will need to gather evidence and other information that allow some decision to be made or conclusion to be drawn.

Information for answering an essay question will most likely come from your textbook, your class or lecture notes, or both. What would happen if (1) you take notes in class that are not detailed enough to provide the relevant facts and reasons you need for an essay response, (2) this information is not found in your textbook, and (3) your instructor asks you an essay question on that material? Most likely, you would not be able to write a good essay response, because you would not be able to find the relevant information and then organize it.

Organizing the relevant information and evidence beforehand can help you come up with an effective plan. You can organize by making lists of related ideas, clustering relevant ideas into categories or assigning them to one or another side of an argument. For example, dividing the evidence into two categories—such as evidence supporting a position and evidence not supporting a position—may be a useful prewriting strategy for you. Also, outlining this information can help you present the information coherently and persuasively. (See the discussion later in this chapter on writing a short term paper for more information on outlining.)

Writing the Response

Some students think that if they do not know the essay question in advance, then there is no need for them to organize the information before they begin writing their in-class essay, as noted by Bond and Magistrale (1987). On the contrary, students in this situation should take a few moments to organize the relevant information in their minds, or on paper if possible, and then begin to write. These few moments of organization and planning are well worth the time spent in terms of the coherence and effective flow of ideas in your essay response. Even though you may not know the essay question in advance, it is often possible to anticipate the subset of questions that your instructor might ask from studying your text or lecture notes and to prepare for some possible questions. This kind of prewriting activity can pay off well, especially when you have limited time to respond in an in-class essay exam.

Also keep the other considerations we have discussed in mind as you write your essay response. Focus your response with the specific purpose for writing in mind, and try to use complete sentences, coherent paragraphs, and clarity in writing your response.

A Short Term Paper That Reviews the Literature

The purpose of the short term paper assignment is to help you learn how to examine critically a very specific question in psychology. State your topic in the form of a question to be answered or a problem to be solved. Develop a discussion that takes alternative positions, opposite sides, or differing viewpoints and presents relevant evidence in support of each position. Finally, evaluate the relative amounts and quality of the evidence for and against each side of the argument in order to draw a sound conclusion about the question.

The literature review for the short term paper assignment is similar to but also differs in important ways from those published in psychology books and journals. Like the reviews in the critical reading passages of this book, the short term paper should present the evidence on various sides of an argument and then evaluate the evidence, drawing a sound conclusion from it. The short term paper differs from published reviews in that published reviews often have very extensive treatment of the evidence relevant to the question under discussion. A good inductive argument should take into account all the relevant evidence. Sometimes an author does an exhaustive review of the literature, citing all the relevant studies—perhaps from 50 to 100 of them. More commonly, however, the author will carry out a selective review, in which the relevant literature is sampled. A selective review should include studies that represent all the relevant and important aspects of the question and sides of the argument in an even-handed way. Obviously, for the short term paper you must do a rather selective literature review; it may be difficult to know whether you have included studies that are representative of all sides of the question. For help, try to find good literature reviews on your question in the literature. They can help you recognize the various controversies related to your question and will even help you to organize and summarize the research evidence.

Writing the Short Term Paper in Three Stages

Consistent with the process approach, the writing of the short term paper can be conveniently divided into three stages. If you follow the instructions for the stages conscientiously, you should end up with a much better paper than had you written the paper all at once. Remember, even if your instructor does not break the assignment of the paper into three stages, you can. The three stages of the short term paper assignment are these:

1. Focusing on a specific question.
2. Organization of relevant information and focused free writing.
3. Writing a final draft and outline that follow product guidelines.

Stage 1: Focusing on a Specific Question

Since your first objective is to find a specific question, you should begin by picking a topic or question you are interested in. Perhaps you will begin with a question you were curious about that motivated you to take a psychology course in the first place. Perhaps a question that you covered in class intrigued you. If neither of these prompts has brought an interesting question to mind, you might browse through your general psychology textbook or another psychology book, looking for a topic that catches your interest.

Once you have found a topical area of interest or a general question, you need to focus that question so that it does not cover too broad a subject area for a short term paper. (Consult with your instructor about the appropriate length and other details of your paper.) Think of your paper as discussing and answering a very specific, well-defined question. For example, the question of how dreams differ from normal waking consciousness is too broad; it could be replaced by the more specific question whether nightmares are different from other dreams. Similarly, the question "What are the causes and treatments of depression?" is too broad and could be replaced by the more specific "What is the primary cause of major depression?" You may be surprised at how focused your question must be in order to discuss it adequately in a short paper. One thing you will probably discover in searching for a specific question is just how broad and extensive our research knowledge base in psychology is.

As you try to focus on a specific question, it is common to have feelings of confusion and a lack of clarity. One of the best ways to reduce this uncertainty is to find information on your topic and read it. Take notes on ideas that seem relevant to your question and study these notes. You will get more focused as you read and learn more. Look at the kinds of questions other people have asked in your area of interest. Discussions in psychology books are often organized around questions. Sometimes, if you try to explain your idea for a question to someone else, this will help you clarify and focus, too. Make sure that the question you decide on lends itself to critical evaluation. For example, a definitional question like "What is intelligence?" could be answered by recalling and elaborating a definition of intelligence. The more specific question "Is there only one kind of intelligence?" would better lead to a discussion in which evidence is raised and evaluated for one position versus another.

Lastly, you should not assume that focusing on your question is a process that stops as you move into the second stage. Rather, you should find that you will become more and more focused even as you write your final draft.

Stage 2: Organization and Focused Free Writing

The purpose of the second stage is to help you organize the information that is going into your paper. It may be useful to put your notes from your reading on notecards. In particular, this makes it easy to organize the evidence you have obtained for one side of the argument or the other by simply separating the cards for the different positions into groups. Then you should copy down this organized evidence under two or more separate headings, such as evidence supporting the claim and evidence against the claim. Study this evidence and think about how it pertains to your question. Make sure that you have a reference to the source of your information and evidence listed on your notecards, because you will need to cite these references in your paper.

After you have organized your evidence, you should think about how to discuss this evidence in your paper. It often helps to create an outline for your paper. An outline can help you plan your paper, giving you an overview of how to organize the major points without having to write it all out. This overview makes it easier to move ideas around in your paper. Keeping your outline in mind as you write can also help you stay focused on your question and the arguments you are making. You should not think of your outline as something carved in stone, but rather as a working outline, to be modified as needed. Use it as a tool to refine your discussion, and change it as you think of better ways to focus your question, to present and evaluate relevant evidence, and to draw a sound conclusion from the evidence.

Another tool for helping you focus your discussion of the question is **focused free writing.** If you have difficulty focusing and organizing your information, it often helps to do some writing. Just begin writing on your topic and try to answer the question you have raised. It is important to get the ideas down. Double space your focused free writing, and use large margins. This makes it easier for you or someone else to write in comments and suggestions for revisions. If possible, do your writing on a word processor, since it is so much easier to make changes on the computer.

After you have written at least three pages, put it aside for a day or two and approach it in a new way. Go back and read it as if it were someone else's writing. Analyze your writing as described in the critical reading exercises from previous chapters of this book. What is your question and the claim it is addressing? Underline it in your draft. If you have not stated this clearly, how can you rewrite it so that it is clear? Identify the evidence you have included and put brackets around each bit of evidence that you are including. Have you used all the evidence that is relevant to the question? Compare this to your list of organized evidence. If not, insert notes saying where this evidence should go in your focused free writing draft and working outline.

Recall that to draw a sound conclusion from an evaluation of the evidence, you need to analyze both the quality and quantity of the evidence supporting the different sides of the question. Inspect the kinds and amounts of evidence you labeled in your list of organized evidence and in your focused free writing. Evaluate this evidence, draw a conclusion consistent with the evidence, and then write this conclusion in your focused free writing draft. Perhaps there is little agreement on your question, and the evidence does not favor one position over another. If so, then this would be your conclusion after you review the evidence. Many questions in psychology do not lend themselves to firm conclusions.

Stage 3: Final Draft and Product Guidelines

For your final draft, you should refer to and try to keep in mind a number of objectives that should make your paper even better. These are written in the form of suggestions for a general outline format and objectives for the final draft.

Outline

Your working outline may have already started to look like the following outline format. Your final outline should incorporate the basic features of the following outline structure in a general way. In other words, it should be moving toward this basic kind of structure; the details of your outline will be specific to the content of your paper. Notice that the following outline structure incorporates important parts of the working definition of critical thinking introduced in Chapter 1 and used throughout the book: critical thinking is reflective thinking involving the evaluation of evidence relevant to a claim so that a sound conclusion can be drawn.

1. Introduction of the basic problem or question
   a. Purpose in writing the paper
   b. How the problem is to be discussed in the paper
   c. Definition of relevant terms
2. Development of the discussion of the problem
   a. Evidence for an idea, position, or claim
      (1) Specific evidence
      (2) Other specific evidence
   b. Evidence against an idea, position, or claim
      (1) Specific evidence
      (2) Other specific evidence
3. Conclusion
   a. Review and summary of main points of the discussion
   b. Evaluation of the evidence or main points of the discussion and conclusion about the question

This outline can be especially effective for making an inductive argument in which you reason from specific bits of evidence to a general conclusion.

Other Product Guidelines for the Short Term Paper

1. The paper should stay focused on the topic and not stray from the chosen question. Develop only closely related ideas.

2. The paper should be well organized. For example, the question or problem is introduced in the first paragraph with mention of the purpose of the paper and an overview of what your discussion will concern. A brief concluding paragraph should summarize the problem discussed, evaluating the arguments you presented earlier.

3. Use the language of argumentation found in Appendix A to signal to the reader what kind of information you are providing and the important parts of your arguments and discussion.

4. Use the psychological terminology correctly in discussing your question.

5. Cite ideas that are supported by research evidence, the statement of authorities, and other sources of evidence. Note that you should cite and reference any idea that is not yours. The *Publication Manual of the American Psychological Association* (1994) gives several options for citations, such as "Hillocks (1986) found . . ." or "It has been claimed by Hillocks (1986) . . ."

6. Your paper should include as many references as needed to represent all positions and evidence relevant to a question. Using references is one way we say where our evidence came from. Journal articles and information from a specialized psychology book are good sources and kinds of evidence. Your references must be listed at the end of the paper. You can use the reference section in this book as a model for writing your own references. Note that you should not use *Time*, *Newsweek*, or other popular magazines as sources unless they are being used to document a relevant news item.

7. Typing your paper in double-spaced form makes your paper look more like a professional product and allows someone else to make critical comments on it.

8. Your final draft should show considerable changes and revisions as compared to your initial draft. To check whether you have made all the changes you intended, you might make a copy of what you think is your final draft, underlining or highlighting your changes. Compare this to your earlier drafts, outline, and the comments on your earlier writing to make sure that you have made all needed changes.

Writing the Introduction to a Research Report

The purpose of a research report is to communicate to a scientifically trained audience about research that was done on a specific question. In a research report, the specific question is investigated through testing a hypothesis. Each part of the research report serves to report a different aspect of the test of the hypothesis. Specifically, the introduction should justify why the hypothesis needs to be tested. The method section describes in detail the method used to test the hypothesis. The results section examines the results of statistical analysis of the hypothesis test. Finally, the discussion section interprets the results of the test of the hypothesis.

This chapter focuses on writing the introduction—that is, providing a justification and context for a particular test of a hypothesis. You should try to use what you have learned from this book about critically reading literature reviews to help you write your introduction. To help you use what you already know, we will examine the introduction to a research report that discusses and proposes an experiment designed to investigate helping behavior. You are already familiar with some of the social psychology literature on helping from our discussion in Chapter 3 of whether people are basically selfish. From that discussion, we learned that people help, not just because they have the trait of altruism, but also because of a number of situational details, such as whether they receive a reward for helping and whether they observe a model who has helped.

In the sample introduction presented in this chapter, we examine one of these factors—that is, the effect of observing a helping model on subsequent helping behavior. One way this sample introduction differs from literature reviews like the one in Chapter 3 is that the literature review for a research report examines a question in order to propose research that will help to answer the question. The sample literature review presented in this chapter identifies a specific question that remains unanswered in the research, tries to isolate what it would take to answer the question, and then justifies the need for a specific study designed to help answer the question. To do this, the sample introduction proposes the test of at least one very specific hypothesis. Whenever possible, the research hypothesis should be derived from a theory directly related to your research question. Recall from Chapter 1 that predictions and hypotheses often are deduced from the relevant theory.

In order to understand the relevant theories, hypotheses, and research related to the research question, you should write a brief historical review of the relevant literature—that is, a selective but representative survey of the research and thinking about the question, from the earliest research to the most recent. You should focus on the need for a particular research project. The introduction should provide the context for understanding what is known and not known in the research literature about the question. In particular, the introduction provides an extended argument that justifies why it was necessary to conduct the particular test of the hypothesis that was conducted. The introduction does not neglect research findings and theories that are inconsistent with the hypothesis tested and described in the research report, however. Rather, you should seek to resolve and understand such discrepancies. In fact, the purpose of the research described is often to test a hypothesis that will help resolve some controversy in the literature regarding previous findings and the theories used to explain them.

So that the reader can understand why you conducted the particular test of the hypothesis, you should explicitly state the purpose of your research project early in the introduction. Common purposes for doing an experiment are (1) to replicate previous studies (which can add support to a hypothesis or theory); (2) to propose a test to resolve a controversy in the literature concerning some hypothesis or theory; and (3) to propose a different kind of test to find out something new about the hypothesis or theory. In any of these cases, your literature review should be relevant to the question and provide a rationale for the specific test of the hypothesis.

As you discuss the relevant literature, you should try to evaluate it critically. You should make comments about problems with other research on your question, especially commenting on limitations in the research relevant to the specific form of the hypothesis you are testing. You should also make positive comments on research methods and approaches that have been productive in helping to answer your question, especially methods and approaches related to your test of the hypothesis.

When you plan and write your introduction, you may find it useful to think of your literature review as like a funnel. As you review more and more of the literature, your question should become narrower and narrower, increasingly well defined, so that by the end of your literature review it should be obvious what hypothesis needs to be tested. Even though it should be obvious, you should still explicitly state the hypothesis you are testing, for added clarity.

Your hypothesis should be stated in "if . . . then" form, or as a prediction based upon a theory. The statement of your hypothesis can also serve to briefly introduce the basic method you used in testing your hypothesis. For example, suppose you are testing the "total time hypothesis" of memory, which states that how well a person remembers depends on the total amount of time the person spent studying. In "if . . . then" form, you might make the following prediction: "If one group of subjects studied a list of words for two minutes and another for only one minute, then the group studying longer should recall more words." Another form of this prediction invokes the theory and might be stated as follows: "According to the total time hypothesis, it was predicted that the group studying the list for two minutes would recall significantly more words than the group studying the list for one minute." (For more information on making predictions from theories, see Chapters 1 and 6.) Putting your prediction in the form of a brief statement of how you tested your hypothesis provides a good transition to the next part of the research report, the method section.

Product Guidelines: Outline

At this point, you may be starting to experience cognitive overload with all these things to remember about writing a good introduction. To help reduce the strain, the following checklist in outline form summarizes and organizes the important information you should include in your introduction.

1. State the purpose of the experiment early in the report.
   a. Describe the basic problem or question the study addresses.
   b. Explain why the research question is important and why your study is worth doing.
2. Write a brief historical literature review—one that does the following:
   a. Examines the research relevant to your question to establish a context for understanding the research.

    b. Presents a more lengthy description of research studies that used methods like your own or that are especially theoretically relevant to your hypothesis.

    c. Has a reference citation for every idea that is someone else's and that is not common knowledge.

    d. Reports findings in past tense ("They found . . ."), and critically examines the relevant studies, making comments about problems with the testing procedures or other limitations in the research reviewed.

3. State your hypothesis in the form of an "if . . . then" statement or as a prediction made from a theory. Your hypothesis must be falsifiable, or stated in such a way that your results can fail to support the hypothesis.

4. Write a *brief* statement of how you tested the hypothesis.

American Psychological Association Format

1. Your report should be typewritten, double-spaced, with 1-inch margins all around.

2. The report should have a page header—a two- or three-word version of your title—in the upper right-hand corner on the same line as the page number. The introduction will begin on page 3, after the title page and abstract.

3. The full title should be centered below the page header.

4. Your references are usually written in one of the following forms. When you use a cited work as a subject or object in a sentence, then the date is in parentheses. For example: "Bensley and Haynes (1995) found that after training in critical writing psychology students' use of the language of argumentation became more like that of experts' in critical thinking." If you cite a document or work at the end of a sentence, then the entire reference citation is in parentheses. For example: "They found substantial increases in the use of the word 'evidence' (Bensley & Haynes, 1995)." Note that you should use "et al." only after you have first mentioned the complete citation with more than two authors.

You should consult the *Publication Manual* of the APA for more details and complete guidelines on APA format (American Psychological Association, 1994).

≈ PRACTICE YOUR THINKING 14.3

Analyzing a Sample Introduction

On the next few pages you will find a sample introduction to a research report. The sample introduction examines factors that affect the likelihood that an observer who watches another person help will also subsequently help a different person. Each day, we observe people open doors for others, pick up something someone has dropped, or engage in other acts of helping. Sometimes, we observe those who are helped thank their helpers, and sometimes they take this help for granted and don't respond. Does observing these mundane acts of kindness affect our own tendency to help, or do we ignore these acts or remain unaffected by them?

The purpose of this exercise is to help you learn how an introduction incorporates each of the product guidelines found in the outline we just went over. Your task is to analyze the sample introduction by identifying each of these product guidelines in the sample introduction. Answer the following questions that correspond to the product guideline format described previously. After you have identified each product guideline in the introduction, then look to see how each one is used in the introduction. This also should help you to better plan and construct your own introduction. Note that an actual introduction should be double-spaced, per APA guidelines.

1. What was the basic purpose of the study described in the introduction? _____

_____

    a. What is the basic problem or question the study addresses?

_____

    b. Why is the research question important?

_____

2. Evaluate the literature review in the introduction.

    a. Does the review examine research that is relevant to the question? Explain. _____

_____

    b. Does the review present a more lengthy description of research studies that are most directly related to the test of the hypothesis? Explain. _____

_____

_____

    c. Does the review have a reference citation for every idea that is someone else's or that is not common knowledge? List any missing ones.

_____

_____

    d. Were research findings presented that critically examined both sides of the question and that noted other problems or limitations in the literature reviewed? Comment. _____

_____

_____

3. What was the hypothesis? Was it in "if . . . then" form or stated as a prediction made from a theory? _____

_____

_____

4. Briefly, how was the hypothesis tested? _____

_____

_____

Answers to these questions appear in Appendix C.

A Sample Introduction

The Effects of Observing Rewarded and Nonrewarded Models on Helping

Several studies have shown that the modeling of altruistic behavior can have considerable impact on subsequent helping in adults (e.g., Bryan & Test, 1967; Rushton & Campbell, 1977; Wilson, 1976) and in children (e.g., Grusec, Kuczynski, Rushton, & Simutis, 1978; Rice & Grusec, 1975; Rushton, 1975; White & Burnam, 1975). Much less research, however, has investigated how observing a model being rewarded in different ways affects the subsequent helping of an observer. The purpose of the present study was to investigate whether observers would be more likely to help another person if they had previously observed a model who received rewards in a more salient or noticeable way than if they observed a model who received rewards in a less salient way. After reviewing the literature on modeling of helping behavior, reward qualities, and the salience of models, we describe an experiment that was designed to investigate this question.

Bandura (1986) identified several ways that observing a model engage in a behavior, such as helping, induces an observer to engage in that behavior. For example, observing a model might draw attention to a potential behavior, making it more salient to the observer and therefore making it more likely to occur. Observing a model could also serve as a cue to remind the observer of an important social norm or valued behavior. If the observed behavior was rewarded, it could signal the possibility of future reinforcement. Or if a rewarded model showed positive affect after engaging in the modeled behavior, then the positive affect could serve as an incentive cue for the observer to engage in future helping behavior.

Several studies have found that rewarding a person for helping increased the incidence of later helping behavior in the observer (e.g., Grusec & Redler, 1980; Midlarsky & Bryan, 1967). For example, Midlarsky and Bryan (1967) found that rewarding children with verbal praise increased the children's donation of candy to other children. After reviewing the literature, Grusec (1991) concluded that social rewards like praise may promote helping in young children, but that intrinsic rewards for helping are acquired later in childhood and may promote the socialization of helping.

Based on social learning theory, Bandura (1986) argued that observers are more likely to engage in modeled behavior when the observed models have been rewarded. Research on vicarious reinforcement has only sometimes supported the idea that observing a helping model who is rewarded will promote helping. For example, Midlarsky, Bryan, and Brickman (1973) found that children who observed a helping model talk about the positive rewards of helping another person later helped more than those observing a model who did not help but only discussed the positive benefits of helping. Rushton and Campbell (1977), however, found that adults who observed a model being praised for giving blood were no more likely to donate blood than those who were not vicariously reinforced. The fact that the Midlarsky et al. (1973) study was done with children and examined donation of money whereas Rushton and Campbell (1977) tested adults donating blood makes these two studies very different. Also, Midlarsky and her colleagues explained their results as due to consistency between the positive comments of the model and the helping behavior, and so this study does not clearly demonstrate the effects of vicarious reinforcement.

Researchers have more consistently found vicarious reinforcement to be effective in producing helping behavior in observers when a helping model demonstrated a positive affective response to being rewarded for helping (Bryan, 1971; Midlarsky & Bryan, 1972). For example, Midlarsky and Bryan (1972) found that children who observed an altruistic model demonstrating positive affect about giving subsequently donated more to a children's fund than a group observing a model who helped while expressing positive affect about winning a game.

Consistent with the results of these experiments with modeling, an experiment by Isen and Levin (1972) not involving modeling found that subjects in a positive mood were more likely to help than subjects not in a positive mood. See Batson (1990) for a review of the effects of positive affect on helping. Other research has found that positive affect could become associated with helping behavior through conditioning. In particular, Parish (1977) found that a group of children shown pictures depicting altruistic scenes along with positive words donated more than either a control group of children who observed no model and were not given the positive words, or another group who observed the model without any positive words.

While the reviewed research suggests that an observer may be more likely to help after observing a helping model who is rewarded or shows positive affect in response to a reward, the results of the studies reviewed could also be interpreted in terms of the salience of the observed interaction between the model and the person helped. When a model is rewarded after helping, then this also makes the interaction more salient or noticeable to an observer than when a model is not rewarded. Similarly, a model who is rewarded for helping and who responds with positive affect should be even more salient than one who is simply rewarded. Along these same lines, a model who helps minimally—that is, one who interacts little— would be at the lowest level of salience. For example, someone who opens a door for another person without looking at the person who is helped, and without being acknowledged for the help, is at the lowest level of salience in the social interaction.

Although the effect of the salience of observed rewards has not been tested directly in the research on modeling of altruistic behavior, Harris (1971) found that the salience of a norm for sharing displayed by a model affected the likelihood of a person's helping. Also, Batson, Fultz, Schoenrade, and Paduano (1987) found that if subjects reflected upon their motives for helping, they would help less. This effect of reflection was especially pronounced when the salience of subjects' self-rewards was greater. Although these results show that self-reflection can reduce helping in adults because it dampens the intrinsic motivation for helping, these results also suggest that adults' helping behavior continues to be influenced by rewards. Also, observing a behavior that is rewarded often increases the frequency of the behavior (Bandura, 1986).

Taken together, this research suggests that the salience of an interaction between a model and a person who is helped may lead to more helping in the observer; in other words, the more salient the interaction between the person helped and the helping model, the more likely a person observing this inter-action would subsequently help. No study has directly tested this hypothesis, how-ever.

To test the hypothesis that observers will tend to help more when the altruistic model they observed was in an interaction in which more salient rewards were provided, we had each of three groups of subjects observe a different kind of social interaction between a helping model and a person being helped. A fourth control group observed no model. First, subjects in the minimal contact modeling group observed a model help open a heavy door for a confederate loaded down with books, and this model merely helped without any other verbal or nonverbal com-munication. A second group observed the same model help, but this time the model was rewarded with eye contact, a smile, and a "thank you" from the person being helped. Lastly, the third modeling group observed a model help who was rewarded as before with the same positive social interaction as the second group, but this time the model reciprocated with "you're welcome!", a smile, and a cheerful tone of voice.

Each of these three groups observing a model differed in terms of the salience of the rewarding situation that subjects observed. The minimal contact group was at the lowest level of salience of reward because they observed an interaction between the model and the person helped in which no external reward was pro-vided. The second group was at a higher level of salience because they observed a model who was rewarded for helping but who did not respond to the reward. The third group was at the highest level of salience because they observed a model who was not only rewarded for helping, but also showed positive affect in response to being rewarded.

Based on the salience hypothesis and the research reviewed, we made the fol-lowing predictions about the degree to which each group of observers would help another person after they observed models that differed in the salience of the rewards in their interactions with the person helped. It was expected that the greater the salience of the observed rewards in the interaction between the model and person helped, the more likely an observer would subsequently help. Specifically, it was predicted that the group observing the most salient interaction—that is, the models who were thanked and then showed a positive response—would then help more than the group who observed the model to be thanked for helping. That group in turn would help more than the group observing the model in the minimal interaction situation.

More generally, we also expected to replicate the basic finding that modeling of helping behavior influences observers' tendency to help. Based on the social learning theory of Bandura (1986), it was expected that if modeling alone was necessary to produce helping, then all three groups observing a helping model would subsequently help more than the control group who observed no model. If, however salience of the interaction was the critical factor, then only the groups observing the more salient interactions would subsequently help more than the minimal interaction modeling group, who in turn might not differ from the control group observing no model.

≈ PRACTICE YOUR THINKING 14.4

Prewriting for Your Introduction

This next exercise is for those students who are planning to write an introduction to a research project of their own. Now that you have had some practice identifying important components of an effective introduction, you should be better prepared to find the components to put into your own introduction. You will have trouble doing this exercise unless you have already focused on an experimental research question and done considerable library research on that question. If you have not already done so, then you can answer these other questions as you become more focused, read more about your research topic, and actually decide upon the hypothesis you want to test. Then, when you have answered the following questions, you should be ready to begin drafting your introduction.

1. What is the basic purpose of the study you are doing?

   _____

   _____

   a. What is the basic problem or question you are addressing?

   _____

   _____

   b. Why is your research question important? _____

   _____

2. Develop and evaluate a literature review in your introduction.

   a. Make a list of at least five reference citations of research studies that are most relevant to your question.

   _____

   _____

_____

_____

_____

_____

b. Now, summarize the results of one or two of the most important studies in terms of their relation to your hypothesis. Include in your summary the hypothesis being tested, the method or design of the study, the basic findings, and any problems or limitations of the study. Include the independent and dependent variables if the study was experimental.

Study 1 citation: _____

Now describe. _____

_____

_____

_____

_____

_____

_____

Study 2 citation: _____

Now describe. _____

_____

_____

_____

_____

_____

c. As you write, think of the ideas you are using. If any of these ideas is not your own or not common knowledge, then find the reference for that idea and cite it after familiarizing yourself with the reference. Do this for every relevant idea.

Someone else's idea: _____

Reference citation for the idea: _____

d. Now examine the research findings and references you are using. Do they help you critically examine your question? Do they represent all sides of the question? Comment.

_____

_____

_____

_____

Are there other problems or limitations in the studies you are reviewing? Comment on individual studies.

_____

_____

_____

3. What is your hypothesis? Put it in "if ... then" form or stated as a prediction made from a theory. Make sure that it is in such a form that it can be falsified. _____

_____

_____

4. Briefly, how is your hypothesis tested? _____

_____

_____

Summary

This chapter was about critical writing—that is, writing in which a person evaluates the evidence relevant to a claim or question in order to arrive at a sound conclusion. For several reasons, writing, especially critical writing, might be expected to improve thinking. Not only do people often have the impression that writing makes their thinking clearer, but writing allows people to externalize their thinking, inspect their reasoning and relation of ideas and improve the communication of these.

Most people have already learned some things that can help them produce effective critical writing in psychology. For example, students should keep their purpose in mind, such as to analyze, evaluate, interpret, or persuade. They should assume that their audience (often, their instructors) are knowledgeable about psychology and then define the terms and concepts most relevant to their specific question. The tone—that is, style and approach—should generally be objective and serious.

Research suggests that novice writers such as students do not plan and revise their writing as much as expert writers do. At the formal level, writers should use a subject and verb in every sentence, introduce paragraphs with a topic sentence that is related to every idea in the paragraph, and use transitions to connect paragraphs. At the more conceptual level, writers should plan and organize their writing so that readers can follow their thinking and line of reasoning. It often helps to organize your evidence before you write, to tell the reader your organization or plan for discussion early in a paper, and then to follow that organization.

Research on writing suggests that taking both a process and a product approach to writing is most effective for improving writing. A process approach involves breaking writing assignments down into stages, such as prewriting, focused free writing, and drafting. Emphasis on product involves keeping in mind product guidelines, or goals and objectives for how your writing should be organized and important ideas that it should communicate.

The chapter also discussed three kinds of writing assignments that require critical writing. In general, the effectiveness of writing and thinking through writing depends on your ability to identify the kind of response requested by the writing assignment, and then following that purpose. For example, on an essay examination, you should be able to use words in the essay question to identify whether it asks for knowledge, comprehension, application, synthesis, or evaluation.

Writing short term papers can be facilitated by focusing on a specific question, then organizing the evidence and other relevant information, often using focused free writing, and then developing an outline that organizes the evidence into a coherent discussion of the questions. The outline of the short term paper preserves much of the working definition of critical thinking in the book: The beginning of the paper introduces the question and how it will be discussed; the middle part of the outline organizes the relevant evidence on all sides of the question; the conclusion summarizes and evaluates the evidence so that a sound conclusion can be drawn from it.

Finally, the introduction to a research report requires critical thinking. The writer should focus on a specific unanswered question in the research literature, present a critical evaluation of the studies relevant to the research question, and provide the rationale for the test of a specific hypothesis.

Review Questions

Does writing improve people's thinking? Why?

How is a critical essay different from some persuasive essays?

How does your purpose for writing affect what you write?

What should you keep in mind about your audience as you write?

What tone should you take in your writing?

Explain how planning and organization are important.

What can you do to make your writing better organized?

What is a process approach to writing? What are the basic steps of the process we discussed?

What are product guidelines? How do they help our writing?

What can you do to focus your response to an essay question?

What clues tell you that a question is asking you to demonstrate knowledge, comprehension, application, synthesis, or evaluation?

What do you do in focused free writing?

How is the outline for the short term paper that we discussed related to the working definition of critical thinking?

How does each part of the research report serve to report on a different aspect of the hypothesis tested in a research project?

References

American Psychological Association. (1994). *Publication manual of the American Psychological Association* (4th ed.). Washington, DC: Author.

Applebee, A. N. (1986). Problems in process approaches: Toward a reconceptualization of process instruction. In A. Petrovsky & D. Bartholomae (Eds.), *The teaching of writing.* Chicago: National Society for Study of Education.

Bandura, A. (1986). *Social foundations of thought and action.* Englewood Cliffs, NJ: Prentice-Hall.

Bandura, A., & Walters, R. H. (1959). *Adolescent aggression.* New York: Ronald Press.

Batson, C. D. (1990). Affect and altruism. In B. Moore & A. Isen (Eds.), *Affect and social behavior.* Cambridge, England: Cambridge University Press.

Batson, C. D., Fultz, J., Schoenrade, P. A., & Paduano, A. (1987). Critical self-reflection and self-perceived altruism: When self-reward fails. *Journal of Personality and Social Psychology, 53,* 594–602.

Bensley, D. A., & Haynes, C. (1995). The acquisition of general purpose strategic knowledge for argumentation. *Teaching of Psychology, 22,* 41–45.

Bond, L. A., & Magistrale, A. S. (1987). *Writers guide: Psychology.* Lexington, MA: D. C. Heath.

Bransford, J., Sherwood, R., Vye, N., & Rieser, J. (1986). Teaching thinking and problem-solving: Research foundations. *American Psychologist, 41,* 1078–1086.

Bryan, J. H. (1971). Model affect and children's imitative altruism. *Child Development, 41,* 2061–65.

Bryan, J. H., & Test, M. A. (1967). Models and helping: Naturalistic studies in aiding behavior. *Journal of Personality and Social Psychology, 5,* 400–407.

Cavender, N., & Weiss, L. (1987). *Thinking/writing.* Belmont, CA: Wadsworth.

Fitzgerald, J. (1987). Research on revision in writing. *Review of Educational Research, 57,* 481–506.

Flower, L., & Hayes, J. R. (1981). Plans that guide the composing process. In C. H. Frederiksen & J. F. Dominic (Eds.), *Writing: Process, development and communication.* Hillsdale, NJ: Lawrence Erlbaum.

Glathorn, A. A. (1985). Thinking and writing. In F. Link (Ed.), *Essays on the intellect* (pp. 67–88).

Alexandria, VA: Association for Supervision and Curriculum Development.

Grusec, J. (1991). The socialization of altruism. In M. S. Clark (Ed.), *Review of personality and social psychology: Prosocial behavior.* Newbury Park, CA: Sage.

Grusec, J. E., Kuczynski, L., Rushton, J. P., & Simutis, Z. (1978). Modeling, direct instruction, and attribution: Effects on altruism. *Developmental Psychology, 14,* 51–57.

Grusec, J. E,. & Redler, E. (1980). Attribution, reinforcement, and altruism: A developmental analysis. *Developmental Psychology, 16,* 525–534.

Harris, M. B. (1971). Models, norms, and sharing. *Psychological Reports, 29,* 147–153.

Hayes, J. R. (1989). Writing research: The analysis of a very complex task. In D. Klahr & K. Kotovsky (Eds.), *Complex information processing.* Hillsdale, NJ: Lawrence Erlbaum.

Hayes, J. R., & Flower, L. S. (1986). Writing research and the writer. *American Psychologist, 41,* 1106–1113.

Hillocks, G. (1984). What works in teaching composition: A meta-analysis of experimental treatment studies. *American Journal of Education, 93,* 133–169.

Hillocks, G. (1986). The writer's knowledge: Theory, practice, research, and implications for practice. In A. Petrovsky & D. Bartholomae (Eds.), *The teaching of writing.* Chicago: National Society for Study of Education.

Isen, A. M., & Levin, P. F. (1972). Effect of feeling good on helping: Cookies and kindness. *Journal of Personality and Social Psychology, 21,* 383–388.

Kellog, R. T. (1992). Creator of symbols: Observations on the psychology of thinking and writing. Address at 38th annual meeting of the Southwestern Psychological Association, Austin, Texas.

Langer, J. A., & Applebee, A. N. (1987). *How writing shapes thinking: A study of teaching and learning.* Urbana, IL: National Council of Teachers of English.

Marzano, R. J., Brandt, R. S., Hughes, C. S., Jones, B. F., Presseisen, B. Z., Rankin, S. C., & Suhor, C. (1988). *Dimensions of thinking.* Alexandria, VA: Association for Supervision and Curriculum Development.

McGuinness, C. (1990). Talking about thinking: The role of metacognition in teaching thinking. In K. Gilhooly, M. Keane, R. Logie, and G. Erdos (Eds.), *Lines of thinking: Reflections on the psychology of thought* (Vol. 2). Chichester, England: John Wiley.

Midlarsky, E., & Bryan, J. H. (1967). Training charity in children. *Journal of Personality and Social Psychology, 5,* 408–415.

Midlarsky, E., & Bryan, J. H. (1972) Affect expressions and children's imitative altruism. *Journal of Experimental Research in Personality, 6,* 195–203.

Midlarsky, E., Bryan, J. H., & Brickman, P. (1973). Aversive approval: Interactive effects of modeling and reinforcement on altruistic behavior. *Child Development, 44,* 321–328.

National Assessment of Educational Progress. (1986). *The writing report card: Writing achievement in American schools.* Princeton, NJ: Educational Testing Service.

Nickerson, R. S., Perkins, D. N., Smith, E. E. (1985). *The teaching of thinking.* Hillsdale, NJ: Lawrence Erlbaum.

Nisbett, R. E., & Wilson, T. E. (1977). Telling more than we can know: Verbal reports on mental processes. *Psychological Review, 84,* 231–259.

Parish, T. S. (1977). The enhancement of altruistic behaviors in children through the implementation of language conditioning procedures. *Behavior Modification, 1,* 395–404.

Perl, S. (1979). The composing process of unskilled college writers. *Research in the teaching of English, 13,* 317–336.

Rice, M. E., & Grusec, J. E. (1975). Saying and doing: Effects on observer performance. *Journal of Personality and Social Psychology, 32,* 384–393.

Roussey, J., & Gombert, A. (1996). Improving argumentative writing skills: Effect of two types of aids. *Argumentation, 10,* 283–300.

Rushton, J. P. (1975). Generosity in children: Immediate and long-term effects of modeling, preaching, and moral judgment. *Journal of Personality and Social Psychology, 31,* 459–466.

Rushton, J. P., & Campbell, A. C. (1977). Modeling, vicarious reinforcement and extraversion on blood donating in adults: Immediate and long-term effects. *European Journal of Social Psychology, 7,* 297–306.

Scardamalia, M., & Bereiter, C. (1991). Literate expertise. In K. A. Ericsson & J. Smith (Eds.), *Towards a general theory of expertise: Prospects and limits.* Cambridge, England: Cambridge University Press.

Scardamalia, M., Bereiter, C., & Steinbach, R. (1984). Teachability of reflective processes in written composition. *Cognitive Science, 8,* 173–190.

Stiggins, R. J., Rubel, E., & Quellmalz, E. (1988). *Measuring thinking skills in the classroom* (Rev. ed.) Washington, DC: National Education Association.

Swartz, R. J. (1989). Making good thinking stick: The role of metacognition, extended practice, and teacher modeling in the teaching of thinking. In D. Topping, D. Crowell, & V. Kobayashi (Eds.), *Thinking across cultures* (pp. 417–438). Hillsdale, NJ: Lawrence Erlbaum.

White, G. M., & Burnam, M. A. (1975). Socially cued altruism: Effects of modeling, instructions, and age on public and private donations. *Child Development, 46,* 559–563.

Wilson, J. P. (1976). Motivation, modeling, and altruism: A person X situation analysis. *Journal of Personality and Social Psychology, 34,* 1078–1086.

APPENDIX A
The Language of Argumentation: Expressions That Identify Parts of Arguments

Defining the Question

All or some _____

Although _____ ,

If it is assumed _____

To clarify _____

In comparison to _____

In contrast to _____

To define _____

Distinction/distinguish between

_____ is different from

_____

For example/for instance, _____

is really _____ is actually

_____

_____ is like or similar to

_____

Seeing that _____

Suppose that _____

Unlike _____

While _____ ,

Language That Signals Relations

_____ causes

_____

_____ contributes to

_____

_____ correlates with

_____

_____ depends on

_____

If _____ , then

_____

_____ is the reason that

_____

_____ is the result of

_____

_____ leads to

_____

_____ is one of the factors

related to _____

_____ most likely;
probably

Making a Claim

argue that _____ or

assert that _____ or

make the assertion _____

claim that _____ or make

the claim _____

expect that _____ or it

would be expected _____

hypothesize that _____

offer _____

predict _____ or make

a prediction _____

propose _____

suggest _____

think _____

Providing Evidence

For a Claim

_____ argues for

Because _____ ,

_____ is consistent with

_____ is evidence that

The fact that _____

On account of _____

_____ is reason to think

_____ shows that

Since _____ ,

_____ supports the claim that

Against a Claim

_____ argues against

_____ contradicts the claim

_____ is in disagreement with

_____ is inconsistent with

_____ does not support

Words that Suggest Kinds of Evidence

After reviewing the evidence, [someone's name] concluded _____ (expert authority)

The case of _____ (case study or perhaps anecdotal)

For example/for instance, _____ (anecdotal)

They found _____ (research study)

They compared _____ (experiment)

A significant effect of _____ (experiment)

They found that as _____ increased, _____ increased (research—correlation)

Drawing a Conclusion

Accordingly, _____

I conclude _____ or

in conclusion, _____

One can deduce _____

One can infer _____

I found _____

Finally, _____

For these reasons, _____

Hence, _____

If _____ , then _____

It is clear that _____

It follows that _____

The implication is _____

indicated that _____

leads one to think _____

Logically, _____

_____ reasoned that

A reasonable evaluation of the evidence suggests _____

A review of the evidence suggests

_____

It has been shown _____

In summary, _____

It stands to reason that _____

So, _____

Then _____

Thus, _____

APPENDIX B
Form for Answering Critical Reading Questions

(You may copy this form as needed for any critical reading exercise.)

1. What is the central question? What claim or claims are being made?

   _____

   _____

2. What is the evidence relevant to evaluating the claim?

   Evidence Supporting the Claim:

   2.1. _____

       Kind of evidence: _____

   2.2 _____

       Kind of evidence: _____

   2.3. _____

       Kind of evidence: _____

   2.4. _____

       Kind of evidence: _____

   2.5. _____

       Kind of evidence: _____

   2.6. _____

       Kind of evidence: _____

   2.7. _____

       Kind of evidence: _____

   2.8. _____

       Kind of evidence: _____

   Add more lines for evidence as needed.

   Evidence Not Supporting the Claim:

   2.1. _____

       Kind of evidence: _____

   2.2. _____

       Kind of evidence: _____

2.3. _____

Kind of evidence: _____

2.4. _____

Kind of evidence: _____

2.5. _____

Kind of evidence: _____

2.6. _____

Kind of evidence: _____

2.7. _____

Kind of evidence: _____

2.8. _____

Kind of evidence: _____

Add more lines for evidence as needed.

3. Evaluate the quality and quantity of the evidence presented so you can draw a sound conclusion.

_____

_____

_____

_____

_____

_____

_____

_____

_____

_____

_____

4. Do any assumptions create problems for this conclusion?

_____

_____

_____

5. What are some implications of this conclusion?

_____

_____

_____

_____

APPENDIX C
Answers

Chapter 4

Critical Reading Question:
Where Is the Mind Located?

- *What is the central question? What claim or claims are being made?* The central question is whether or not mental processes can be attributed to the activity of specific brain areas. The localization of function hypothesis claims that specific functions and behaviors are supported by particular areas of the brain.

- *What is the evidence relevant to evaluating the claim?*

Evidence Supporting the Claim of Localization of Function

1. Hippocrates thought that the mind resided in the brain (cited in Kolb & Whishaw, 1990). (authority)

2. Galen tested the heart versus brain hypothesis and found the brain to be the source of voluntary control. (early experiment—early surgeon)

3. The case of Phineas Gage showed that severe brain damage resulted in personality and other "mental" changes (in secondary source—Blakemore, 1977). (case study-as reported by his doctor)

4. Gall, Spurzheim, and other phrenologists observed traits related to characteristics of skull and brain. (authority and case data)

5. Flourens, using ablation, found evidence for the brain's regulating functions and abilities; brain was the seat of intelligence but not localized to one area. (experiments with animals)

6. Broca found that the ability to produce coherent speech was localized in the left frontal region of the brain. (case studies)

7. Wernicke found language ability to be in the brain, but not strictly localized to one specific brain area. (case studies)

8. Goltz found that function was not specifically localized in the cortex, but that the more tissue removed, the more impairment. (experiments with dogs)

9. Lashley (1929), using ablation, found that memories for running a maze were not stored in a specific place, but after destroying a considerable area the animal could no longer run the maze. (experiments with rats)

10. H. M. showed problems getting information into long-term memory from localized destruction of the hippocampus. (case study)

11. Fritsch and Hitzig found that electrical stimulation of specific brain areas would produce particular behaviors. (experiments and demonstrations)

12. Penfield (1975) stimulated the brains of patients and found changes in mental experience. (case studies with patients undergoing surgery for epilepsy)

13. Electrostimulation of specific areas of the brain produced aggression and feelings of pleasure, and was rewarding. (experiments mostly with animals)

Evidence Not Supporting the Claim of Localization of Function

1. Sumerians thought the soul resided in the liver. (common sense—folk "theory")

2. Aristotle, the Greek philosopher, thought the heart was more important than the brain. (authority)

3. Many people believe heart is where love and emotion reside. (common sense)

4. Magendie tested Spurzheim to see whether he could use phrenology to identify a person's characteristics, and he couldn't (Krech, 1960). (anecdote of a small experiment)

5. Lashley may not have precisely destroyed the specific areas that he thought he had. (scientific authority)

- *Evaluate the quality and quantity of the evidence presented so you can draw a sound conclusion.* There is a great deal of evidence based on authority, clinical case studies, and experiments and demonstrations with both ablation and electrostimulation of the brain in both humans and other animals that supports the claim that mental function is supported by and depends upon brain function. Also, case studies with brain-damaged persons have shown that mental experience becomes much more limited following brain damage. It has not been shown, however, that brain damage causes mental experiences; this would be harder to demonstrate.

The evidence against the claim that the mind is located in the brain is limited to the statements of authorities from centuries past. The evidence for the more specific claim that mental function is localized to specific parts of the brain is sometimes supported by experiments and sometimes not.

Based on the evidence reviewed, it can be concluded that the bulk of the evidence, much of which is experimental, supports the claim that the brain supports and is necessary for many different kinds of mental processes and behaviors. After reviewing the evidence for the localization of function, however, we may conclude that not all functions are localized. In fact, some mental processes and abilities, such as memory and intelligence, do not appear to be localized; however, some may be.

- *Do any assumptions create problems for this conclusion?* One assumption that might influence our evaluation of the evidence is the fact that much of the strongest evidence for the mind depending upon the brain is experimental evidence with nonhumans, especially with rats and dogs. Some psychologists would be unwilling to admit that animals other than primates—monkeys, apes, humans—have mental processes. This assumption could influence how we view the evidence, since according to these people we would not expect rats and dogs to have mental experiences.

- *What are some implications of this conclusion?* One implication of the conclusion that the brain is necessary for mental processes is that when someone is demonstrated to be brain-dead, they no longer have mental functioning. Another implication of the more weakly supported localization of function theory is that brain damage to specific areas may produce specific kinds of behavioral and mental deficits. In either case, it would be a good idea to wear a helmet when you ride a bicycle.

Chapter 5

Critical Reading Question: Does Hypnosis Improve Memory?

Note that italicized words are from the language of argumentation (see Appendix A) and help identify and classify parts of the argument.

- *What is the central question? What claim or claims are being made?* Often, the claim in a passage will take different forms as the discussion proceeds, becoming more and more refined and focused. In this passage, the major claim to be evaluated is in the title. The claim is that hypnosis improved memory. In the first paragraph, however, the claim is stated more generally. It is placed within the context of the popular claim that hypnosis gives people extraordinary abilities. Psychologists call this hypnotic hypermnesia: the phenomenon in which hypnosis helps a person to recall information that he or she did not previously recall. Notice that this term and claim refer to improving recall of information already learned. The question whether hypnosis helps a person to learn new information is a different question, not relevant here. Later in the passage, the claim is transformed further and addressed in terms of research and practical questions

such as whether people who are age-regressed remember more and whether hypnosis can help witnesses to remember more details from a crime.

- *What is the evidence relevant to evaluating the claim?* Once again, you should have organized the evidence and classified it as to kind or source.

Evidence That Hypnosis Improves Memory

1. There is a *popular view* that individuals have extraordinary abilities while under hypnosis, such as "super memory." (common sense)

2. The *case* of People vs. Woods, et al. (1977), better known as the Chowchilla kidnapping (Smith, 1983). (documented case)

3. In a *review of the literature, Smith (1983)* cited other *cases* in which hypnosis has later improved memory of events and crimes. (unspecified cases mentioned by scientific authority)

4. There have been many *examples* from the stage and in the laboratory that an adult who is given suggestions to "return" to an earlier age will show changes in speech and facial expression appropriate to that younger age. (anecdote)

5. Some early *research* showed that hypnosis did enhance memory for information from a person's past, but these *studies* were often poorly controlled according to a *literature review by Relinger (1984).* (scientific research of low quality according to scientific authority)

6. *Relinger (1984)* argued that hypnotic hypermnesia tended to occur in *studies* of memory for meaningful mate-

rial but not for material of low meaningfulness. (experiments reviewed by scientific authority)

7. Sometimes, however, *well-controlled studies* have shown beneficial effects on memory that were thought to be due to hypnosis. For example, Dhanens & Lundy (1975) conducted an *experiment* in which subjects who were motivated and hypnotized recalled the best. (experiment)

Evidence That Hypnosis Does Not Improve Memory

1. Nonsense syllables and other items of low meaningfulness failed to show any benefits from hypnosis according to a *literature review by Relinger (1984)*. (scientific authority)

2. Mingay (1985) *found* no better recall of meaningful material for hypnotized than nonhypnotized subjects. (experiment)

3. When *researchers* checked memories of events in age-regressed subjects they *found* the subjects did not accurately remember details. (experiment by Nash, 1987)

4. Summary of *literature review showed* age-regressed memory not accurate. (scientific authority)

5. *Experimental studies* done under heightened arousal and more realistic conditions, in general, have not *resulted* in subjects' showing better memory than nonhypnotized subjects according to a *review of these studies by Smith (1984)*. (experiments—reviewed by scientific authority)

6. Other *research by Erdelyi & Becker (1974)* showed that what looks like a hypermnesic *effect* due to hypnosis instead may be due to repeated

attempts at recall. Even under other recall *conditions* without hypnosis, subjects will remember things they did not previously recall. (experiment)

7. In a *review of the literature*, Erdelyi (1994) *concluded* that it is the repeated attempt at recalling ... and not hypnosis, per se. (scientific authority)

8. *Researchers* like Laurence and Perry (1983) have shown *experimentally* that a hypnotized person may be given a false suggestion while trying to recall some event and will incorporate this false suggestion into memory, thus creating a pseudo-memory, and they will be very confident in their false memories. (experiment)

9. Spanos and McLean (1985) produced pseudo-memories in all 11 highly hypnotizable subjects they tested, but under special reporting conditions, almost all subjects acknowledged the memories were imagined. (research demonstration—no actual manipulation)

10. Spanos, Burgess, and Burgess (1994) *argued* that people form pseudo-memories of alien abduction through hypnotic and structured interviews. (scientific authority—literature review)

11. Pseudo-memories were created in a woman by police using a suggestive interrogative technique. (case study)

• *Evaluate the quality and quantity of the evidence presented so that you can draw a sound conclusion.* The passage summarizes the evidence well. We can add to this an evaluation of the quality and the quantity of the evidence. Some of the evidence in support of the claim comes from documented cases, but these must be interpreted with care since they are not directly comparable and we do not know what other extraneous variables could have caused the apparent hypermnesic effect. Also, results were mixed from the early studies, and these often did not have proper experimental controls. Some better-quality experiments have been done, but these positive effects on memory have often depended on other variables such as subjects' motivation and the meaningfulness of the material to be remembered. Sometimes hypnotized subjects recall inaccurately, as in age-regression and the formation of pseudo-memories. Finally, hypnotic hypermnesia may sometimes be explained as really due to ordinary hypermnesia—improvement in memory that results from repeatedly trying to recall the same material. The conclusion in the evaluation of the evidence relevant to this claim is that true hypermnesia due to hypnosis has not been clearly demonstrated.

- *Do any assumptions create problems for this conclusion?* Case studies and anecdotes have frequently shown hypnotic hypermnesia, but experiments often do not. In some of the research it was assumed that realistic conditions had been simulated. Perhaps this assumption was wrong. It is actually quite difficult to simulate in the artificial environment of the laboratory the actual, natural conditions within which hypnotic hypermnesia would occur.

- *What are some implications of this conclusion?* An implication is that those using hypnosis to investigate crimes should be wary, since careless use of leading questions might actually make recall more inaccurate following the use of hypnosis. Perhaps hypnosis should be used as an investigative tool for obtaining evidence, but testimony obtained through hypnosis should not be admissible as evidence in trials. Note that we would be overgeneralizing if we concluded that, because memory is not supernormal under hypnosis, other claims about hypnosis are false. For example, people have, indeed, had major surgeries performed on them without an anesthetic other than hypnosis.

Chapter 8

Critical Reading Question: Is Human Memory Accurate?

- *What is the central question? What claim or claims are being made?* The main question may be stated: "Is memory accurate?" But a more specific form of the question is stated in this form: "Is memory reconstructive or reproductive?"

- *What is the evidence relevant to evaluating the claim?*

Evidence That Memory Is Reconstructive (Inaccurate)

1. Bartlett (1932) found subjects made systematic errors in recall such as omissions, intrusions, and recalling gist, due to schemas and reconstruction (experiments and later scientific authority)

2. Loftus and Palmer (1974) found estimates of speed and seeing broken glass reconstructed from leading questions. (experiment)

3. Sulin and Dooling (1974) found recognition memory reconstructed

from knowledge of famous people cued by title. (experiment)

4. Brewer and Treyens (1981) found memory of places reconstructed from schema of how a professor's office looks. (experiment)

5. Most people are familiar with stories that circulate that change and so agree that memory is inaccurate. (common sense)

6. Father Paggano was falsely identified from eyewitness memory. (anecdote)

7. Memory is reconstructed, according to review of literature. (scientific authority)

8. While John Dean's memory of his meetings was accurate in terms of the gist of what happened, he was inaccurate about several details that occurred (Neisser, 1981). (case study)

9. Events that were not originally viewed as sexual harassment later came to be conceptualized as such (Kidder, LaFleur, & Wells, 1995). (interviews)

10. Rebuttal to the claim that electrostimulation of the brain can lead to accurate recall of experiences: These memories were not verified to be accurate, and research on memory shows that memories even when vivid may be inaccurate. (scientific authority—literature review)

11. Rebuttal to the claim that people may recall accurately through hypnosis. (scientific research)

Evidence That Memory Is Reproductive (Accurate)

1. Actors can remember word for word. (anecdote)

2. Rajan the mnemonist could remember pi out to the 38, 100th digit. (anecdote)

3. The mnemonist studied by Luria could remember long lists of nonsense syllables accurately for at least four years. (case study and single-subject experiment)

4. Penfield (1975) electrostimulated brains and recovered apparently accurate memories of music played. (case study or single-subject experiment)

5. Eyewitness memory of Chowchilla kidnapper's license plate was refreshed by hypnosis. (anecdote)

6. Two experiments—one by Alba, Alexander, Hasher, and Caniglia (1981) and another by Bates, Masling, and Kintch (1978)—showed subjects could recognize accurately. (experiments)

7. Hasher and Griffin (1978) gave different wrong title for passage, and subjects reconstructed, but when later given correct title they could recall accurately. (experiment)

8. A literature review by Alba and Hasher (1988) found that reconstruction depended on the kind of memory test and criticized Bartlett's methods. (scientific authority)

• *Evaluate the quality and quantity of the evidence presented so that you can draw a sound conclusion.* A number of experimental studies, including data from memory for text, eyewitness memory, and memory for places, all showed that memory is reconstructive. This position was further bolstered by statements of scientific authorities and people's common-sense experience; however, common sense is not a very strong form of evidence.

Supporting the other side of the argument were numerous pieces of anecdotal evidence, including examples of how mnemonists, actors, and hypnotized persons could remember quite accurately. But these were individual, perhaps unique, cases that might not be true of memory in general. Similarly, the case study of Penfield may be unique to the individual; there is no way to verify the accuracy of the memory produced under electrostimulation conditions. Some experiments showed that right after being presented with some materials, subjects can recognize accurately or recall when given appropriate cues. Also, authorities on the subject argued that whether or not memory was reconstructed often depended on memory testing conditions.

In conclusion, the evidence suggests that memory need not be reconstructive under the right study conditions, as with actors, or under the right memory testing conditions. Much evidence, however, demonstrates that memory frequently is reconstructive. Under ordinary learning and testing conditions, memory will likely be reconstructive. There is no experimental evidence that an exact replica of an experience exists in memory.

Chapter 10

Critical Reading Question: Do Emotions Make Thinking Irrational?

- *What is the central question? What claim or claims are being made?* The central question is whether or not our emotional states cause us to think irrationally. Other claims

include the ideas that depression reduces our ability to make inferences and positive moods make people more creative.

- *What is the evidence relevant to evaluating the claim?*

Evidence That Emotions Make Thinking Irrational

1. That emotions make us behave irrationally is a popular idea (common sense)

2. Emotions oppose reason. (Plato and Socrates—philosophical authorities)

3. That emotion interferes with judgment is reflected in the popular saying "love is blind" (Fischer & Jansz, 1995). (common sense)

4. Most people associate emotion with a disruption in thinking (informal survey by Parrott, 1995). (common sense)

5. Emotions are viewed by legal system as involuntary while reason is thought to be a voluntary function. (Oatley, 1990). (legal opinion and authority reported by scientific authority)

6. Ellis (1977a, 1977b) argued that people become depressed because they hold irrational beliefs about themselves and the world. (clinical, scientific authority)

7. People who endorse irrational beliefs tend to show greater dogmatism and to make less critical inferences (Tobacyk & Milford, 1982). (correlational research)

8. Subjects who were experimentally induced to be in a depressed mood performed significantly more slowly on an inductive reasoning task than those induced to be in a neutral

mood (Palfai & Salovey, 1993). (experiment)

9. Camp and Pignatiello (1992) found subjects induced to be in a depressed mood failed to show any impairment in their inferential reasoning. (experiment)

10. Keinan (1987) found that when subjects were induced to be fearful by the threat of an electric shock they were less likely to examine alternatives to an anagram problem than subjects who were not made fearful.

11. Anxiety may produce thinking problems during tests (Hembre, 1988). (literature review by scientific authority)

12. Wright (1974) found that subjects under extreme time pressure may have weighed negative evidence disproportionately. (scientific research)

13. Johnson and Tversky (1983) found that subjects whose mood changed as a result of reading a tragic newspaper story increased their judgments of the frequency of other risks and undesirable events, as compared to subjects in a positive mood, who decreased their estimates of the frequency of risks. (experiments)

14. Happy subjects were willing to bet more on a long shot than subjects not made happy (Isen & Patrick, 1983). (experiment)

15. Happy subjects tend to rate the likelihood of good weather as greater than bad weather.

16. Isen and Daubman (1984) found that positive mood causes people to be overinclusive in grouping things into categories. (experiment)

17. Schwartz and Bless (1991) argued that when people are in positive moods, they are likely to use a processing strategy that lacks logical consistency and attention to detail. (scientific authority in literature review)

18. For example, Bless, Bohner, Schwartz, and Strack (1990) found that happy subjects were just as persuaded by weak arguments about a message opposite to their own attitudes as by strong arguments about the same message. (experiment)

Evidence That Emotions Do Not Make Thinking Irrational

1. Subjects experimentally induced to be in an elated mood performed significantly more slowly than depressed and neutral condition subjects on a deductive reasoning task (Palfai & Salovey, 1995). (experiment)

2. Some experts think emotions do not necessarily have negative effects on thinking (Scherer, 1984). (scientific authority)

3. Thorndike's law of effect is that organisms are more likely to engage in a behavior in the future when it leads to a pleasant outcome. (scientific authority)

4. The functions of emotion are different from reason, but not necessarily irrational, and thinking errors occur outside of emotion, too. (Oatley, 1990). (scientific authority)

5. Nathanson (1985) pointed out that the ideal of rationality and emotion originating with Plato is wrong. (authority)

6. Positive mood may actually help a person on creative kinds of tasks

(Isen, Johnson, Mertz, & Robinson, 1985). (experiment)

7. A study of Isen and Means (1983) found that subjects in a positive mood were more efficient in their decision making than were control subjects not put in a positive mood. (experiment)

8. Sad subjects were found to be more influenced by strong arguments than weak ones (Bless, Bohner, Schwartz, & Strack, 1990). (experiment)

- *Evaluate the quality and quantity of the evidence presented so that you can draw a sound conclusion.* Evidence on the question is mixed. Considerable evidence from experiments, anecdotes, and authorities suggests that negative emotion may interfere with thinking, causing us to behave irrationally. Some experimental evidence and statements from authorities on emotion also suggests that positive moods may lead people to be more creative and to maintain their motivation on a task. At the same time, other experimental research evidence suggests that positive mood may lead people to be overinclusive in their use of categories. In conclusion, considerable evidence supports the idea that negative emotions like depression and anxiety may interrupt thinking, interfere with thinking, and lead to poorer inferences. Sometimes, however, negative emotion leads to relatively better evaluation of evidence. Positive emotions and moods may also lead to benefits in thinking under certain conditions and to decrements under other conditions. Therefore, emotions have complex effects on thinking, and we cannot

conclude that they necessarily lead to irrational thinking.

- *Do any assumptions create problems for this conclusion?* The literature reviewed was selective. It did not examine the research on all negative moods and emotions. Depression, anxiety, fear, and anger were examined, but it may be that the conclusions would not hold for other negative emotions such as shame or guilt. At the same time, the conclusion is already that emotion has complex effects on thinking; this conclusion would probably not be overturned by the missing evidence.

- *What are some implications of this conclusion?* One implication of the conclusions drawn from this review is that some types of emotional states may interfere with people's thinking on certain kinds of tasks. People should, therefore, be careful about certain kinds of thinking errors when they are in certain moods. We might also expect that if one is in a positive mood, then one will be better able to do creative types of tasks.

Chapter 12

Case 1: "It's Not Good Enough Yet"

Answering the questions from Table 12.1 provides us with substantial evidence of the seriousness of Bill's problem. His behavior is unusual in that most people do not become severely agitated when working on almost every project they attempt and then stop the project to move on to something else. His behavior is very maladaptive in that he is unable to finish his work or pay his bills on time and his boss is threatening to fire him. Finally, Bill comes to therapy complaining of stress, suggesting that he finds his situation is personally distressing. All three indicators from Table 12.1 are present, suggesting that Bill has a serious problem and quite possibly a psychological disorder.

Answering the questions in Table 12.2 allows us to eliminate a number of disorders and to identify a likely candidate disorder. Bill does not appear to show signs of substance abuse. Nor does he report other physical symptoms. He converses normally, not revealing a part of himself that he is unaware of (which would be dissociation); nor does he show severe thought disturbance (psychosis). Unusual sexual practices have not been observed or reported.

Changes in his emotional state may be part of his problem, however. He gets uncomfortable, agitated, and nervous every time he works on a project, and this prevents him from completing it. These three emotion descriptors suggest anxiety may be involved. Bill engages in a number of ritualized behaviors in relation to his work, repeatedly stacking up his papers, neatening his desk, sharpening his pencil, reading and rereading what he has written, and repeatedly correcting his punctuation. He even keeps old drafts of articles he has completed with the idea of making them better. The anxiety related to his work, his indecisiveness, his repetitive behavior, his perfectionism, his preoccupation with details, and his inability to discard worthless objects suggest an obsessive-compulsive disorder.

On the other hand, sometimes he gets discouraged by his job, but he fails to apply for a new one. His procrastination, discouragement, and inactivity might suggest depression. This depression, however, may be secondary since it may be his perfectionism and ritualistic behaviors that prevent him from acting on his discouragement and writing for a new job.

Finally, the fact that Bill has been slow and perfectionistic for many years may suggest a personality disorder. Taking all of this evidence into account in our analysis, the best diagnosis for Bill would be **obsessive-compulsive personality disorder.**

Case 2: "The Walls Have Earrings"

Some of the evidence found in this case could be explained as eccentricity. Some writers, who are not psychotic, use unusual language in their everyday conversations. It is also true that writers may have a flight of ideas in creative inspiration and may seek to be alone for prolonged periods to write. Other substantial evidence, however, suggests that Jim has a severe problem. His behavior is very unusual in that most people do not hear the thoughts of other people plotting against them through the walls, unless someone is speaking these thoughts through the thin walls of an adjacent room. His behavior is very maladaptive in that he is not completing his assignments and he has stopped attending classes. Finally, Jim comes to therapy complaining of an inability to concentrate, suggesting personal distress. All three indicators from Table 12.1 are present, suggesting that Jim has a serious problem and quite possibly a psychological disorder.

Answering the questions in Table 12.2 allows us to eliminate a number of disorders and to identify a likely candidate disorder. We do not know whether Jim has some sort of organic disease or nervous system damage that might cause his severe thought disturbances. This possibility is worth pursuing since some diseases may cause severe cognitive and perceptual disturbances. He shows no other physical symptoms, however. Also, he does not appear to have a substance abuse problem that could lead to thought disturbance; but this possibility should be examined. His problem does not apparently involve sexual practices or dysfunction. Also, he does not seem to be dissociating part of himself or his experience. The changes in his thinking and perception are not attributed to another personality. Rather, these dramatic changes in his thinking seem to be happening to him. Also, his hearing thoughts through the walls (auditory hallucinations) and his bizarre use of language suggest psychotic-like thought disturbance, a primary symptom of schizophrenia. Consistent with this hypothesis is his blunted affect or almost total lack of emotion. Rather than experiencing an unusual or dramatic change in emotion, he doesn't appear to express any emotion in later sessions. Also consistent with the schizophrenia hypothesis is his social withdrawal. Taking note of the kind of delusions (false beliefs) he has about his girlfriend conspiring to make him fail suggests that he is paranoid. Since these changes came on him recently, they are not likely part of the development of a personality disorder, like paranoid personality disorder. Rather, the thought disturbance (paranoid delusions and hallucination of his ex-girlfriend's voice), his blunted affect, and his social withdrawal all suggest the development of **paranoid schizophrenia.**

Case 3: "I'm Not Ready"

Karen is experiencing a number of conflicts related to making an important decision in her life. These kinds of conflicts often lead to stress and anxiety. She is experiencing anxiety in making her decision, but this is a normal response. Her distress has lasted only a little while and may pass. Also, her symptoms are not of high magnitude, suggesting that while she may be upset, she is not suffering from a mental disorder. Similarly, she is engaging in some adaptive behaviors in trying to deal with her boyfriend about her conflicts. She does seem to be experiencing enough personal distress to lead her to consult her physician. So although she does not seem to fit the criteria in Table 12.1 to be having a mental disorder, her personal distress and confusion might nevertheless be helped if she sees a clinical psychologist or counselor.

Case 4: "What's the Use?"

Marilyn meets all three criteria from Table 12.1 for having a serious problem. Her long bouts of crying are high-magnitude signs, suggesting a serious disorder, as are her extreme swings in mood. Her behavior is maladaptive since she is having trouble with her schoolwork, and she has essentially given up. Finally, she is experiencing considerable personal distress. All of these suggest she has a mental disorder.

Inspecting Table 12.2, we might form the initial hypothesis that Marilyn has a problem with her moods. She shows signs of depression, such as lack of energy, helplessness, and profound sadness. Although she does show some anxiety, her primary state is depression, and sometimes she also gets energized and becomes manic, apparently feeling as if she is on top of the world. Her mood swings from depression to mania are consistent with a diagnosis of bipolar-affective disorder or what used to be called manic depression. At the same time, several hypotheses can be eliminated. She does not appear to be using a drug to have thought disturbances, dissociative experiences, or sexual problems. In conclusion, the best diagnosis of Marilyn's problem seems to be **bipolar disorder.**

Chapter 13

Interaction 1

There are a number of threats to the soundness of the conclusion that Jennifer suffered sexual abuse as a child. First of all, her therapist may be making a premature decision on this. Early on, he suggested to her that her pattern of symptoms is consistent with a diagnosis of sexual abuse, when it also is consistent with a number of other psychological problems. The therapist should have explored these explanations, as well. Also, his statement to her about the pattern of symptoms could create a confirmatory expectancy leading to her own premature conclusion that she was abused. In addition, his use of base rate information is inaccurate and misleading. He should have taken more seriously her statement that she did not remember being abused. His use of a guided imagery technique in which he focused on an anger incident may have helped to reconstruct her memory of her father. It appears that she may be very suggestible to hypnosis and so go into a hypnotic state even though not formally hypnotized.

Furthermore, there are other explanations for the memories she begins to reconstruct besides sexual abuse. Many people can remember their fathers yelling at them, holding their hand tightly, or standing over them, and many people have at one time or another seen their fathers naked. Her father's drinking problem and anger control problems do not necessarily mean that he abused her. Suggesting that she go to a survivors' group in which there are great incentives for labeling experiences as sexual abuse could lead her to draw the wrong inference about her memories. Her body memory of the weight of her father's body is ambiguous, and research on childhood amnesia suggests that the part of her abuse extending back to six months of age is confabulated. Finally, the fact that neither of her sisters recall anything related to her alleged abuse should increase one's skepticism. In conclusion, there are many problems with the methods used to find out about possible childhood sexual abuse. The therapist's conclusion that Jennifer was sexually abused is likely to be wrong, and he risks misrepresenting her problem, which could result in inappropriate treatment.

Interaction 2

In this interaction, the therapist did not use inappropriate recovery methods. By using relaxation therapy with suggestions to focus on her client's sexual problems and her bod-ily feelings while encouraging her to reflect upon her problems, the therapist opened up the possibility that her client would recover her own memories of abuse. She also provided a supportive therapeutic environment as she encouraged her client to explore her own feelings and memories without unduly interpreting her client's experience. Her use of a sexual abuse inventory along with a number of other instruments in assessment and her direct questioning about abuse helped identify sexual abuse in her client's history. When her client finally did identify an experience of sexual abuse, she allowed her client to verify that it was her memory. In conclusion, based on the therapist's careful use of methods for recovering memories, the client's own recovery of her memory of sexual abuse without the use of suggestion or confirmation by the therapist, her brother's corroboration of abuse, and her mother's supporting statements, the conclusion that the client was sexually abused as a child seems sound.

Chapter 14

Analyzing a Sample Introduction

1. *What was the basic purpose of the study described in the introduction?* The purpose was to investigate whether observers would be more likely to help another person if they had previously observed a model who received rewards in a more salient way rather than a less salient way.

   a. *What is the basic problem or question the study is dealing with?* Will the salience of observed interactions between models and helped persons be a factor that leads to observers' subsequently helping more?

   b. *Why is the research question important?* Every day, we

observe people helping others; they are either rewarded or not rewarded. Do these observations affect our tendency to help even when we do not pay much attention to them?

2. *Evaluate the literature review in the introduction.*

   a. *Does the review examine research that is relevant to the question? Explain.* Yes. The literature review gave a brief historical review of the relevant studies from a number of relevant areas, such as the effect of reward on helping, modeling and helping, and the salience of rewards.

   b. *Does the review present a more lengthy description of research studies that are most directly related to the test of the hypothesis? Explain.* Yes. A study on modeling and rewards (Midlarsky, Bryan, & Brickman, 1967) was discussed more, as was a similar study that obtained a negative outcome (Rushton & Campbell, 1977).

   c. *Does the review have a reference citation for every idea that is someone else's or that is not common knowledge? List any missing ones.* Yes, but perhaps there could be more information about the effects of intrinsic versus extrinsic rewards.

   d. *Were research findings presented that critically examined both sides of the question and that noted other problems or limitations in the literature reviewed? Comment.* Yes. In the studies mentioned above, two opposing findings were presented. Similarly, the seemingly conflicting findings of Batson et al. (1987), Harris (1971), and Bandura (1986) were presented.

3. *What was the hypothesis? Was it in "if . . . then" form or stated as a prediction made from a theory?* The hypothesis was put in the following form: It was expected that the greater the salience of the observed rewards in the interaction between the model and the person helped, the more likely the observer would help.

4. *Briefly, how was the hypothesis tested?* Four groups of subjects were tested. Three differed in terms of the salience of the interaction between the model and helped person. One group observed the model without any other interaction. One was rewarded with a thank-you, and the other was rewarded after helping and then showed positive affect in response. A fourth control group observed no model helping the person.

Index

TO THE OWNER OF THIS BOOK:

I hope that you have found *Critical Thinking in Psychology* useful. So that this book can be improved in a future edition, would you take the time to complete this sheet and return it? Thank you.

School and address: _____

Department: _____

Instructor's name: _____

1. What I like most about this book is: _____

_____

_____

2. What I like least about this book is: _____

_____

_____

3. My general reaction to this book is: _____

_____

4. The name of the course in which I used this book is: _____

_____

5. Were all of the chapters of the book assigned for you to read? _____

If not, which ones weren't? _____

6. In the space below, or on a separate sheet of paper, please write specific suggestions for improving this book and anything else you'd care to share about your experience in using the book.

_____

_____

_____

_____

_____

Optional:

Your name: _____ Date: _____

May Brooks/Cole quote you, either in promotion for *Critical Thinking in Psychology* or in future publishing ventures?

Yes: _____ No: _____

Sincerely,

D. Alan Bensley

FOLD HERE

- -

BUSINESS REPLY MAIL

FIRST CLASS   PERMIT NO. 358   PACIFIC GROVE, CA

POSTAGE WILL BE PAID BY ADDRESSEE

ATT: *D. Alan Bensley* _____

**Brooks/Cole Publishing Company
511 Forest Lodge Road
Pacific Grove, California 93950-9968**

FOLD HERE